CONTENTS

INTRODUCTION   I

1   UNDERSTANDING POVERTY – THE CONCEPTS AND MEASURES   9

2   POVERTY: THE FACTS   30

3   CIRCUMSTANCES LEADING TO POVERTY   77

4   EFFECTS OF POVERTY AND DEPRIVATION   110

5   CHILDREN AND POVERTY   142

6   WOMEN AND POVERTY   163

7   ETHNICITY AND POVERTY   187

8   UNEQUAL SHARES   206

9   GEOGRAPHICAL DIVISIONS   227

10   INTERNATIONAL COMPARISONS   249

CONCLUSION   271

APPENDIX   274

INDEX   283

ACKNOWLEDGEMENTS

Poverty: the facts is a flagship publication for CPAG. Our aim is to raise the level of the debate and to provide an accessible resource of facts, figures and analysis to inform discussions over the nature, causes and impacts of poverty. In terms of authorship, John Veit-Wilson was responsible for Chapter 1, Jan Flaherty for Chapters 2 through 10 and Paul Dornan for the Introduction and Conclusion.

We are very grateful to all the people who contributed to this book. Thanks to Fran Bennett and Usha Brown for reading and commenting on the draft version. Thanks are also due to Pauline Phillips at CPAG for managing the production of this edition, Paula McDiarmid for proofreading the text and Sylvia Potter for compiling the index.

Jan is also grateful to Lily, Eden and Mike for their help in various ways.

We are thankful to Carey Oppenheim, the creator of this book, and all the contributors to previous editions.

ABOUT THE AUTHORS

Jan Flaherty holds an Economic and Social Research Council studentship and her research interests are poverty and discourse. She has worked as a research assistant for Professor Ruth Lister at Loughborough University.

John Veit-Wilson is Emeritus Professor of Social Policy at Northumbria University and Visiting Professor in Social Policy in the School of Geography, Politics and Sociology at the University of Newcastle upon Tyne. He has been engaged in research into poverty measures and their relationships with income maintenance systems since 1964, and was a founding member of CPAG in 1965.

Paul Dornan is CPAG's Policy and Research Officer. Before joining CPAG he was studying for a PhD in the Department of Social Policy and Social Work at the University of York. His research and writing has focused on pensioner poverty, with a specific interest in means testing and the non-take-up of entitlements.

Introduction

For all those passionate about the need to end poverty in general, and child poverty in particular, these are heady times. In March 1999, the Prime Minister, Tony Blair, got to his feet in Toynbee Hall, East London to deliver a speech on Sir William Beveridge and his legacy. An unexpected high point of the speech was a commitment to end child poverty within 20 years.[1] The route to this endpoint has since been elaborated, with a promise to reduce child poverty by a quarter by 2004/05 and to halve it by 2010. Since that speech we have seen real increases in the level of resources focused on reducing poverty. To cite only a few initiatives: new working and child tax credits, Sure Start, the national minimum wage and increases in both child benefit and the child elements of income support. These measures, and many others, have shown official resolve in the fight to reduce child poverty. It was in this climate, in the run-up to the 2001 general election, that CPAG published *An End in Sight?*,[2] which analysed progress towards this aim. Child income poverty has been falling. Nevertheless we find ourselves in a position where in 2001/02, 30 per cent of the children in Great Britain were living in income poverty.[3] In 1979, at the start of Margaret Thatcher's first term as Prime Minister, the chances of a child being in income poverty stood at 14 per cent (see Chapter 2). If the chances of a child being in income poverty in 2001/02 were the same as they were in 1979, we would have had two million *fewer* children living in income poverty.

The resolve to tackle poverty has not been restricted to children; in particular, concern has encouraged action on pensioner poverty. At the Labour Party's autumn conference in 2003 Gordon Brown expounded the goal of creating 'a Britain where child and pensioner poverty can be eradicated'.[4] Examples of this concern have included substantial increases in the value of the income support for pensioners, reformed into the minimum income guarantee and then the guarantee element of the new pension credit. The effect of these measures is to increase generosity of, and the proportion entitled to, benefit – although problems of non-take-up have persisted. Though not all is attributable to policy, there has been an impact on the rate of pensioner income poverty. Between 1996/97 and 2001/02 the proportion of pensioners measured as living in income poor households[5] grew slightly on the before housing costs (BHC) measure (up 1 per cent to 22 per cent of pensioners) but fell after housing costs (AHC) (from 27 per cent to 22 per cent).[6] Sutherland et al model the changes beyond 2001 as having a much greater effect in reducing pensioner income poverty. They suggest that by 2003/04 the proportion of pensioners taken out of income poverty may have been more substantial, leaving 18 per cent of pensioners in income poverty on the BHC basis and 15 per cent AHC.[7]

This book is about poverty and so it ought to start off with a clear statement about what CPAG believes poverty is. Poverty is sometimes couched in terms of 'absolute' and 'relative' notions. Absolute poverty can be defined in reference to some kind of basic – usually biological – requirement. Relative poverty is about the relationship of the individual to the society in which s/he lives.[8] Using these terms, CPAG believes in an explicitly relative concept of poverty. Poverty is not only about basic needs and material deprivation but also about engagement and participation in society. If an individual finds her/himself locked out of participation in the activities of a society, because of a lack of means, then s/he should be considered to be in poverty. This is discussed further in Chapter 1, which analyses the conceptualisation of poverty and what is often implied by the use of the term.

CPAG is particularly concerned about child poverty because of its demonstrable effects on the lived experience of children (see Chapter 5) and because of the outcomes to which it often leads in later life. The body of evidence that underlies this belief is discussed in Chapter 4. A word is useful here, therefore, on the link between the negative effects felt by poorer children and the causes of poverty itself. The ultimate cause of poverty is an imbalance of power. This imbalance plays itself out through the most powerful having a disproportionate control of the society's resources, at the expense of the least powerful. Poverty, the consequence, is a lack of financial resources, pure and simple. Other explanations that are from time to time offered, such as labour market problems, benefit inadequacy or behavioural explanations (see Chapter 3), are the mediators which make powerlessness lead to poverty. Establishing the causal chain is critical: unless the causes are properly understood policy makers will not be in a position to design effective responses.

MEASURING POVERTY

Discussing what is meant by poverty opens up the thorny issue of how it may be measured. Chapter 1 discusses the nature of poverty measurement, both why and how this is done. As argued in the chapter, the issue of measurement cannot be thought of as value-neutral; how poverty is defined and measured affects the prevalence that we will find and thus the sorts of policy interventions made to tackle it.

Where they are available, the statistics discussed in this book use living in households with equivalised incomes below 60 per cent of the median AHC as a proxy for poverty, here termed 'income poverty'. This is an imperfect proxy for poverty, but one which has been used widely in research and in international comparisons, especially across Europe, and so one on which we need to rely. There is no alternative that has been universally accepted as better than the 60 per cent of median measure. The words 'where they are available', at the start of the paragraph, are important because the collection of statistics that allow us to understand the prevalence of poverty is inconsistent between geographic areas and over time. Reading, and using, statistics therefore requires care. Not only is there no overriding poverty measure used by research but measures are dependent on the data made available by research. The practical implication of this is that concepts of poverty and low[er] income are often run together. When data does not exist on the precise level of income, 'flags' of likely income, or social position, are often used, such as occupational or social class.

THE IMPACT OF POVERTY

Poverty is something that we should rightly get very angry about indeed. Chapter 4 shows that poverty is associated with demonstrable effects on living standards, on opportunity, on morbidity and on mortality. It is usually the poor who suffer the worst impact. Not only this, the worst effects of poverty are often felt by those people least able to defend themselves: people who are young, old, disabled or sick. The data and analysis in this book are presented in a dispassionate and considered fashion; they must be, given the seriousness of the issue. Research must be rigorous, we must have the evidence. But solving poverty is not just about research. Tackling the injustice of poverty – an injustice that means those in poverty live lives which are usually shorter and more brutal than is the case for the majority – requires both political will and political action.

With this in mind it is worth setting out some of the social conditions, discussed later in this book, which are associated with measures of low income:

- **Higher mortality**: In England and Wales in 2001, infants born to fathers in the lowest social class were twice as likely to die within one year of birth as those born into the highest social class.[9]
- **Lower educational outcomes**: Of the 100 schools with the highest proportions of pupils eligible for free school meals (a proxy for deprivation) in England, only three attained the national average GCSE point score.[10]
- **Less decent homes**: 42 per cent of the poorest quintile of English households, compared to 23 per cent of those in the richest quintile, lived in homes not deemed decent in 2001.[11]
- **Financial exclusion**: In Great Britain one in five poorer households, defined as having a household income lower than 60 per cent of the median AHC, did not have a bank account in 2001/02. The average for the population was 7 per cent.[12]

Poverty is highly patterned; certain groups suffer systematically more than others. For this reason Chapters 5 (children), 6 (women) and 7 (ethnic minorities) are devoted to exploring the experience of specific groups which have been shown to have a higher risk of being poor. Chapter 9 explores a further aspect to this patterning, analysing the geographical dimensions of poverty.

This book demonstrates that there is a strong case to answer to reduce poverty. As we document here, poverty has demonstrable effects on both lived experience and on outcomes. Reducing poverty is the best way to counter the social ills discussed in Chapter 4. Poverty in the UK is embedded in extreme inequality. In very general terms, those in extreme poverty suffer the worst, followed by those whose poverty is less extreme and so on up the income scale. CPAG retains its focus on income poverty because it is the manifestation of extreme inequality. As Chapter 2 illustrates, between 1979 and the mid-1990s inequality grew sharply, and a sizeable and growing group of the population – in which children were over-represented – were locked out of the mainstream living standards of society.

ERADICATING CHILD POVERTY WITHIN A GENERATION

Although this book is not just about child poverty, that is the reason why CPAG was founded and so this final section of the Introduction examines progress in this area. At the time of writing we are a couple of months off the first 'crunch' year for the tracking of progress against the income poverty targets. After Tony Blair promised to end child poverty within 20 years the first milestone target set was to reduce by a quarter the number of children in income poverty. This was formalised in a Public Service Agreement (PSA) target[13] set between the Treasury and the Department for Work and Pensions. For this to be met, income poverty will have to have fallen by a quarter between the base year of 1998/99 and the first milestone year of 2004/05 on both the before and after housing costs measures. In practical terms, this requires a numerical reduction on the BHC measure from 3.1 million to about 2.3 million and on the AHC measure from 4.2 million to 3.1 million. In 2001/02 (the most recently available data), the number of children in income poverty stood at 2.7 million and 3.8 million[14] on the before and after housing costs measures respectively. A greater number of children will therefore have to be removed from income poverty to meet the target than has been achieved up to now.

It is difficult to say with confidence whether or not the Government will meet its first milestone; falls in child poverty result not solely from policy but from its interaction with concurrent social trends (most notably employment levels). We are able to say that it will be easier to meet the target on the BHC measure than the AHC measure because it is the lesser of the two reductions. In 2003 the Joseph Rowntree Foundation (JRF) brought out encouraging findings[15] which used policy simulation techniques to suggest that, if all else remains equal, the Government may hit its target. The Institute for Fiscal Studies (IFS) has produced research which suggested that more needs to be done to reach the milestone.[16] It was after some of this research had been conducted that CPAG began to campaign for a £5 rise in the weekly rate of income for poorer children in order to reach this target. The December 2003 pre-budget report[17] announced, from April 2004, an extra £885 million spending on the child element of child tax credit, equivalent to £3.50 per child, or £2.50 having taken account of earnings inflation.[18] This increase was counterbalanced by a freezing of the child tax credit thresholds and of the family element, which both make the reform less generous overall whilst focusing resources on the poorest recipients of child tax credit. The overall effect is progressive. Though the extra spending announced in December 2003 is a little less than the IFS had argued for to ensure the first milestone is reached,[19] this does get us closer to a goal well worth achieving. Whether or not the Government reaches the first target, both the IFS and JRF analysis emphasise that the second target – that of halving child poverty by 2010 – is a much more difficult proposition.

The complicating factor here is that the JRF study, as with analysis from the IFS, was premised on the continuation of the use of having an equivalised household income of below 60 per cent of the contemporary median as being in income poverty. This measure has now been reviewed with the new regime of three indicators, of which a restricted version of the 60 per cent of contemporary median is one, so things are a little more complex. The measures which will apply after 2004/05[20] will contain three indicators:

- Absolute low income: Children are counted as poor on this measure if they live in household with a BHC equivalised income of less than 60 per cent of the 1998/99 median income, uprated for inflation.
- Relative low income: Children are counted as poor on this measure if they live in a household with a BHC equivalised income of less than 60 per cent of the contemporary median.
- Material deprivation and low income combined: Children are counted as poor on this measure if they live in a household with a BHC equivalised income of less than 70 per cent of the contemporary median and if they both lack material necessities and could not afford them.

We have no targets of precisely how these indicators will be used to track poverty reduction. We also do not have data on the first and third indicators on which to establish a baseline number of children in poverty. We are able to see from the second indicator that the new measure appears to substantially reduce the number of children in income poverty, down from 3.8 million in 2001/02 (the highest of the BHC and AHC measures) to about 2.9 million using the new measure.[21] Further, although most would view the eradication of child poverty as meaning no children being left in income poverty, this has now been (re)defined as meaning that relative incomes would be amongst the 'best in Europe'.[22] Calculation, based on the figures available in the report and comparable income poverty rates in other European countries, suggests that this could leave between 900 thousand and 1.2 million children still in relative income poverty. This is a watering down of Blair's historic promise. We welcome the serious effort which has gone into tackling child poverty but to redefine income poverty so it is less difficult to tackle is unacceptable − more ought to be done for the sake of Britain's children and, through them, for the nation's own future. Much has been done, but much remains to be done if the corrosive effects of poverty, detailed in this book, are to be reduced.

NOTES

1 The speech is reproduced in R Walker (ed), *Ending Child Poverty*, The Policy Press, 1999

2 G Fimister (ed), *An End in Sight? Tackling child poverty in the UK*, Child Poverty Action Group, 2001

3 Defined as living in a household with an equivalised income after housing costs of below 60 per cent of the median

4 G Brown, speech to conference, 'The NHS only truly safe with us and our values', Labour Party conference, 29 September 2003

5 With equivalised incomes less than 60 per cent of the concurrent median

6 See Office for National Statistics, *Households Below Average Income 1994/5–2001/02*, Department for Work and Pensions, 2003, p114

7 H Sutherland, T Sefton and D Piachaud, *Poverty in Britain: the impact of government policy since 1997*, Joseph Rowntree Foundation, 2003

8 As Chapter 1 notes, the distinction between absolute and relative is simplistic − all measures of poverty are relative to something since understandings of minimum biological needs depend on a particular time and place

9 Infant mortality defined as death within one year of birth. Analysis of Department of Health, *Mortality statistics childhood infant and perinatal. Review of the Registrar General on deaths in England and Wales 2001*, London: Office for National Statistics, 2003, p62, Table 12

10 R Lupton, *School Quality, Free School Meals and Area Deprivation: reading between the lines*, CASE, London School of Economics, 2002

11 'Not decent' is defined as in disrepair or in need of modernisation or providing insufficient thermal comfort; Office of the Deputy Prime Minister, *English House Condition Survey*, 2003, p10

12 Office for National Statistics, *Households Below Average Income 1994/5–2001/02*, Department for Work and Pensions, 2003, p31

13 Department for Work and Pensions, *Public Service Agreement (PSA) Technical Note for the Department for Work and Pensions*, Department for Work and Pensions and HM Treasury, 2002

14 Office for National Statistics, *Households Below Average Income 1994/5– 2001/02*, Department for Work and Pensions, 2003, p65

15 See note 7

16 M Brewer and G Kaplan, 'What do the child poverty targets mean for the child tax credit?', in R Chote, C Emmerson and H Simpson (eds), *The IFS Green Budget, Institute for Fiscal Studies*, 2003; M Brewer, A Goodman and A Shephard, *How has child poverty changed under the Labour government? An update*, Institute for Fiscal Studies, 2003; M Brewer, *What do the child poverty targets mean for the child tax credit? An update*, Briefing Note 41, Institute for Fiscal Studies, 2003

17 HM Treasury, *Pre Budget Report 2003: the strength to take the long-term decisions for Britain: seizing the opportunities of the global recovery*, December 2003, para 5.19

18 Institute for Fiscal Studies, *IFS analysis Pre Budget report analysis*, Press release, December 2003, note 2

19 See M Brewer, *What do the child poverty targets mean for the child tax credit? An update*, Briefing Note 41, Institute for Fiscal Studies 2003

20 Department for Work and Pensions, *Measuring Child Poverty*, December 2003, DWP, pp7–14. The implication of the measurement review is discussed more fully in P Dornan, 'Defining income poverty out of existence?', *Poverty 117*, February 2004, p12

21 The difference is between the higher of the old relative income measures, 60 per cent of after housing costs equivalised household income (3.8 million children are measured as poor) and the new measure, 60 per cent of before housing costs equivalised household income, together with a change in the equivalisation formula (2.9 million children are measured as poor). See Office for National Statistics, *Households Below Average Income 1994/5– 2001/02*, Department for Work and Pensions, 2003, p65 and p258, author's calculation.

22 Department for Work and Pensions, *Measuring Child Poverty*, December 2003, DWP, p20, para 71

Understanding poverty –
the concepts and measures

INTRODUCTION

What poverty is this book about? The word is used in so many ways with so many meanings across so wide a range of different kinds of poverty that perhaps we should instead talk about poverties. At one end of the range of ideas about poverty are deprived lives, stunted and constrained by exclusions from what society defines as decency and dignity. At the other end are statistical assertions that poverty is having a cash income at some point below the household average. What connections do such disparate ideas of poverty have to each other, or to what the society we live in itself sees as poverty? How can they be conceptualised, defined or measured? What distinguishes poverty from *inequality* and when is inequality a problem? What are the similarities to and differences from the two related expressions which describe unsatisfactory conditions, *deprivation* and *social exclusion*? What do the statistics of poverty, deprivations and social exclusions within and between countries really tell us? What are the implications of these issues for government policies dealing both with the wider social evils and the adequacy of benefits under the income maintenance system?

Questions like these have led to many arguments which often muddle the situation rather than clarifying it. Both the academic literature and the political debates are full of disagreements, contradictions and confusions. Commentators often use one approach as if it were the only one, rather than seeing which is most appropriate for the topic in hand. They sometimes deny the possibility of being objective and treat the whole matter as no more than the clash of subjective opinions. This is misleading, since social science allows us to discover what are reliable objective facts about societies and what their beliefs are by collecting a mass of individual opinions – this is, after all, a foundation of democracy. In any case, studying the facts about poverty is not a matter of playing word games but of confronting realities about the avoidable suffering of millions of people, both in the UK and around the world. But some governments or politicians have other agendas than relieving the suffering poverty causes, for instance preferring to keep wages and benefits low for political ends such as offering electors cheaper goods and services and lower taxes. We must not assume that everyone wants to carry through the action needed to abolish poverty.

This chapter aims to explain the variety of approaches taken to understanding poverty, and what follows from such understandings in terms of the different measures and statistics quoted in later chapters. Although this variety seems to be connected by nothing more than the word 'poverty', each example may validly reflect some aspect of the causes, conditions or consequences of this kind of human suffering, or the ambivalence which some governments seem to feel about acting against it. The chapter tries to address these questions more broadly than is possible where research findings by one method are presented or a political argument is promoted. A short chapter can aim only to outline the key issues about such a complicated subject and offer some tools with which to make sense of the arguments about different approaches. As the subject is constantly developing, the current methods and data change, and government responses and initiatives rarely remain constant or focused on any one aspect.

TO START WITH

What idea are we talking about? There is no agreement on what the concept of 'poverty' means in practice. Some attempts to frame the concept in formal definitions leave it both vague and broad, including the conditions of life in which people suffer all kinds of deprivations, social exclusions and social evils, or cause them to other people. For instance, some kinds of crime are seen as symptoms of poverty. The Blair Government in the UK favours this vague and broad approach in some of its statements. Others favour a definition of poverty which is more precise and narrow, often in terms of whatever a particular kind of measurement produces. For example, UK governments since the

1990s have identified 'people in poverty' as being those living in households whose disposable income fell below a certain percentage of average household incomes. In earlier years, UK governments identified 'low income families' as being people who lived in households with incomes below or close to the lowest means-tested benefit levels (national assistance, supplementary benefit or income support). These official definitions of poverty are not based on any evidence that the income levels are enough to avoid the condition of being poor. People poor by one definition may not even be poor by another.[1]

Whether the idea of poverty is understood as the *condition* of suffering intolerable deprivation, or its *cause* in having inadequate resources, especially income, needed to avoid the deprivations, or even as suffering the variety of adverse *consequences* of deprivation in life, depends on the context, the observer, and the observer's purpose in wanting a definition. The way it is expressed in a definition also depends on which of a range of ways of talking about poverty observers or their audiences find more plausible. For example, what people experience and see is often expressed in social and psychological terms, but what politicians and governments are concerned about is political problems and policies. By contrast with these perspectives, researchers need precise tools for analysis and measurement. They may try to capture the essence of the social and political perspectives, or they may disregard them in favour of some different theoretical perspectives, like those of economics.

A RANGE OF APPROACHES TO TALKING ABOUT POVERTY

We talk about poverty in many ways. Paul Spicker identified eleven clusters of meanings surrounding the word poverty,[2] while John Veit-Wilson's cross-national research found seven different ways being used to talk about poverty.[3] Spicker classified the meanings into those which clustered around ideas of bad material conditions (multiple deprivations, unmet needs, low levels of living), around aspects of people's economic position (inequalities, class position, power over resources) and their social position (lack of entitlements, lack of security, exclusions, dependencies), and saw all of these as connected with the idea of unacceptable hardship. Veit-Wilson used the word 'discourses' because it covers not only the scientific idea of a paradigm, which is an explanatory system, but also the taken-for-granted way of talking about a subject, its vocabulary and all the habits of thought which go with that.[4]

The seven discourses Veit-Wilson found in use in the 1990s can be divided into the four humanistic discourses which treat poverty as an aspect of human society, how it operates, how people behave and who is excluded, and three which treat it as simply an abstract and formal position in a statistical distribution, an economic theory or a legal status. Use of each of these discourses implies that this is the right way of talking about poverty and that other ways are wrong – in effect discourse usage implies a closure on some other aspects of poverty.[5] Thus seeing poverty as a matter of deviant behaviour, for instance, neglects the 'invisible poor' who lack resources for participation but try to live outwardly conventional lives. The denial that poverty exists in a country closes off debate over what degree of divergence is intolerable, and to whom. Social exclusion discourses overlook both deprived people who are not members of 'excluded' categories or areas, or who have low incomes but are 'integrated' into non-poor society, and discussion of how the exclusion comes about – who is doing the excluding, and why are they doing it? Being poor by statistical income distribution begs the question of the adequacy of incomes to avoid deprivations or ensure participation. Economic theories that people need only sufficient funds for food, clothing and housing – the 'minimum subsistence' approach – close off social values and psychological and altruistic motives for action (which in fact may be even more rational than the self-interest assumed by such theories), or the expenses of participation in society. Poverty as a legal status excludes those who are poor but are not recipients of social assistance.

All of the ideas expressed in these clusters or through these discourses are represented in the data reported in this book, but that does not mean that CPAG endorses the appropriateness of such usages. All of us, publics and politicians alike, have to deal with the ideas and discourses which other people use, and use those available to us and which we find convincing. The problems in discussion and action arise when these conflict with each other, or when facts on one kind of poverty are presented using data on another kind. Agreement that any one approach is the only right one may not be desirable since we want to describe so many differing aspects of unacceptable human hardship. The question is whether this helps or hampers the search for solutions, since, as David Piachaud put it, 'the term "poverty" carries with it an implication and moral imperative that something should be done about it', adding that its definition is always a value judgement.[6]

Whichever approach is taken, we must always be sensitive to who is overlooked by that definition of poverty, and what hardship would remain if that kind of poverty were abolished. They do not all carry similar implications for action even though they too embody value judgements.

IDENTIFYING POVERTY

These many ways of approaching the variety of poverties leads naturally to as many ways of identifying them. To list what they look like is not the same as defining poverty, although they are often confused with each other: to describe an elephant is not to define it, still less to measure it. This section looks at some of these descriptive attempts to identify poverty.

At the global level, the World Bank defined poverty as 'the inability to attain a minimal standard of living'.[7] To give this some depth and in an attempt to give international guidance on what was meant by poverty, the United Nations World Summit for Social Development meeting in Copenhagen in 1995 agreed that the condition of poverty, in the broadest sense wherever it occurs in the world, could be described as follows (note that it draws on many of the meanings identified by Spicker). This is sometimes called the UN definition of overall poverty, though the UN did not use that word about it:

> Poverty has various manifestations, including lack of income and productive resources to ensure sustainable livelihoods; hunger and malnutrition; ill-health; limited or lack of access to education and other basic services; increased morbidity and mortality from illness; homelessness and inadequate housing; unsafe environments and social discrimination and exclusion. It is also characterised by lack of participation in decision-making and in civil, social and cultural life. It occurs in all countries: as mass poverty in many developing countries, pockets of poverty amid wealth in developed countries, loss of livelihoods as a result of economic recession, sudden poverty as a result of disaster or conflict, the poverty of low-wage workers, and the utter destitution of people who fall outside family support systems, institutions and safety nets.[8]

It goes on to describe many of the groups who are especially vulnerable to poverty. Within this broad description of what its idea of poverty covers, what it calls absolute poverty has a more limited and extreme form:

Absolute poverty is a condition characterised by severe deprivation of basic human needs, including food, safe drinking water, sanitation facilities, health, shelter, education and information. It depends not only on income but also on access to social services.[9]

As the research carried out at the University of Bristol has shown during the 1990s, if poverty is identified in this way then such 'absolute' poverty can be found even in the UK.[10] Similarly, the UN Administrative Committee on Coordination issued a statement of commitment for action to eradicate poverty in 1998 which aimed to identify poverty in very broad terms which can apply equally to the most deprived people in the most deprived countries as well as to those in richer countries:

> Fundamentally, poverty is a denial of choices and opportunities, a violation of human dignity. It means lack of basic capacity to participate effectively in society. It means not having enough to feed and clothe a family, not having a school or clinic to go to, not having the land on which to grow one's food or a job to earn one's living, not having access to credit. It means insecurity, powerlessness and exclusion of individuals, households and communities. It means susceptibility to violence, and it often implies living on marginal and fragile environments, without access to clean water and sanitation.[11]

Such lists of universal identifying conditions help to fill out the assumptions contained in simple definitions of poverty such as that of the World Bank economist, Martin Ravallion, who stated that:

> 'Poverty' can be said to exist in a given society when one or more persons do not attain a level of material well-being deemed to constitute a reasonable minimum by the standards of that society.[12]

The problem is then to discover what that society's standards are and how it ranks them in importance, so that we can see the difference between, for example, the UN's overall poverty and its absolute poverty in a country. We should not expect the list of precisely what people need for their well-being to be the same in different countries. The economist Amartya Sen proposed[13] that we should instead consider poverty in terms of unfulfilled *capabilities*, meaning how far in practice people are capable of achieving the well-being that their societies define as a reasonable minimum. Thus the individual capability of access to clean water can be met by a variety of different means in different contexts, ranging from piped water at home to enough money to pay for bottled water from elsewhere. Similarly, the individual capability of mobility beyond what is customarily walked (if the individual can walk – if not, the capability demands further resources) can be met by individual or collective forms of transport, or the incomes needed to pay others to provide them. However, this approach brings out the fact that meeting capabilities is not an individual matter and collective provision for them is indispensable, whether for social use or commercial profit. The availability of clean water implies that a source has been found, the water has been purified and made available in pipes or bottles at charges which consumers can pay without causing other deprivations. Similarly, the capability of mobility can only be met if forms of pathway (road, rail, airport) and vehicle (bicycle, car, bus, train, aeroplane) have been made available collectively.

'ABSOLUTE' AND 'RELATIVE', 'PRIMARY' AND 'SECONDARY' POVERTY

The UN's use of the term 'absolute' poverty should not lead us to suppose that it has some independent agreed scientific meaning. The problem with this word, and with its opposite, 'relative' poverty, is not only that neither of them have any agreed meaning, but that the people who use them do so for very different and even incompatible purposes. The terms cannot be said to represent any 'real' kind of poverty as it is experienced and can be studied, but only reflect what various commentators have at various times felt is a useful distinction to argue a particular case.

One common version of the idea of absolute poverty is that it represents the minimum needed to sustain physical life, a state of lacking all but a given list of physiological requirements ('minimum subsistence' measures). Some economic theorists assume that this can be done reliably, an assertion which (given the continued absence of any evidence) sociologists and psychologists would generally dispute. Attempts to measure absolute needs quickly show that no humans live only a physical life; indeed, we should not be human if we did. It is impossible to separate the physiological needs from the social needs since they are not only closely intertwined but the physical needs, for example for nutrition or warmth, are expressed in terms of the foodstuffs we conventionally eat or the clothes conventionally worn, or the houses and heating systems available. What is minimally acceptable to society in food and clothing, and all the other necessities for taking part in social life, is inevitably relative to that society, time, place and observer – it cannot be otherwise. That is what the idea of relative poverty was meant to express. However, a very unusual, perhaps even original, use of the term 'absolute poverty' has been by the Blair Government to describe a statistical measure of current household income inequality compared with 1997 when it came into power, while it uses 'relative poverty' to mean household income inequality by current measures. This has an obvious political purpose, but it is not what others have meant by the terms.

When the pioneer of empirical poverty research, Benjamin Seebohm Rowntree, devised his 'primary' poverty measure based on the cost of a basket of necessities for 'merely physical efficiency' a century ago, it was not because he thought this reflected what any family could live on. He knew that no one could live a minimally decent social life on that income but he wanted to show the non-poor classes that a large proportion of the poor (whom he identified and counted by the appearance of their deprived lifestyles) had too little money even to meet physical, let alone social, requirements. 'Secondary' poverty was merely his name for the condition of those who had more income than those in 'primary' poverty but who still suffered poverty lifestyles.[14] When Rowntree came to study the minimum incomes needed for social life, in order to recommend minimum wage rates, he abandoned these terms as unhelpful, but some people still use them.

Relativity is a very broad notion. One must always ask 'relative to what?' Answers may include relative to society's present or past standards, relative to other people or groups in this country or in others, or other aspects of comparison such as the degree of inequality in society. W G Runciman's research into relative deprivation showed that people judged their positions by comparison with other people's (their reference groups) or with their own at some previous point in time.[15] A pensioner might, for example, feel relatively deprived by comparison with those in work today but well off by comparison with her/his own earnings in the past. Thus both observer and time could change the content and quality of the subjective judgement about an objective position.

Sen argued that in spite of the meaninglessness of the absolute/ relative and primary/secondary distinctions commonly made, the idea of 'an irreducible absolutist core in the idea of poverty' lives on. Using a narrow version of 'relative' he stressed that 'If there is starvation and hunger then, no matter what the relative picture looks like there clearly is poverty', admitting that this absolutist core is itself relativist in a wider sense.[16] This is clear if we think about how the UN's description would be put into practice in the UK. However, if we cannot agree what they mean, the use of words like absolute and relative does not help our understanding of poverty. Similarly, the distinction between primary and secondary poverty refers to a debate a century ago which took for granted middle class judgements about working class lifestyles and the ability of science to measure 'minimum subsistence', assumptions which would not be supported today.

POVERTY AS SOCIAL EXCLUSION

Social exclusion has attracted a large literature since the term first attracted attention in the 1980s, often as a synonym for poverty. The official uses of the word 'poverty' at that time were so narrow that many wanted a broad term to cover all the deprivations and social ills (many described in this book) which rightly need attention if deprived human lives are to be liberated. But the broader the approach taken to describing what poverty is, the harder it is to define it precisely. The harder it is to see your target clearly, the harder it is to hit it. This suits those governments and others who want to express concern about the wide range of deprivations and social ills but without having to do anything substantial because the problem is too large, it is hard to see where to intervene to make a difference, or any intervention on the scale suggested would be too difficult.

In the UK poverty debate the idea of exclusion was first used influentially by Peter Townsend in his celebrated definition of poverty in 1979:

> Individuals, families and groups in the population can be said to be in poverty when they lack the resources to obtain the types of diet, participate in the activities and have the living conditions and amenities which are customary, or are at least widely encouraged or approved, in societies to which they belong. Their resources are so seriously below those commanded by the average individual or family that they are, in effect, excluded from ordinary living patterns, customs and activities.[17]

What is notable is that the word 'excluded' is used here to express not the condition of poverty but the process – *lack of resources causes the exclusion*. In later formulations of this definition, Townsend changed the formulation to read: 'If they lack or are denied resources to obtain access to these conditions of life and so fulfil membership of society they may be said to be in poverty',[18] again implying that poverty can be caused by exclusion from access to resources.

A second influence came from the European Community. It had promoted national member states' initiatives to combat poverty in the 1970s, but in the 1980s the governments of Germany, France and the UK refused to accept the continued use of the word in these plans because of the implication that 'poverty' in the severe 1930s sense persisted in their countries, and because they saw the problem for governments as being far more multifaceted than lack of income resources alone. Instead, the EC adopted the French usage of 'social exclusion' and policies for 'insertion', which came from a traditional view of society as an organic and inclusive but hierarchical whole. Nevertheless, the EC description of poverty reflected Townsend's approach:

> For the purposes of this Decision 'the poor' shall be taken to mean persons, families and groups of persons whose resources (material, cultural and social) are so limited as to exclude them from the minimum acceptable way of life in the Member States in which they live.[19]

While the limited resources were seen as causing the exclusion, the subsequent policy developments in both Europe and the UK have tended to focus on the consequences, stressing the behavioural aspects of lack of cultural and social resources rather than the structural aspects of lack of material resources. The discourse used plays down the role of material resources such as income, which is odd in what one may call marketised societies: those in which money can buy many of the goods, services and experiences needed to avoid almost all deprivations and exclusions.

The most relevant aspect of the idea of social exclusion to poverty is thus *market exclusion*. But this does not mean that social exclusion is not a serious political issue in its own right. This is a both/and issue, not an either/or issue. Governments should indeed have policies to deal with the wide range of unsatisfactory social conditions and their causes and consequences which are embraced by the very broad idea of social exclusion, but this must not be confused with the identification of poverty and policies to deal with it in its own right. The people affected by each are not necessarily the same people: by no means everyone who is poor is also socially excluded,[20] while it is clear that many who are seen as socially excluded because of, for instance, their gender, sexuality, ethnicity, ability, age or location are not poor.

POVERTY AS DEPRIVATION

Most of the many attempts to define social exclusion treat it as a description of unsatisfactory and deprived social conditions and their consequences, leaving open the question of what caused the conditions in the first place. We therefore need to consider what is meant by deprivation. Townsend suggested:

> Deprivation may be defined as a state of observable and demonstrable disadvantage relative to the local community or the wider society or nation to which an individual, family or group belongs. The idea has come to be applied to conditions (that is, physical, environmental and social states or circumstances) rather than resources and to specific and not only general circumstances, and therefore can be distinguished from the concept of poverty. For purposes of scientific exposition and analysis both ideas are important and their relationship has to be clarified.[21]

The distinction Townsend suggested is to rephrase his definitions of poverty so that failing to achieve the range of conditions for full participation in society is deprivation, while lacking or being denied the resources to achieve these conditions is poverty.[22] In other words, deprivation describes the condition and poverty describes the cause of that condition, the lack of sufficient resources.[23]

POVERTY AS INEQUALITY

The condition of being unequal is not the same as the condition of being deprived or the causes of that deprivation. Poverty carries the implication that something must be done[24] but inequality does not necessarily do so: some experiences of inequality may be seen as problems, but there is no necessary connection between measures of income inequality and the poverty which is an inadequate income.

Nevertheless, in the UK and across much of the EU, people in poverty are counted using income inequality measures, identifying poverty as an income below some statistical percentage of the average. In the 1980s the UK governments changed the statistical basis of counting what they called 'low incomes' (avoiding the use of the word 'poverty') from the legalistic identification of all those households with incomes below or close to the minimum income social assistance levels (Low Income Families or LIF), to the statistical inequality identi-fication of the households with incomes at or below half of the average household income (later changed to 60 per cent of the median), adjusted for differences in household size and composition and the age of members (*Households Below Average Income* or HBAI). The reason for the change was political – governments deplored poverty counts based on benefit rates, where each time the benefit rate was raised the people counted as in poverty by that measure would also rise. By contrast, inequality measures avoided this disadvantage, and statistical lines were believed to embody no judgements about the adequacy of benefits or other incomes.

There had in fact been lengthy technical argument about these measures. One issue was whether to use measures of income inequality around the average (mean) or the median. The mean average, formerly used, divides the total income of a population by the number of people in it. Because it takes into account the size of very high incomes, a few more rich people can drag the average upwards and make more people seem to be poor by this measure. This problem is avoided by the median measure, which simply divides the population into two, irrespective of the size of incomes above or below the median. The other argument revolved around what percentage of the median to use as the statistical poverty line. In Europe the debate had ranged across 40, 50 or 60 per cent of the median, and some research is still reported using poverty lines of 50 per cent. In the UK the decision was taken more recently to move from 50 per cent of the mean to 60 per cent of the median because the accuracy of the mean measure was affected by small numbers of low income and high income households surveyed, and during the 1990s 60 per cent of the median measure was a figure very close to 50 per cent of the mean and thus made little difference to the numbers in poverty.

The influence in all these debates of political expediency rather than evidence of what poverty means to people is very apparent. There is as yet no evidence that any of these lines, at whatever percentage of the mean or median household income in a country, tells us anything about the level of household or individual income which is in fact needed in that society to avoid what it sees as deprivations and social exclusions. The danger of this method of defining poverty is the implication that people who live in households with incomes above the percentage taken are not recognised as 'really' poor, or are blamed for their deprivations and exclusions because it is assumed that their incomes are 'high enough to avoid poverty'. Governments could sponsor or carry out the research needed to discover at what percentage of median income people in reality manage to avoid deprivations and exclusions, but this has not yet been done even though the sources of data exist.

Whether or not income inequality is seen as a social or political problem is a different matter from considering the causes, conditions and consequences of deprivations and exclusions. However, there are some ways in which the degree of inequality may affect the social ills in a country. Richard Wilkinson's research has over many years illustrated the close connection between inequality and many aspects of ill-health, even if the causal mechanisms remain unclear.[25] They may lie in the lack of a feeling of solidarity, a sense of being a member of the inclusive (even if unequal) society which some traditional ideologies aim for, resulting in feelings of alienation and experience of distress. Many commentators have remarked on how, for example, inequalities in educational provision work their way through to success or failure achieved later in life, irrespective of children's abilities at the outset. The often severe problems of debt and even crime are ascribed by some to the aspirations set up by commercial advertising for consumption, then criticised by those who have already acquired the desired lifestyles as 'the politics of envy'. The key issue in all these arguments is whether or not everyone in society has access to the resources needed not to be deprived or excluded from participation as society defines it, whatever the inequality is beyond that point. For decades in the mid-twentieth century the Nordic countries claimed to have reached this situation, to have abolished poverty in its severe deprivation sense even if acknowledging that some inequalities were still too great. It therefore remains a political challenge to other governments to achieve the same situation for their peoples.

CAUSE, CONDITION OR CONSEQUENCE?

The discussion of the ideas of exclusion, deprivation and inequalities emphasises how many disparate issues have become bundled together in the whole discussion of poverty, and makes it hard to see what can be done. What may be a consequence of childhood deprivations becomes a cause of further problem conditions in adult life in a circular system which some policy-makers want to break. Much of the debate in the UK has long centred on the idea of dealing with the 'causes of poverty', but these have only been seen in behavioural terms (misuse of resources wrongly believed to be adequate), or in terms of the common characteristics found among people in poverty. Chief among these in the UK Government's policy agenda are people without paid work, lone mothers, people with low educational qualifications or lacking skills, sick and disabled people, and old people. The identification of these characteristics with causes of poverty is not as simple as the Government suggests, since it is immediately obvious that some of the richest people in the UK, even the Royal Family, share some or all of these characteristics. Evidently it is not these characteristics in themselves which cause poverty, but the fact that most people who have them have not got enough money to buy their way out of their deprivations and exclusions. Even describing the characteristics as engendering the risk of poverty implies that government could not ensure adequate incomes for people who cannot work because none is on offer or they are unfit or old. Such social security and pension policies have been effectively used before and are feasible again.

WHOSE NEEDS? WHOSE STANDARDS?

What we need, therefore, is methods to measure how much income is enough to avoid the deprivations and exclusions which society defines as unacceptable. But there are serious problems around discovering what the idea of an adequate income is. The question 'how much is enough?' can be answered only by asking further, 'enough for what?' 'sufficient for how long?' 'adequate for whom?' and 'who says?'[26] It is obvious that answers will differ depending on whether they are about short-term or lifetime needs, and for everyone in society or only for those in poverty now.

When Joanna Mack and Stewart Lansley defined 'poverty in terms of an *enforced* lack of socially perceived necessities',[27] they were focusing on the condition of deprivation as well as its causes in lack of income, but their idea of how to find out what were the necessities which no one in society should be without differed from Townsend's methods, and these differences still arise in debate. Townsend was concerned that, when asked to specify what necessities were, people might not be aware of all the physical, social and psychological needs they really have, and so he tended to include items which social scientists identified as essential and which might not be purchasable.[28] By contrast, Mack and Lansley said they took simply what their sample of the whole population rightly or wrongly told them were necessities, and took account only of those which could be bought, so that they could find out how much money was needed not to be deprived and who had too little money to buy them if they wanted to.[29]

The argument about human needs is as old as the Greeks[30] and cannot be reviewed here. The key issue has always been who shall have authority to decide what people need. For instance, scientists know about nutrients, but it is societies which determine conventional foodstuffs. These differences have affected all the methods developed to identify and count people in poverty. But the methods have also been directly affected by what people want poverty measures for.

DIFFERENT PURPOSES NEED DIFFERING POVERTY MEASURES

There are several different reasons[31] why governments and researchers may want a method of distinguishing people in poverty from those who are not. They include:

- describing poverty and who is poor;
- explaining why they are poor;
- counting people in poverty;
- comparing groups over place and time;
- reporting what people describe as poverty;
- discovering what a poverty income is and who is poor by it;
- prescribing action to deal with poverty.

Each of these distinct purposes leads to a distinct kind of measure, and there is no point in arguing about measures without being clear what they are intended for.

Historically, people developed the measures for the purposes they had in mind, and within the different discourses they chose to use. At the end of the nineteenth century, Seebohm Rowntree used the long-standing conventional middle-class visual measure of a squalid lifestyle to *identify* poor households and *count* them, but for the purpose of *explaining* why people were poor he devised the minimum subsistence 'primary poverty' budget to show that at least one-third of those visibly poor had too little money even for physical necessities. Because Rowntree's 'primary poverty' tool seemed to be an objective measure, unlike the visual measure of domestic squalor which was interpreted subjectively, it became very popular as a means of counting and comparing the poor in the first half of the twentieth century. Indeed, the fact that it was deliberately chosen to be too little to live on socially was overlooked and instead it became used as a measure of what was minimally adequate for participation.[32] Peter Townsend queried this;

first, he proposed research to discover the income levels at which people *in practice* actually did not achieve the recommended nutritional intakes,[33] and later he and colleagues carried out research to discover what the population itself defined as the characteristics of poverty, and the income levels at which such poor levels of living in fact occurred.[34] This involved surveying random samples of the population as a whole to discover what the majority thought were the necessities which nobody should be without, which has led it to be called the *deprivation indicator* approach, and then analysing the findings about incomes. The poverty measure which this produced is therefore derived from the survey findings and not from anyone's ideas of how much it should be.

Public opinion has also been used as the basis of measures designed by economists at the Universities of Leyden, Antwerp and elsewhere. These allow sample surveys of the population itself to report on the income levels which it felt were needed 'to make ends meet' or similar phrases suggesting minimal adequacy for participation.[35] Such reports were subject to complex statistical procedures to produce national average minimum income figures for households of varying size and composition. These reported income levels are in effect proxies for the levels of living which they could support according to the varied conditions of what is marketed and what is 'free' (such as health or education) in each country in which they have been used. The methods show how different perspectives affect what is seen as poverty. Attitudinal surveys have found poverty reported at income levels higher than those which some economists wanted to accept as 'real' poverty, which they thought should involve much greater hardship than the population itself did.[36]

The *budget* approach has been revived by Jonathan Bradshaw and colleagues in the Family Budget Unit, not as developed by Rowntree to create an impossibly low figure, but instead to use the evidence from many national surveys and databases of the British population's patterns of consumption of goods and services.[37] Also using the evidence from the deprivation indicator research findings of Gordon, Townsend *et al*,[38] they have calculated the total costs over time of what, by these current British standards, reflects a 'modest but adequate' or a 'low cost but acceptable' level of living. Each item in these measures is specified and so can be adjusted to whatever open discussion suggests is the right standard to reflect minimally decent participation in society. A variant of this approach is the *focus group* method of discovering what people report, to ask much smaller groups, representative in type but not necessarily statistically, to discuss the issues surrounding the definitions of poverty, deprivation and exclusions and to come to conclusions about what these terms and experiences mean to them, and what income levels are needed to avoid them. Such groups may represent the population as a whole, or selected sections of it, such as families with children.[39]

Here we have four kinds of objective, scientific survey-based poverty measure – one derived from social survey statistics, one based on mass public opinion and one on small group discussion, and one calculated from national surveys of levels of living and social values. But these are not the only measures of poverty being used and reported in this book. Other types of 'poverty' measure are prescriptive – that is, they state what poverty is to be taken as being, which may not be the same as what the population as a whole would say – and usually based on social or political objectives. These include the common statistics of income inequality, as used by the UK Government and in many international comparative studies,[40] which assume that household incomes at or below 60 per cent of the median represent poverty in the countries under comparison. Other comparative poverty studies are based on the number of people receiving means-tested social assistance benefits. The count of recipients is carried out on a cross-sectional basis (the total number on one day) in some countries, and on a longitudinal basis (the total during a year) in others. Since many years of research in industrial countries have found that far more people receive social assistance benefits over time than are doing so on one day, care must be taken to see whether the statistics report the number of recipients at one time or the number of different people who have been recipients, and for how long.[41]

Another kind of measure used in some countries (ten were found by research in the 1990s[42]) is the governmental minimum income standards (MIS), which are based on some kind of publicly and politically credible measure of poverty. These are used to carry out one or more of the functions of poverty measures:

- identifying individuals and groups 'in poverty' by this measure, counting them and calculating how far below the line they fall;
- acting as criteria of the adequacy of the various income maintenance measures – minimum wage rates, tax thresholds, long-term and short-term social security and social assistance benefits;
- acting as guidelines against which to calibrate the relations of the tiers of income maintenance.

A key difference between MIS and social science poverty measures is that MIS must be politically credible for use by governments for these purposes, while the findings of social science about the realities and extent of poverty may be unwelcome. The US National Academy of Sciences review of the MIS in USA in 1995 pointed out that political credibility involves public acceptability, methodological defensibility and administrative feasibility.[43] There is a contradiction between political measures – which have to be precise even if they are not reliable as reflections of poverty incomes – and research findings, which are reliable but rarely precise. Some commentators therefore do not treat these political measures as indicators of poverty in a country, but only of political reactions to it.

Finally, agencies such as the World Bank and the Organisation for Economic Co-operation and Development (OECD) use various measures for making global comparisons of what they define as poverty. Some of these are statistical and refer to the degree of inequality in countries' measurable income distributions (as described above, or the Gini co-efficient which reflects income inequalities) or the gross domestic product per head of population. Others are based on some arbitrary notion of a given cash income, such as the World Bank's one or two US dollars per day per head, or variations on this approach. Measures of this kind are not based on the realities of each country's own society and domestic economy, and pay no attention to differences between and within countries in people's need for cash among the various resources to meet human needs. International measures like these do not allow who is poor in a country to be identified reliably, nor show what should be done to relieve that poverty. The problem of who is poor, where, and which distinct elements of their deprivations need policy attention, each have to be studied with appropriate measures separately. That is too large and contentious a subject to touch on here.

CONCLUSIONS: WHAT ANTI-POVERTY POLICY NEEDS

This chapter has touched on some of the difficulties about understanding the many facts about poverty reported in the chapters which follow. It is easy to get lost in the thicket of what all these definitions and measures refer to, but it is important always to question the source of the standards being used, society's own or some elite within it, and for what purpose they are being used. Since many more people experience poverty at some point in their lives than are poor at one time, choosing the minimum standards which the whole population thinks are right can be justified because it represents people who have been or may become poor. This is distinct from the often argued case that people currently in poverty should have more voice than policy makers generally give them, since in a democratic society the minimum acceptable standards of resources and treatment should be those which people not in poverty would find acceptable if they were to experience them.

What deprived and excluded people need is enough of the necessary resources (whether tangible and intangible, personal and collective) to allow them to take part in society to the extent that – according to its standards – they are no longer deprived or excluded. Money is only one of these resources, but it is the most central in modern industrial societies and, as William Beveridge wrote, 'freedom to spend is part of essential freedom'.[44] Approaches to poverty which do not acknowledge the centrality of enough disposable income to overcome market exclusion should be treated very sceptically, since they usually reflect the unwillingness of non-poor people to pay the price of redistributing resources. So whichever idea of poverty you hold, deprived lifestyle or inadequate resources, you still have to make sure that everyone has sufficient resources to avoid poverty before you condemn the lifestyle. As Mack and Lansley noted in their research, 'the rich do not choose the lifestyles associated with the lack of necessities'.[45] Can you be confident that everyone has enough money not to be poor?

NOTES

1 See for example J Bradshaw and N Finch, 'Overlaps in Dimensions of Poverty', *Journal of Social Policy*, vol 32, no 4, 2003

2 P Spicker, 'Definitions of Poverty: eleven clusters of meaning', in D Gordon and P Spicker (eds), *The International Glossary of Poverty*, Zed Books and CROP, 1999

3 J Veit-Wilson, *Setting Adequacy Standards: how governments define minimum incomes*, The Policy Press, 1998; see also R Levitas, *The Inclusive Society?*, Macmillan, 1998, for three discourses of social exclusion

4 Drawing on Michel Foucault's work on the history of ideas of madness, criminality and sexuality

5 J Veit-Wilson, 'Horses for Discourses: poverty, purpose and closure in minimum income standards policy', in D Gordon and P Townsend (eds), *Breadline Europe: the measurement of poverty*, The Policy Press, 2000

6 D Piachaud (1981) quoted in P Townsend, *The International Analysis of Poverty*, Harvester Wheatsheaf, 1993, p119

7 See note 5, *Breadline Europe: the measurement of poverty*, p83

8 United Nations, *Report of the World Summit for Social Development, Copenhagen 6–12 March 1995, Annex II: Program of Action of the World Summit for Social Development*, Chapter II: Eradication of Poverty, United Nations, 1995, para 19

9 See note 8

10 P Townsend, D Gordon, J Bradshaw and B Gosschalk, *Absolute and Overall Poverty in Britain in 1997: what the population themselves say: Bristol Poverty Line Survey*, Report of the Second MORI Survey, Bristol Statistical Monitoring Unit, University of Bristol, 1997; see note 5, Breadline Europe: the measurement of poverty

11 See note 5, *Breadline Europe: the measurement of poverty*, p37

12 M Ravallion, *Poverty Comparison: a guide to concepts and methods*, Living Standards Measurement Study Working Paper No 88, The World Bank, 1992, p4

13 A Sen, 'Poor, Relatively Speaking', *Oxford Economic Papers*, 35, 1983

14 B S Rowntree, *Poverty: a study of town life*, Macmillan, 1901; see also J Veit-Wilson, 'Paradigms of Poverty: a rehabilitation of B S Rowntree', *Journal of Social Policy*, vol 15, no 1, 1986, pp69–99, and 'Paradigms of Poverty: a reply to Peter Townsend and Hugh McLachlan', *Journal of Social Policy*, vol 15, no 4, 1986, pp503–507

15 W G Runciman, *Relative Deprivation and Social Justice*, Routledge, 1966

16 See note 13; P Townsend, 'A Sociological Approach to the Measurement of Poverty: a rejoinder to Professor Amartya Sen', *Oxford Economic Papers*, 37, 1985, pp659–668

17 P Townsend, *Poverty in the United Kingdom*, Penguin, 1979, p31 (emphasis added)

18 P Townsend, *The International Analysis of Poverty*, Harvester Wheatsheaf, 1993, p36

19 European Economic Community, 'On Specific Community Action to Combat Poverty' (Council Decision 19 December 1984), 85/8/EEC, *Official Journal of the EEC*, 2/24, 1985, Article 1.2 (emphasis added)

20 C Whelan, quoted in N Yeates and E McLaughlin (eds), *Measuring Social Exclusion and Poverty*, NI Government Department for Social Development, 2000, p69

21 P Townsend, *The International Analysis of Poverty*, Harvester Wheatsheaf, 1993, p79

22 P Townsend, *The International Analysis of Poverty*, Harvester Wheatsheaf, 1993, p84

23 J Veit-Wilson, 'Measuring Poverty', *New Society*, vol 58, no 986, 1981, p76

24 D Piachaud (1981) quoted in P Townsend, *The International Analysis of Poverty*, Harvester Wheatsheaf, 1993, pp119–120

25 R Wilkinson, *Unhealthy Societies: the Afflictions of Inequality*, Routledge, 1996

26 S Dubnoff, 'How much income is enough? Measuring public judgements', *Public Opinion Quarterly*, vol 49, no 3, 1985, pp285–299, augmented for duration

27 J Mack and S Lansley, *Poor Britain*, Allen and Unwin, 1985, p39 (emphasis added)

28 P Townsend, *Poverty in the United Kingdom*, Penguin, 1979

29 J Mack and S Lansley, *Poor Britain*, Allen and Unwin, 1985; see also discussion by J Veit-Wilson, 'Consensual Approaches to Poverty Lines and Social Security', *Journal of Social Policy*, vol 16, no 2, 1987, pp183–211

30 P Springborg, *The Problem of Human Needs and the Critique of Civilisation*, Allen and Unwin, 1981

31 See note 5, pp142–146

32 Noted as long ago as 1946 by B Woolf, 'Poverty Lines and Standards of Living', *Proceedings of the Nutrition Society*, vol 5, nos 1 and 2, 1946, pp71–84

33 P Townsend, 'Measuring Poverty', *British Journal of Sociology*, vol 5, no 2, 1954, pp130–137. UK governments have still not published the relevant data.

34 P Townsend, *Poverty in the United Kingdom*, Penguin, 1979

35 K Van den Bosch, *Identifying the Poor: using subjective and consensual measures*, Ashgate, 2001

36 H Deleeck, K Van den Bosch and L De Lathouwer, *Poverty and the Adequacy of Social Security in the EC*, Avebury, 1992, pp37–38

37 J Bradshaw (ed), *Budget Standards for the United Kingdom*, Avebury, 1993; H Parker, *Low Cost but Acceptable: a Minimum Income Standard for the UK: families with young children*, The Policy Press, 1998; S Middleton, 'Agreeing Poverty Lines: the development of consensual budget standards methodology', in J Bradshaw and R Sainsbury (eds), *Researching Poverty*, Ashgate, 2000

38 D Gordon and C Pantazis (eds), *Breadline Britain in the 1990s*, Avebury, 1997

39 See D Gordon, A Adelman, K Ashworth, J Bradshaw, R Levitas, S Middleton, C Pantazis, D Patsios, S Payne, P Townsend and J Williams, *Poverty and Social Exclusion in Britain*, Joseph Rowntree Foundation, 2000; see note 37, 'Agreeing Poverty Lines: the development of consensual budget standards methodology'

40 For instance those of the Luxembourg Income Study

41 L Leisering and S Leibfried, *Time and Poverty in Western Welfare States*, Cambridge University Press, 1999

42 See note 3, *Setting Adequacy Standards*

43 C F Citro and R T Michael (eds), *Measuring Poverty: a new approach, US National Research Council Panel on Poverty and Family Assistance Report*, National Academy Press, 1995

44 William Beveridge to Seebohm Rowntree, letter dated 18 August 1942, Joseph Rowntree Foundation Library Archives SR/B6

45 See note 29, *Poor Britain*, p96

2 Poverty: the facts

*How we think and speak about poverty and what we do (or don't do)
about it emerges as much from a mix of ideology and politics as from the
structure of the problem itself.*

(M B Katz, *The Undeserving Poor:
from the war on poverty to the war on welfare*)[1]

INTRODUCTION

At the end of the twentieth century, the British government began for
the first time in many years to admit the existence of poverty and to
sanction the use of official measures to tackle it, attaching these to
public targets for the elimination of child poverty. However, despite the
political recognition of poverty as a significant and enduring social
problem there is still no one, official poverty line – no government-
sanctioned marker as there is in, for example, the United States. Instead,
a combination of indicators of poverty has been adopted – these are
examined in more detail on p66. To estimate the extent of poverty,
though, some form of poverty line needs to be established that
differentiates the poor from the non-poor. This chapter will look first at
a possible income poverty line and then at a broader measure of
poverty and social exclusion.

The first poverty line is based on the *Households Below Average Income*
(HBAI) statistics. The HBAI presents data on a number of income
thresholds. The 60 per cent of median income after housing costs,
adjusted for family size, is a measurement tool used as a proxy for

income (and other forms) of poverty, and is referred to here as **income poverty**. It is an explicitly 'relative' measure, which looks at how people at the bottom of the income distribution have fared in relation to the median. This measure is the 'headline' indicator of income poverty used by the current British Government and also as an income poverty threshold within the European Union to gauge those 'at risk' of poverty.

A second poverty line, based on the *Poverty and Social Exclusion in Britain* (PSE) survey, is not an income poverty line but adds an independent measure of deprivation showing items people lack or cannot afford despite the fact that they are considered to be necessities by the majority.

Each approach has its strengths and weaknesses, and by examining each side by side a more comprehensive picture of poverty is presented.

KEY RESULTS

Despite their different approaches, the figures reveal that:

- In 2001/02, 12.5 million people in Great Britain (22 per cent of the population) were living in households with below 60 per cent of median income after housing costs.[2] In 1979, 7.1 million (13 per cent of the population) were living in households below 60 per cent of median income after housing costs.[3]
- At the end of 1999, 14.5 million people in Great Britain (26 per cent) were living in poverty according to the PSE survey (defined as lacking two or more socially perceived necessities). A comparison with earlier *Breadline Britain* surveys shows that in 1983, 14 per cent of households lacked three or more socially perceived necessities, rising by 1990 to 21 per cent and by 1999 to over 24 per cent – roughly one in four households.[4]

So, whatever generally accepted method you use to measure it, poverty has grown significantly over recent decades and, even with a slight decline in the latest figures, nearly a quarter of the British population were living in poverty in 2001/02.

CONTEXT

The HBAI figures cover the period 1979 to 2001/02. During this time there have been major economic and social changes that have shaped poverty trends. As a result of such changes poverty levels rose in the 1980s, fell, and then rose again in the 1990s. Between 1979 and 2001/02, such changes included those in the following lists.[5]

ECONOMIC

- There was a rise in the Gross Domestic Product (GDP); real household disposable income per head (ie, adjusted for inflation) increased one and a quarter times between 1971 and 2001,[6] although the rise was not consistent over this period and real GDP fell by 3 per cent between 1979 and 1981 and by more than 1 per cent between 1990 and 1992 because of recession.
- There were very substantial rises in average (mean) incomes – a rise of around 80 per cent in real personal disposable income between 1979 and 1999/2000.[7]
- There was a rise in average earnings, although the earnings of the rich and poor became more dispersed; by 2002 pay rises for the top earners had pulled the average wage upwards, with the result that nearly two-thirds of the workforce currently have weekly earnings below the average.[8]
- There were bonuses for the average earner and windfalls for the rich through reductions in income tax. However, national insurance contributions and indirect taxes were increased.

EMPLOYMENT AND UNEMPLOYMENT

- There was an increase in employment in service industries and a decline in manufacturing jobs.
- There was a change in employment patterns, with the growth of part-time, temporary, flexible and self-employed work.
- A downward trend in male employment rates was apparent, and slower recovery after the two recessions, whereas female employment rates rose and recovered more quickly. However, in the three months to June 2003 the employment rate for people of working age, at 74.7 per cent, was at a 13-year high.[9]

- There was a rise in the proportion of households with no one in paid work from below 10 per cent in the mid-1970s to 17.5 per cent in 1998. The fastest rises took place in the mid-1970s and early 1980s. The May 2003 figures show a fall to 15.9 per cent – representing over three million households without paid work.[10]
- A very sharp rise took place in the number of people unemployed and seeking paid work, from just over one million in 1979 to more than three million in 1986. Levels fell in the late 1980s to peak again at just under three million in 1993. In 2001 the number of people unemployed and claiming benefits fell below one million for the first time in over 20 years. In July 2003 the claimant count was 939,200.[11]
- More than three million people were unemployed according to the International Labour Organization (ILO) definition in the 1980s and again in 1993. In June 2003, 1.46 million people were unemployed by this definition.[12]
- Between 1979 and 2002 the numbers of people on incapacity benefits more than trebled to 2.7 million. That is greater than the combined total of lone parents and unemployed people on benefit[13] and may suggest a significant amount of hidden unemployment.

BENEFIT CHANGES

- The weakening of some contributory parts of the social security system, such as sickness, incapacity and unemployment benefits, left many more people to fall back on means-tested benefits.
- There were increases in the proportion of the population receiving means-tested benefits, from 17 per cent in 1979 to 25 per cent in 1999.
- Since 1997 benefit expenditure has undergone significant changes. Between 1996/97–2001/02 expenditure on disability benefits has risen in real terms[14] by 23.8 per cent and on pensions by 15.1 per cent but the cost of unemployment-related benefits has fallen in real terms by 55.1 per cent over this period.[15]

SOCIAL CHANGES

- There were increases in the number of single adult households below pension age without children, pensioners and lone-parent families – all these groups tend to have lower than average incomes.

- There were decreases in the number of couples with children and of children in general.

The persistence of high unemployment, coupled with increased average incomes for most of these two decades, have forged a much wider gap between the people who were dependent solely on benefits (which generally rise by the level of inflation only) or reliant on low wages, and those on average earnings and above.

WHAT THE FIGURES MISS OUT

The HBAI figures up to 1994/95 are derived from the *Family Expenditure Survey* (FES) and from 1994/95 onwards from the larger *Family Resources Survey* (FRS), an annual government survey of around 24,000 private households in Great Britain. Analysis of incomes within HBAI is also supplemented by the use of longitudinal data from the *British Household Panel Survey* (BHPS). Overlapping figures are available for the years 1994/95 to 1996/97. Both surveys only cover Great Britain (not Northern Ireland) although data for Northern Ireland will be included in the FRS from 2002/03. The FRS and the BHPS include only private households and therefore do not collect information on:

- people living in residential institutions – eg, hospitals, nursing homes, barracks, student accommodation, residential homes and prisons;
- homeless people or those in bed and breakfast accommodation.

The exclusion of homeless people and people living in institutions means that all the figures presented below are likely to be an underestimate. This is because homeless people and people living in institutions often have very little money.

The recognised assumption in HBAI that household incomes are shared equally, to the benefit of all members, may also give rise to an additional underestimate of people living in poverty. There is a significant body of research to suggest that resource-sharing within households is uneven and consequently 'hidden poverty' may exist for individual members, whose combined figure for household income does not indicate poverty[16] – see Chapter 6.

HOUSEHOLDS BELOW AVERAGE INCOME STATISTICS

WHAT ARE THE HOUSEHOLDS BELOW AVERAGE INCOME STATISTICS?

Households Below Average Income (HBAI) was published for the first time in 1988. It is now the major source of official information about people living on a low income. The latest edition, *Households Below Average Income 1994/5–2001/02*, was issued in March 2003. For comparisons dating back to 1979, the earlier *Households Below Average Income, a statistical analysis, 1979–1996/97* is used.[17] HBAI replaced the previous Low Income Families (LIF) statistics – see p56. It examines the living standards of people in the lower half of the income distribution. The series shows:

- the number of individuals in households[18] with incomes below various thresholds of the average (mean), from 40 per cent up to the average (mean) household income;
- the number of individuals in households with incomes below various thresholds of the median, from 40 per cent up to the median household income;
- the number of individuals living in households in the bottom 10 per cent, 20 per cent, 30 per cent, 40 per cent and 50 per cent of the income distribution (these are known as decile groups), and the rises in real income for each of these groups;
- the number of individuals ranked into five equal-sized groups (or quintiles) where the lowest quintile is the bottom 20 per cent of the income distribution; *and*
- the number of dependent children below various thresholds and within certain income distributions.

WHAT IS THE POVERTY LINE IN THE HOUSEHOLDS BELOW AVERAGE INCOME STATISTICS?

HBAI does not contain an obvious poverty line – it provides data on both the average (mean) and median (or mid-point) income thresholds. The income poverty line adopted here is 60 per cent of median disposable income,[19] a definition used by the British government to measure its own performance when looking at low-income households. Below 50 per cent of average (mean) income was formerly favoured as the income poverty threshold but has now been replaced by the 60 per cent of median income measure.[20] It is argued that, in times of rising prosperity, the average (mean) can be inflated and affected by the incomes of small numbers of rich people at the top of the income distribution. Comparing people at the bottom to the median of the income scale is less vulnerable to this effect (although results would be skewed if a large proportion of the population were predominantly either rich or poor). The common usage of below 60 per cent of median income as an income poverty threshold also allows for easier comparisons across European countries. Paul Spicker offers a clear explanation of the median measure:

> The threshold of poverty has been taken as 60 per cent of the median income. The median income is technically an 'average', but it is calculated differently from the mean, which most people understand by the term 'average'. The median is the midpoint average: the level of income at which half the population have more, and half the population have less.[21]

HBAI presents figures both before and after housing costs. There are arguments for using both measures.[22] In most cases the figures presented here show numbers and income *after housing costs* for the following reasons. First, the figures are more comparable with income support, which does not include an allowance for rented housing (although it does contain an element for some owner occupation housing costs). Second, housing expenditure is different from other kinds of expenditure, varying widely between geographical areas and different stages of life. Third, it is also a fixed cost for many families, particularly those on low incomes, who have little choice about the amount they spend on their housing and therefore about the money they have left, for example, to meet their children's needs.

Table 2.1 shows the income poverty line, defined as 60 per cent of median income after housing costs. In 2001/02 (the date of the latest set of figures) a two-parent family with two children aged five and eleven were living in poverty if they had an income (after paying for their housing costs) of less than £242 a week.

TABLE 2.1: **The income poverty line in 2001/02: defined as 60 per cent median income (after housing costs, including the self-employed),**[23] **£ per week**

	2001/02 £
Single person	91
Lone parent with child aged 3	120
Lone parent with two children (aged 3 and 8)	158
Lone parent with two children (aged 5 and 11)	168
Couple	165
Couple with one child aged 3	195
Couple with two children (aged 3 and 8)	233
Couple with two children (aged 5 and 11)	242
Couple with three children (aged 3, 8 and 11)	282

Source: Derived from Department for Work and Pensions, *Households Below Average Income 1994-5–2001/02*, Corporate Document Services, 2003

WHAT DO THE HOUSEHOLDS BELOW AVERAGE INCOME FIGURES SHOW?

HBAI presents the official figures on low income. HBAI shows that in the UK in 2001/02 12.5 million people were living in income poverty (below 60 per cent of median income after housing costs) – 22 per cent of the population. This is nearly twice the number in 1979 – 7.1 million, or 13 per cent of the population.[24]

WHO IS IN POVERTY?

The figure of 12.5 million hides within it important patterns. We can look at the composition of the poor – ie, which groups make up the bulk of those in poverty; as well as an assessment of those at risk of poverty – ie, which groups are most likely to be poor. These two things are different – for example, lone-parent families make up only a small proportion of the total number of people in poverty as they are a small group, but they have a high risk of poverty.

Figure 2.1 illustrates how income poverty is distributed among different groups, showing the composition of people in poverty, by

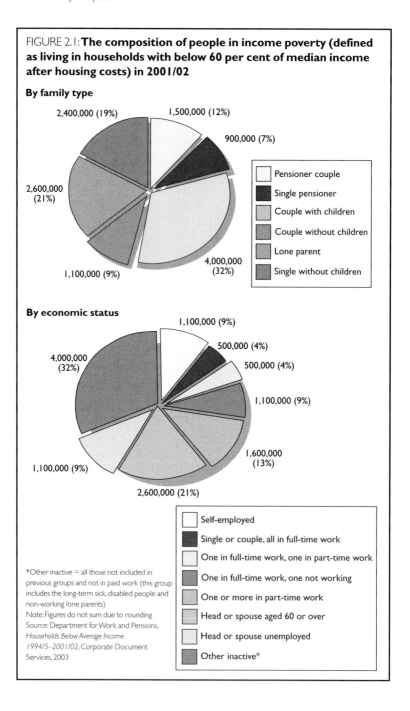

FIGURE 2.1: **The composition of people in income poverty (defined as living in households with below 60 per cent of median income after housing costs) in 2001/02**

By family type

2,400,000 (19%)

1,500,000 (12%)

900,000 (7%)

2,600,000 (21%)

1,100,000 (9%)

4,000,000 (32%)

Pensioner couple

Single pensioner

Couple with children

Couple without children

Lone parent

Single without children

By economic status

1,100,000 (9%)

500,000 (4%)

500,000 (4%)

4,000,000 (32%)

1,100,000 (9%)

1,100,000 (9%)

2,600,000 (21%)

1,600,000 (13%)

Self-employed

Single or couple, all in full-time work

One in full-time work, one in part-time work

One in full-time work, one not working

One or more in part-time work

Head or spouse aged 60 or over

Head or spouse unemployed

Other inactive*

*Other inactive = all those not included in previous groups and not in paid work (this group includes the long-term sick, disabled people and non-working lone parents)

Note: Figures do not sum due to rounding

Source: Department for Work and Pensions, *Households Below Average Income 1994/5–2001/02*, Corporate Document Services, 2003

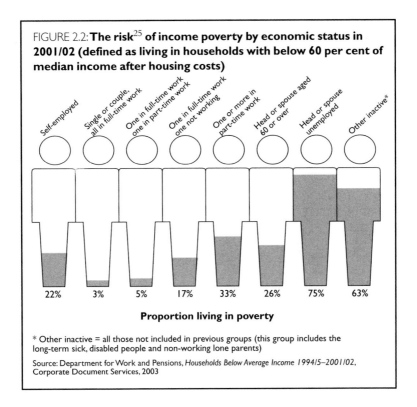

FIGURE 2.2: **The risk[25] of income poverty by economic status in 2001/02 (defined as living in households with below 60 per cent of median income after housing costs)**

Proportion living in poverty

* Other inactive = all those not included in previous groups (this group includes the long-term sick, disabled people and non-working lone parents)

Source: Department for Work and Pensions, *Households Below Average Income 1994/5–2001/02,* Corporate Document Services, 2003

economic status and family status. A family here is taken to be a single adult or couple together with any dependent children.

Looking at economic status first, absence of full-time employment is clearly linked with low income. People in families where one or more members are in part-time work constitute 13 per cent of those living in income poverty. Households with only one member working full time and one not at all make up 9 per cent of those in income poverty, the same percentage as unemployed households. Couples where both partners are working full time make up only 4 per cent of those in income poverty, illustrating the growing importance of a dual income to protect families against poverty.

Turning to family status, couples with children account for the largest group in income poverty - 32 per cent. The next largest group is lone parents who make up 21 per cent. Poverty among lone-parent families has increased dramatically in recent years. A large proportion (45 per cent) of all poor children now live with a lone parent and

FIGURE 2.3: **The risk of income poverty by family status in 2001/02 (defined as living in households with below 60 per cent of median income after housing costs)**

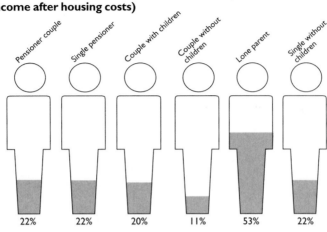

Proportion living in poverty

Source: Department for Work and Pensions, *Households Below Average Income 1994/5–2001/02*, Corporate Document Services, 2003

FIGURE 2.4: **The risk of income poverty for men, women and children in 2001/02 (defined as living in households with below 60 per cent of median income after housing costs)**

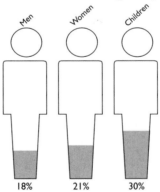

Proportion living in poverty

Source: Department for Work and Pensions, *Households Below Average Income 1994/5–2001/02*, Corporate Document Services, 2003

43 per cent of all poor children live with a lone parent who is not in full-time paid work.[26]

The risk of income poverty for different groups is illustrated clearly in Figures 2.2 and 2.3. The group with the highest risk (by economic status) is the unemployed – three quarters are in income poverty. A significant proportion (63 per cent) of the 'other inactive' group, which includes the long-term sick, disabled people and lone parents not in paid work (but not classified as unemployed) are at risk of income poverty. People in families where there is only part-time work also carry a high risk of income poverty – more than one in three.[27]

Looking at risk by family status shows that lone-parent families are the group most vulnerable to income poverty (53 per cent), followed by pensioners and single people without children. The risk of income poverty for single pensioners has reduced fairly dramatically in recent years, from 33 per cent in 1999/2000 to 22 per cent in 2001/02, currently the same risk as pensioners living in a couple. However, single female pensioners have a much higher risk of income poverty (24 per cent) than single male pensioners (18 per cent).[28] Figure 2.4 shows the risk of income poverty for men, women and children.

HOW MANY CHILDREN?

Children living in poverty are of primary concern within the current British Government's anti-poverty agenda. Figure 2.5 shows that children have been more vulnerable to poverty than the population as a whole throughout the period from 1979 to 2001/02.

In 2001/02, a higher proportion of children were living in income poverty than of the GB population as a whole[29] – 3.8 million children were living in poverty (defined as living in households with below 60 per cent of median income after housing costs), equating to 30 per cent of all children. This compares to 1.9 million in 1979 – 14 per cent of all children.

WHICH CHILDREN ARE IN POVERTY?

Of the 3.8 million children living in income poverty (defined as living in households with below 60 per cent of median income after housing costs) in 2001/02:

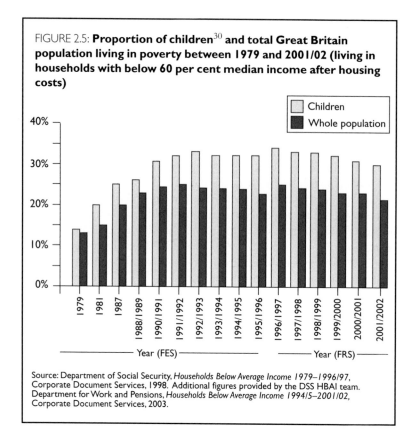

FIGURE 2.5: **Proportion of children[30] and total Great Britain population living in poverty between 1979 and 2001/02 (living in households with below 60 per cent median income after housing costs)**

Source: Department of Social Security, *Households Below Average Income 1979–1996/97*, Corporate Document Services, 1998. Additional figures provided by the DSS HBAI team. Department for Work and Pensions, *Households Below Average Income 1994/5–2001/02*, Corporate Document Services, 2003.

- 2 million were living in families where there were one or more workers – 52 per cent of all children living in poverty;
- 1.8 million were living in families where there was no full-time worker – 48 per cent of all children living in poverty;
- around one in three lived in workless lone-parent families and around one in five in workless couple families.

Children at greatest risk of income poverty were those living in families where there was no full-time worker:

- 81 per cent of children in couples with no full-time worker were living in income poverty;
- 75 per cent of children in lone-parent families with no full-time worker were living in income poverty.

The risk of income poverty is also much greater for large families – half of all children in large families (those with three or more children) were living in income poverty.[31]

WHAT HAS HAPPENED SINCE 1979?

HBAI only provides comparative data as far back as 1979, so comparisons over a longer time span cannot be made.[32] Poverty increased dramatically between 1979 and 1999, whether measured before or after housing costs. Since 2000 there has been a slight decline in the income poverty figures (see Table 2.2).

TABLE 2.2: **Numbers and proportion of individuals living in households with below 60 per cent of median income before and after housing costs**

Year	Before housing costs		After housing costs	
	Number (millions)	%	Number (millions)	%
1979	6.5	12	7.1	13
1981	6.9	13	8.1	15
1987	9.3	17	11.1	20
1988/89	10.9	19	12.6	23
1990/91	11.4	20	13.5	24
1991/92	11.7	21	13.9	25
1992/93	11.4	20	13.9	24
1993/94	10.5	18	13.5	24
1994/95	9.8	18	13.2	24
1995/96	9.4	17	13.0	23
1996/97	10.3	18	13.9	25
1997/98	10.3	18	13.5	24
1998/99	10.2	18	13.4	24
1999/2000	10.0	18	13.3	23
2000/01	9.7	17	12.9	23
2001/02	9.7	17	12.5	22

Note: Figures for individuals include children

Source: Department for Work and Pensions, *Households Below Average Income 1994/5–2001/02*, Corporate Document Services, 2003

Although presented as a continuous series, the HBAI figures suffer from a degree of discontinuity due to the change in methodology in 1994/95.[33] However, it is still possible to draw broad conclusions about changes in the poverty figures over time.

By considering the poorest 10 per cent (decile) of the population in 1979 and 2001/02 (after housing costs), one can see how the *composition* of the poorest groups has changed in Great Britain.[34] Figure 2.6 shows how:

- pensioners made up a much smaller proportion of the poorest 10 per cent in 2001/02 than in 1979 (down from 20 per cent to 6 per cent of the bottom 10 per cent for a pensioner couple and from 11 per cent to 5 per cent for single pensioners);
- couples with children also made up a smaller proportion (down from 41 per cent to 34 per cent);
- couples without children increased (up from 9 per cent to 14 per cent);
- lone parents made up a significantly larger proportion of the poorest (up from 9 per cent to 15 per cent); *and*
- the proportion of single people under pensionable age without children in the bottom 10 per cent increased by two and a half times between 1979 and 2001/02 (from 10 per cent to 25 per cent), a fact rarely commented on in the recent debate.

In relation to *economic status*, the situation of households with a head/ spouse aged over 60 has improved dramatically; comprising 33 per cent of those in the poorest 10 per cent in 1979, this figure had decreased to 14 per cent in 2001/02. However, the proportion of self-employed and households with one or more part-time workers in the poorest 10 per cent increased over this period (from 10 per cent in 1979 to 14 per cent and 13 per cent respectively by 2001/02.

GROWING DIVISIONS?

The figures also show a stark picture of poor people falling further and further behind the rest of society since 1979 (see Chapter 8). Over the last four decades median equivalent incomes have almost doubled in real terms but the incomes of the richest 10 per cent before housing costs have risen almost twice as fast (up 137 per cent) as those of the poorest tenth (up 74 per cent).[35] The greatest increase in inequality was during the Thatcher Governments (1979–1990), when the income

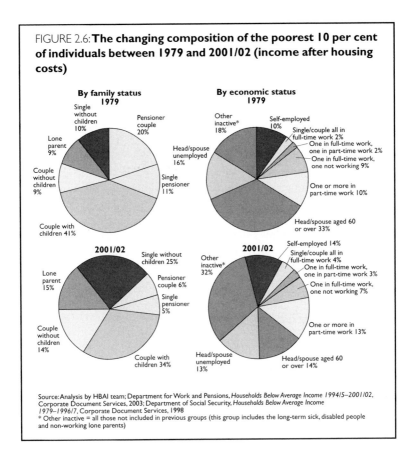

FIGURE 2.6: **The changing composition of the poorest 10 per cent of individuals between 1979 and 2001/02 (income after housing costs)**

Source: Analysis by HBAI team; Department for Work and Pensions, *Households Below Average Income 1994/5–2001/02*, Corporate Document Services, 2003; Department of Social Security, *Households Below Average Income 1979–1996/7*, Corporate Document Services, 1998
* Other inactive = all those not included in previous groups (this group includes the long-term sick, disabled people and non-working lone parents)

growth of the richest group was over eight times that of the poorest.[36] The economic downturn of the 1990s led to little income growth overall and was one reason why inequality stabilised at this time. However, using a popular measure of inequality, the Gini coefficient, it can be seen that income inequality over the two years 2001/02 has increased and is higher than at any time during the past four decades.[37]

Between 1996/97 and 2001/02 the poorest 10 per cent saw an increase in real income after housing costs of between 9 per cent and 21 per cent, while the rise for the average was 21 per cent. In terms of incomes before housing costs, the range of increase for the poorest tenth of the population was 10 per cent compared with 17 per cent for the average. The latest figures indicate income gains overall (19 per cent for the median) with strongest growth in the lowest two quintiles

(25 per cent), followed by the richest group.[38] Other figures from the Institute of Fiscal Studies also indicate a gain in income for the poorest groups, whilst the richest experience a loss of around 3 per cent of net income.[39] Such signs of improvement are to be welcomed but the disparity in income between the rich and poor remains vast.

Reviewing a slightly earlier period and comparing the poorest 10 per cent in 1979 with the poorest 10 per cent in 1995/96, a fall in real income after housing costs of 9 per cent can be seen, while the richest 10 per cent saw a real terms increase of 70 per cent over the same period. These figures include the self-employed. If the self-employed are excluded,[40] the real income of the poorest 10 per cent shows a fall of 5 per cent.[41]

Another way of examining inequality is to look at the distribution of total income. Poor people's share of total income after housing costs fell between 1979 and 1995/96. The share of the bottom 10 per cent fell from 4 per cent to 2.2 per cent, and the share of the bottom 50 per cent fell from nearly a third (32 per cent) to one-quarter (25 per cent).[42] Between 1994/95 and 2001/02 the income share of the poorest tenth of the population remained at 2 per cent, compared to the richest tenth whose share rose from 27 per cent to 29 per cent.[43] The bottom half of the population retained a quarter share of total income (25 per cent) (see Chapter 8).

A look at individual gross incomes from paid employment shows a similar picture of income inequality; between 1992 and 2002 the earnings of the top 10 per cent rose by 53.7 per cent while the lowest tenth of earners saw an increase of only 45.6 per cent.[44] In 2002, employees in the top bracket were earning £752.40 a week, more than three times that of the lowest earning bracket.[45] The problem of very low pay was addressed, to some extent, by the introduction of the statutory national minimum wage in 1999. The minimum wage has had a positive impact on the lowest 10 per cent of workers, representing a significant increase in earnings for low-paid employees, and has been particularly beneficial to women and part-time workers (groups which make up a large proportion of the very low paid).[46] However, although some effect on wage distribution is evident the minimum wage has had little impact on overall inequality.[47]

DO PEOPLE STAY POOR?

> From a dynamic perspective, one may distinguish three groups: the persistently poor, the recurrently poor, and the temporarily poor.
>
> (S P Jenkins *et al, The Dynamics of Poverty in Britain*)[48]

The length of time in poverty and the frequency of spells in poverty are key to explaining the intensity of the experience of poverty and its long-term effects. Short-term poverty occurs in households that still have resources to fall back on, whereas longer periods in poverty are characterised by debt, difficulty in replacing worn items, uncertainty, and increasing powerlessness, exclusion and disadvantage (see Chapter 4). It is therefore important to look in more detail at the frequency and persistence of poverty.

HBAI looks at what has happened to the equivalised incomes of the poorest 20 per cent (the bottom quintile). It is important to remember that the people who were in the bottom quintile in 2001/02 are not necessarily the same people who were in the bottom quintile in 1979. The figures do not mean that any one person has stayed in the bottom quintile since 1979 with the same real income.[49] But if the person who was in this situation in 1979 has moved up, then someone else has had a *fall* in real income. Recent figures show that over a 10-year period from 1991, just under half of all individuals spent at least one year in households with an equivalised income below 60 per cent of the median, 15 per cent of individuals spent at least five years, with 2 per cent spending all ten years in such households.[50] Researchers working on the *British Household Panel Survey* (BHPS) and others have begun to look at poverty over a longer period, examining the dynamics of movement in and out of poverty, in some cases over a lifetime. Once a longer interval of time is considered, the number of people touched by poverty increases significantly.[51]

Recent evidence on income dynamics shows considerable mobility from one year to the next, although the change in income is not always great. Jenkins *et al*'s analysis of the BHPS (1991–1999) found: 'Between one-third and two-fifths of those who are poor one year, are no longer poor the next'.[52] After two years, 70 per cent of those who had become poor left poverty and after three years only one-fifth remained poor. However, 12 per cent remained poor for at least five years and 8 per cent remained poor for at least seven years. The pattern that emerges is 'one of relatively short poverty spells for the majority, but relatively long spells for a significant minority'.[53] These findings have challenged policy makers to adopt a more dynamic approach to tackling frequent or chronic spells in poverty. New evidence is bringing to light the different life 'events' likely to give rise to movements in and out of poverty.[54] These can be related to income, such as gaining or losing a job, or family and demographic change such as gaining or losing a partner. For many, exit from family poverty is most likely to come about through entering paid work (62 per cent) rather than demographic changes (44 per cent). However, for lone parents, changes in household composition accounted for more exits from poverty than changes in labour market income (see Chapter 3).[55]

WHO IS AT RISK OF PERSISTENT POVERTY?

As well as looking at movements in and out of poverty it is also important to look at the experience of poverty, particularly for those people who experience persistent and/or prolonged spells in poverty. Being female, a child, a pensioner or a member of a lone-parent or workless family increases the likelihood of experiencing persistent poverty.[56] Research by Jenkins *et al* found that over one-third (35 per cent) of individuals in lone-parent families are in persistent poverty.[57] In addition, large families, those with low levels of educational attainment, people from minority ethnic groups, those living in areas of high unemployment or who are themselves unemployed, retired, disabled or on maternity leave are at greater risk of persistent or prolonged spells in poverty.[58] While these factors may increase vulnerability, the risk of persistent poverty appears to peak at either end of the life cycle, with the very young and the very old most vulnerable to long-term poverty.[59] The latest HBAI data shows that 16 per cent of children lived in poverty for at least three out of four years between 1998 and 2001.

Very young children are at particular risk of being poor for long periods, even when income is averaged over six years to take account of temporary spells of low income. A study for UNICEF has shown that around one-tenth of young children in Great Britain were poor in every year – 14 per cent of children under five and 8.2 per cent of primary aged children – compared to 6.1 per cent of adults.[60] Pre-schoolers were most at risk of repeated spells of poverty, with 20.9 per cent poor at least three times in six years. On average, 15 per cent of children were poor and 9 per cent chronically poor over the six-year period compared with rates of 12 per cent and 7 per cent for adults.[61]

A recently published study, using data from the *Poverty and Social Exclusion in Britain* (PSE) survey and the BHPS, examined both the severity and persistence of child poverty in Great Britain.[62] The study found that 8 per cent of British children were severely poor in 1999 and 13 per cent were severely poor for at least one out of the five years under analysis. Between 1991 and 1999, 9 per cent of children experienced income poverty that was both persistent and severe.[63]

Recent Government indicators acknowledge the damaging effects of prolonged or repeated poverty by setting as a target the reduction of persistent poverty in addition to reducing the extent of poverty.[64] The measure is the proportion of children and working age adults living in households with incomes below 60 per cent median income (before housing costs) in at least three out of four years.[65] On this measure, persistent child poverty fell little, from 20 per cent in 1991–1994 to 16 per cent in 1998–2001, showing no change since 1995–1998. For adults of working age, the proportion fell from 8 per cent to 7 per cent over the same period.[66]

THE POVERTY AND SOCIAL EXCLUSION IN BRITAIN SURVEY

[The PSE] measures poverty by looking at both deprivation and income level: whether people lack items that the majority of the population perceive to be necessities, and whether they have incomes too low to afford them ... its main data are derived from the investigation of socially perceived necessities.

(D Gordon *et al, Poverty and Social Exclusion in Britain*)[67]

WHAT IS THE POVERTY AND SOCIAL EXCLUSION IN BRITAIN SURVEY?

The *Poverty and Social Exclusion in Britain* (PSE) survey was based on research by a team of academics and published by the Joseph Rowntree Foundation.[68] It extends the approach used in previous *Breadline Britain* surveys and attempts to measure both the scale and severity of poverty and the relationship between poverty and social exclusion. While the *Households Below Average Income* (HBAI) measure is a convenient tool for gauging income poverty, some people below the defined poverty line may have a relatively good standard of living, while some above it may be severely deprived of essentials. The PSE survey attempts to measure this deprivation more objectively, in order to capture the wider reality of poverty. Although the PSE survey is not part of a continually updated or internationally comparable series like the HBAI, the evidence adds significantly to income measures, such as the HBAI series, because it tells us more about what poverty and social exclusion mean in people's lives.

WHAT IS THE POVERTY LINE IN THE PSE SURVEY?

The PSE survey used a consensual definition of poverty derived from public assessment of a range of items identified as 'necessary, which all adults should be able to afford and which they should not have to do without'.[69] The list of necessities came from the *Omnibus Survey*, conducted in 1999 by the Office for National Statistics (ONS), which had asked a sample of the general population which items and activities they deemed to be necessities.[70] The PSE survey also used two further data sets: the *General Household Survey* (GHS) (1998–99) which provided information on the socio-economic circumstances of respondents; and a follow-up survey, conducted with a subset of respondents from the GHS (weighted towards those with lower incomes) who were interviewed to establish how many necessities they lacked, in addition to other information on poverty and social exclusion.[71]

A poverty threshold was established by charting the incomes and living standards of the PSE sample and finding the optimum poverty threshold between those with high incomes and living standards and those with low incomes and living standards. In the PSE survey the poverty line was set at the point where an individual was unable to afford at least two socially defined necessities. The researchers further defined some people as having recently 'risen out of poverty' (eg, by getting a job) or as being 'vulnerable to poverty' (eg, having recently lost a job but still retaining certain necessary items), thus providing helpful additional evidence on the nature of chronic and persistent poverty. Once account is taken of those who are vulnerable to, or rising out of poverty, in Great Britain, classifications emerge – see Table 2.3.

There was a very close association between actually being poor and a person's own subjective assessment of the adequacy of her/his income – 85 per cent of those who said their income was a lot below what they needed to stay out of poverty were found to be poor in the PSE survey.

TABLE 2.3: **PSE poverty classifications, 1999**

	Number ('000s)	%
Poor	393	25.6
Vulnerable to poverty	158	10.3
Risen out of poverty	28	1.8
Not poor	955	62.2
Total	1,534	100.0*

*Figures do not sum due to rounding

Source: D Gordon et al, Poverty and Social Exclusion in Britain, Joseph Rowntree Foundation, 2000

The research shows:

- At the end of 1999, 14.5 million people (26 per cent) were living in poverty according to the PSE survey (defined as lacking two or more socially perceived necessities and having a low income).
- In a comparison with earlier *Breadline Britain* surveys, 14 per cent of households in 1983 lacked three or more socially perceived necessities. This rose to 21 per cent by 1990 and to over 24 per cent by 1999 – roughly one in four households.[72] (In order to make comparisons over time, the poverty line used here is households lacking three or more socially perceived necessities taken from the 1983 *Breadline Britain* survey.)

THE RISK OF POVERTY

Although the proportion of people who are defined as poor (lacking two or more socially perceived necessities and having a low income) in the PSE survey is around 26 per cent, some groups have a greater *risk* of poverty – for example, unemployed people (77 per cent), those on income support (70 per cent), lone parents (62 per cent), local authority tenants (61 per cent), sick or disabled people not in paid work (61 per cent) and housing association tenants (57 per cent). Men have a 22 per cent chance of being poor compared with 29 per cent for women. Young people and those with younger children were also more likely to be poor. Table 2.4 and Table 2.5 show the risk of poverty by employment status and household composition.

TABLE 2.4: **The risk of poverty in the PSE survey by employment status**

	Poverty rate (% in poverty)	Poverty proportion (% of all in poverty)	Number ('000s)
One worker	28	26	361
Two workers	14	19	520
Three workers	23	8	141
No workers – retired	23	21	354
No workers – sick/disabled	61	10	62
No workers – unemployed	77	10	48
No workers – other	76	8	38

Source: D Gordon et al, Poverty and Social Exclusion in Britain, Joseph Rowntree Foundation, 2000

WHAT DO THE RESULTS OF THE PSE SURVEY SHOW?

From the PSE survey it is possible to tell who is poor because they are deprived of socially perceived necessities. This information, together with income data, can be used to formulate a poverty threshold. In addition, the subjective experience of poverty is assessed.

Certain items were regarded as necessities by a high proportion of respondents. For example, 'beds and bedding for everyone', 'heating to warm living areas of the home', 'a damp-free home', 'visiting friends or family in hospital' and 'medicines prescribed by doctor' were deemed essential by over 90 per cent of people. Fewer than 10 per cent regarded a dishwasher, a mobile phone, internet access or satellite television as necessities.

Looking specifically at the proportion of those people who could not afford necessities:

- 27.7 per cent of respondents lacked at least two socially perceived necessities;
- 14.2 per cent lacked one;
- 72.3 per cent of individuals did not lack any necessities.[73]

From the results, it is possible to tell neither which combination of items were lacked by any given deprived individual nor which items are most commonly lacked by those defined as poor – it is safe, therefore, to assume that the effects of poverty are different from one

TABLE 2.5: **The risk of poverty in the PSE survey by household composition**

	Poverty rate (% in poverty)	Poverty proportion (% of all in poverty)	Number ('000s)
Single adult	32	22	274
Lone parent with 1 child	66	5	29
Lone parent with 2 children	62	3	21
Lone parent with 3+ children*	89	2	9
Couple	15	18	485
Couple with 1 child	24	7	108
Couple with 2 children	26	11	172
Couple with 3 children	39	6	57
Couple with 4+ children	29	2	21
Two or more adults no children	34	6	71
Two or more adults with children	52	4	33
Couple with one or more adults no children	21	9	159
Couple with one or more adults and 1 child	13	2	56
Couple with one or more adults and 2+ children	37	4	41

* Based on 20 cases or fewer and not reliable

Source: D Gordon *et al, Poverty and Social Exclusion in Britain,* Joseph Rowntree Foundation, 2000

individual to the next. However, a higher proportion lacked certain items than others. For example, over 10 per cent lacked 'regular savings (of £10 per month) for rainy days or retirement', 'a holiday away from home once a year (not with relatives)', 'money to keep home in a decent state of decoration', 'a small amount of money to spend on self weekly not on family', 'replace or repair broken electrical goods and replace worn out furniture'.

Poor people were also able to comment on the degree to which they felt socially excluded by answering questions about their experience of poverty, their perception of poverty in Great Britain, their sense of security in their own neighbourhood, participation in civic life and the effect of money on well-being. Eighty-six per cent of those who felt poor 'all the time' were also poor by the definition used in the survey (lacking two or more socially perceived necessities). Those feeling most dissatisfied with their neighbourhood or very unsafe in their own home tended to be poor (48 per cent and 45 per cent respectively of those who described themselves as poor). The people most likely to say that they did not participate in civic life tended to be the poorest group (43 per cent).

HOW MANY CHILDREN ARE POOR IN THE PSE IN BRITAIN SURVEY?

Twenty-seven items were thought to be necessities by over half the parents in the *Omnibus Survey*. A child was considered poor in the PSE survey if s/he lacked one or more of the items on the list. By this definition, 34 per cent of children are poor. If defined by lacking two or more items, then 18 per cent were poor. The item lacked by the highest proportion of children was 'a holiday away from home at least one week a year'.

Children were more or less deprived depending on the household they lived in. A higher proportion of children lacking socially perceived necessities were deprived of items in households with only part-time workers or no paid worker (52 per cent and 63 per cent lacking at least one item respectively). Children in lone-parent households were deprived to the same extent as 'workless' households (52 per cent). Thirty-seven per cent of children aged 2 to 4 were deprived with a significantly higher chance of lacking two or more items than other age groups. Larger families, those in local authority or other rented property and those in receipt of income support or jobseeker's allowance were also more likely to be deprived.

POVERTY AND SOCIAL EXCLUSION IN NORTHERN IRELAND

The PSE survey in 1999 only looked at the situation in Great Britain. A recent study has replicated the PSE research to examine poverty and social exclusion in Northern Ireland.[74] As with the PSE survey, a consensual measure of poverty was established using a list of the items and activities that were regarded as necessities by a representative sample of the population in Northern Ireland in 2002. A second major survey, conducted between October 2002 and January 2003, looked at the extent to which households went without these socially defined necessities, in addition to collecting data on income and aspects of social participation. A poverty threshold was then established by combining the findings on deprivation with an income measure of poverty. A household was defined as poor if they lacked at least three 'necessary' items and had an average equivalised income of £156.27 a week. The *Poverty and Social Exclusion in Northern Ireland* (PSENI) survey found that in 2002/03:

- 29.6 per cent of households in Northern Ireland were poor;
- 12.1 per cent were vulnerable to poverty;
- 2.1 per cent had 'recently risen out of poverty' (those households who lacked three or more necessities but had relatively high incomes).[75]

As with the PSE survey, the PSENI showed that some groups in Northern Ireland had much higher rates of poverty:

- 37.4 per cent of children (aged 15 or under) were living in a poor household;
- 67 per cent of lone-parent households were living in poverty;
- 67 per cent of social housing (Housing Executive) tenant households were living in poverty;
- 56 per cent of households containing one or more persons with a disability were living in poverty.

Looking at deprivation only (those households lacking three or more socially defined necessities) considerable inequalities are apparent:

- half of all households (50.7 per cent) lacked no necessities;
- one-third (30.7 per cent) lacked three or more items;
- 7 per cent of households lacked 12 or more necessities because they could not afford them.[76]

Such findings indicate significant levels of poverty and deprivation in Northern Ireland in 2002/03, 4 per cent greater than poverty levels found in the British PSE survey of 1999.

THE POVERTY LINE: A FULLER PICTURE

The PSE and PSENI surveys highlight the deprivation of families living in poverty. This, together with the HBAI thresholds, presents a more comprehensive picture of poverty. Other poverty indicators can also shed light on the type of income and expenditure that gives rise to such high levels of deprivation. This section looks first at benefit levels for out-of-work families and second at family budgets and spending as indicators of need.

CLAIMING INCOME SUPPORT

Prior to 1995, although not adopting an official poverty line, successive governments produced figures based on supplementary benefit/income support levels. These Low Income Families (LIF) figures were originally published by the Department of Social Security (for the years 1972–85), subsequently by the independent Institute for Fiscal Studies and then under the auspices of the House of Commons Social Security Committee until 1995.[77] The figures showed the numbers of people living on and below the supplementary benefit/income support level. Those people living between 100 per cent and 140 per cent of the supplementary benefit/income support level were described as living on the *margins* of poverty. This followed a similar approach to the pioneering work of Peter Townsend and others, though Townsend defined people living on, or 40 per cent above, supplementary benefit levels as in poverty, not just on the margins.[78] A 'constant' or 'fixed' threshold was also used in the LIF figures to scale down the income support threshold to its real 1979 level.

Income support replaced supplementary benefit as part of the 1988 social security changes. Like its predecessor, supplementary benefit, it is a means-tested benefit for people who are not in full-time paid work. However, it has a different structure from supplementary benefit. Instead of scale rates and extra weekly additions for certain needs such as heating and diet, income support consists of personal allowances and premiums for certain groups such as families with children, pensioners, lone parents, disabled people and carers. This change in the social security system created some difficulties in looking at these figures over time – income support statistics are unable to reflect the detrimental effect of these changes on some groups.

The LIF figures were used until 1995 by CPAG and others as a proxy for the poverty line and all those living on and below supplementary benefit/income support levels were defined as living in poverty. This allowed for an assessment of how many people were living on or below what the state deemed a minimum level of income for people not in full-time paid work. Income support (and supplementary benefit before it)

TABLE 2.6: **Numbers of people dependent on supplementary benefit, income support and income-based jobseeker's allowance, children, adults and all individuals, 1979–2003***

Year	Number of children ('000's)	Number of adults ('000s)	Number of individuals ('000s)
1979	955	3,416	4,370
1981	1,550	4,571	6,122
1983	1,868	5,370	7,238
1985	2,033	5,696	7,729
1987	2,236	5,969	8,205
1988**	2,196	5,193	7,388
1989	2,139	4,885	7,021
1990	2,151	4,871	7,022
1991	2,497	5,250	7,747
1992	2,874	5,979	8,853
1993	3,163	6,659	9,822
1994	3,185	6,667	9,852
1995	3,158	6,616	9,774
1996	3,123	6,465	9,587
1997***	2,919	6,005	8,924
1998	2,727	5,629	8,356
1999	2,660	5,482	8,141
2000	2,577	5,326	7,904
2001	2,530	5,358	7,824
2002	2,438	5,337	7,717
2003	2,394	5,357	7,770

Figures for all individuals may not sum due to rounding

* All estimates relate to a point in time. In 1979 the month was November, for 1981 and 1983 the month was December, for 1987–2003 it was May.

** Income support replaced supplementary benefit in 1988

*** Income support for the unemployed was replaced by jobseeker's allowance in October 1996

Source: Most figures supplied by the Department for Work and Pensions, Analytical Services Division, rounded to the nearest thousand; Department for Work and Pensions, *Income Support Quarterly Statistical Enquiry* and *Job Seeker's Allowance Quarterly Statistical Enquiry*, August, 2003

acts as a 'safety net'; but benefit rates usually rise year on year by inflation only and thus do not completely reflect rising living standards. Also, if over time this minimum standard increases, the number of families deemed to be living on minimum income will also rise. Thus, raising benefit rates increases the number of people deemed to be poor. For this reason these figures are no longer produced or used as the basis for poverty estimates. Here benefit statistics are used simply to add another dimension to the picture of poverty detailed in the HBAI and PSE survey evidence above.

WHAT DO THE INCOME SUPPORT/JOBSEEKER'S ALLOWANCE FIGURES SHOW?

Today, 7.8 million people live on income support/income-based jobseeker's allowance (see Table 2.6). Income-based jobseeker's allowance replaced income support for unemployed claimants in October 1996. The proportion of the population relying on supplementary benefit/ income support/jobseeker's allowance has risen from 8 per cent in 1979 to a peak in 1993 of 15 per cent. In 2003, the proportion living on income support/jobseeker's allowance is 13.9 per cent. As well as telling us the number and proportion of people living on the state minimum, the figures show that reliance on income support increased for certain groups and family types – most notably children in general and lone-parent families. Both the number and proportion of children in families on income support has been falling since a peak year in 1993/94. For lone parents too, after a peak year in 1995, the number and proportion on income support have been falling.

The figures in Table 2.7 show that for most people, benefit levels have risen substantially over the past five years. But one group, lone parents, saw a real-terms cut in income support in 1998 through the abolition of the lone-parent rate of the family premium. Benefit increases for children in subsequent years have largely compensated for this, although the premium has not been restored.

HOW MANY CHILDREN?

Around 2.2 million children under 16 rely on income support today. In 1979, only 7.3 per cent of children in Great Britain lived on income support (then supplementary benefit) but this proportion rose

TABLE 2.7: Income support levels (after housing costs)

Family type	Income support rates (£ per week)*						
	Apr '97–Mar '98	Apr '98–Mar '99	Apr '99–Mar 2000	Apr 2000–Mar '01	Apr '01–Mar '02	Apr '02–Mar '03	Apr '03–Mar '04
Non-pensioners							
Single person aged 18–24	38.90	39.85	40.70	41.35	42.00	42.70	43.25
Aged 25+	49.15	50.35	51.40	52.20	53.05	53.95	54.65
Lone parent with one child (aged under 11)*	81.80 From Nov '98: 81.20	85.50 From Oct '99: 90.20	93.05 From Oct 2000: 97.40	99.00 From Oct '01: 100.00	103.35 From Oct '02: 106.85	109.05	
Couple**	77.15	79.00	80.65	81.95	83.25	84.65	85.75
Couple with two children (aged under 11)	121.75 From Nov '98: 129.65	124.65 From Oct '99: 144.35	134.95 From Oct 2000: 158.10	149.25 From Oct '01: 162.65	160.65 From Oct '02: 173.40	166.40	178.50
Pensioners (aged 60–74)*							
Single person	68.80	70.45	75.00	78.45	92.15	98.15	102.10
Couple	106.80	109.35	116.60	121.95	140.55	149.80	155.80

Notes

These figures were the levels of income support paid at the time and are cash figures not adjusted for inflation

* Lone parent is aged 18 or over and is a new claimant. The enhanced lone-parent rate of family premium was abolished for new claimants in April 1998 – these figures are based on the new claimant rate.

** At least one member of the couple is aged 18 or over. If one member is aged 16–17 her/his personal allowance is lower. Single 16–17-year-olds and lone parents aged 16–17 also receive a lower allowance than those aged 18 or over.

*** Pension rates are for the pension credit, which replaced the minimum income guarantee in October 2003

Source: National Welfare Benefits Handbook, 1997/1998, 1998/1999, Welfare Benefits Handbook, 1999/2000, 2000/2001, 2001/2002, 2002/2003 and Welfare Benefits and Tax Credits Handbook 2003/2004, CPAG

to 25.7 per cent by 1993. In 2002, the figure stood at 17.2 per cent – a fall of about one-third in nine years compared with a two and a half-fold increase in the 14 years from 1979. The fact that this fall has been less steep than the rapid rise in the 1980s reflects a rise in the number and proportion of workless households amongst other factors (see Chapter 3).

LIVING BELOW INCOME SUPPORT LEVELS

Entitlement to benefits does not always guarantee a minimum standard of income and many people live below these levels. One of the principal reasons why people are living below the income support level is that they are not taking up the means-tested benefits to which they are entitled. Table 2.8 shows the latest take-up figures for the main means-tested benefits, produced by the Department for Work and Pensions; it reveals that between £2 billion and £4 billion of means-tested benefits went unclaimed in 2000/01.[79] Pensioners in particular miss out on their full entitlements; although 2 million pensioners were

TABLE 2.8: **Estimates of take-up of means-tested benefits by caseload and expenditure**[80] **in 1999/2000**

	% take-up by caseload (range)	% take-up by expenditure (range)	Total unclaimed (millions)* (range)
Income support	86–95	91–97	240–860
Housing benefit	87–94	91–96	360–960
Council tax benefit	70–76	73–80	590–860
Jobseeker's allowance (income-based)	62–71	69–78	650–1,040
Minimum income guarantee	68–76	78–86	470–820
Working families' tax credit (all families with children)	62–65	73–78	data not available

* Rounded to the nearest ten million

Source: Department for Work and Pensions, *Income-related Benefits: estimates of take-up in 2000/01*, The Stationery Office, 2003; Inland Revenue, *Working Families' Tax Credit: estimates of take-up in 2000/01*, Analysis and Research Inland Revenue, 2002

living in low-income households in 2001/02, probably between a quarter and one-third entitled to claim the minimum income guarantee failed to do so.[81]

The lack of benefit take-up highlights one of the problems inherent in targeting help on poor households. It also provides a warning against relying too heavily on assumptions about the actual income received by many families. For many it is not safe to assume that they receive all to which they are entitled.

LIVING ON THE POVERTY LINE

Comparing the poverty lines represented by both the HBAI and PSE survey, it appears that the income level represented by each measure cannot provide an adequate standard of living in Great Britain today. Some suggest that the vast numbers in poverty are due to over-generous poverty lines. The evidence suggests that the level of income measured by both poverty lines is unquestionably meagre in an affluent society such as this.

The Family Budget Unit has drawn up a 'low cost but acceptable' (LCA) budget standard for different family types, drawing on a panel of experts and consumer groups and using expenditure data.[82] The budget standard estimates the income needed by a particular family type or household to reach a benchmark living standard. This is achieved by identifying a basket of key goods and services and estimating the quality, quantity and cost of each over a given lifetime. The LCA budget standard can be seen as representing a level of income that allows people to reach only a minimum income standard or poverty threshold. No childcare costs or costs of seeking employment are included. Expenditure on rent and council tax are also excluded – on the grounds that these are paid in addition to income support. Gas central heating is assumed for the lower floor only – costs may in fact be higher in poor-standard accommodation without central heating. Travel costs include bus fares, two emergency taxi journeys a year, the purchase of second-hand bikes for each adult and a journey by coach to a holiday destination (about 40 miles away) and a theme park twice in three years. Pocket money, Christmas and birthday presents are incorporated into the leisure budget for each child.

In Table 2.9 the living standard represented by income support is compared with the LCA budget standard. It shows that in 1998, both poverty lines still fell well below this standard for families with

TABLE 2.9: **Value of the income support (IS) scales over time and comparison with the Family Budget Unit (FBU) low cost but acceptable (LCA) budget**

	Lone parent plus two children under 11			Couple plus two children under 11		
	IS per week	FBU LCA budget per week*	Difference per week between IS and LCA	IS per week	FBU LCA budget per week*	Difference per week between IS and LCA
January 1998	£98.70	£122.21	−£23.51	£121.75	£154.04	−£32.29
February 2001	£119.95	£126.37	−£6.42	£158.10	£158.16	−£0.06
April 2002	£135.70	£129.53	+£6.17	£166.40	£162.11	+£4.29

* FBU LCA budget for families with a boy aged 10 years old and a girl age 4. The budget excludes alcohol expenditure and the value of milk tokens and free school meals. The LCA calculated for 2002 was based on families living in the East End of London.

Source: Family Budget Unit website (www.york.ac.uk/res/fbu); *National Welfare Benefits Handbook 1997/1998, Welfare Benefits Handbook, 1999/2000, 2002/2003* and *Welfare Benefits and Tax Credits Handbook 2003/2004*, CPAG

children. For example, income support for a couple with two children represented 79 per cent of the LCA budget. By 2001, the shortfall had been much reduced due to increases in income support for children. By 2002 income support levels had overtaken the LCA standard for the first time. While this change is encouraging it must be remembered that the budget represents a very basic standard of living in the twenty-first century.

The Family Budget Unit also produces a 'modest but adequate' (MBA) budget. This represents a level of income that allows people to participate fully in society rather than merely exist. According to the Family Budget Unit: 'Households at MBA level can afford to live comfortably, run a car, avoid debt problems and take an annual holiday. In the Netherlands, Scandinavia and Finland, a similar standard, called reasonable, is widely used'.[83] It is set well below an affluent standard of living. Income support levels would fall well short of this standard.

EVIDENCE ON FAMILY SPENDING

Important evidence on family spending also comes from the Centre for Research in Social Policy at Loughborough University. This evidence shows that in 1997, on average, food accounted for 63 per cent of spending on children and that parents spend far more on their children than is allowed in income support allowances for children.[84] In fact, income support provided only 70 per cent of the actual spending on children, with younger children costing only slightly less than older children. Clearly, this evidence influenced government thinking on benefit levels for children, which have been significantly increased, especially so for children under 11 since 1997 (see Table 2.7).

This study also revealed the efforts made by parents to protect their children from the effects of poverty. For example, economic circumstances and family type were a poor predictor of spending on children, although the most significant chance of lower spending occurred in families with no one in paid work. Children in lone-parent families were more likely to go without regardless of whether the parent was in paid work, although lone parents and families on income support spent almost as much at Christmas as other parents. But most revealing was the evidence of the practical consequences of managing on such an inadequate income. Significantly, mothers reported going without clothes, shoes and entertainment to provide for their children. One in 20 mothers in the study went without food to meet a child's needs and lone mothers on income support were 14 times more likely to go without food than mothers in non-claimant, two-parent families.

PROGRESS SINCE 1997

> We are making progress. Not on every front, but in important ways... But there is much more to do. Our aim is and remains to abolish child poverty in a generation, so that in time everybody, no matter what their background or class, can share in the nation's rising prosperity.
>
> (Tony Blair, Prime Minister's speech on tackling poverty and social exclusion, 18 September 2002)

The historic commitment made in 1999 by the Prime Minister, to end child poverty in a generation, makes it important to assess any progress made to date. This commitment relates only to ending child poverty so in this section we concentrate solely on this aspect of the evidence. Since 1997 a number of policy changes have been made with the aim of reducing child poverty and encouraging the move from 'welfare to work'. The policies include:

- the New Deal programmes (for young people, the over-50s, lone parents and disabled people);
- working families' tax credit and disabled person's tax credit, introduced in 1999 and replaced in April 2003 by the working tax credit in combination with the child tax credit;
- increases in means-tested benefit rates for children under 11;
- increases in child benefit, an increase in income support earnings disregards, of up to £25 a week for lone parents;
- reductions in the basic rate of income tax.

Assessments made by the Treasury and research by David Piachaud and Holly Sutherland estimated that policy changes would reduce child poverty by one million by 2002.[85] However, despite contentious claims that 1.2 million children had avoided income poverty owing to government initiatives,[86] estimates of the actual change between 1996/97 and 2000/01 indicate a fall of only half a million.[87] From 1996/97 to 2000/01 there was a reduction in income poverty within the whole population for between 0.8 million and 1.1 million individuals, the biggest falls occurring among families with children. The numbers for child income poverty show a reduction of 540,000 on the before housing costs (BHC) measure and 450,000 after housing costs (AHC). Piachaud and Sutherland account for the discrepancy between the original estimate and most recent figures by pointing out that not all of the policy changes in their earlier analysis had come into effect by March 2001, as well as the fact that poverty levels are subject to economic and social changes and not just policy initiatives alone.[88] Piachaud and Sutherland suggest that changes in the employment situation, with many more adults in full-time employment and a fall in unemployment, have been central factors in poverty reduction between 1997 and 2001. The effect of tax credit and benefit changes was also identified as significant in the reduction of child poverty.[89]

While the combination of policy changes has meant that many children have moved out of income poverty it is argued that 'Few children in inactive and unemployed families have moved over the poverty line, though there is some evidence that unemployed families have moved nearer the poverty line'.[90] Other recent research, part of the ongoing *Families and Children Study* (FACS), has found general improvements for low-income families.[91] This study examined the living standards (including income, health, material well-being and hardship) of a nationally representative sample of British families in 2001 and looks at changes of living standards within cross-sections of lone-parent and low/moderate-income families since 1999. FACS has found general improvements in family incomes, material well-being and in the reduction of hardship for both working and non-working families between 1999 and 2001.[92]

Although tax credits and benefit increases for families with children appear to be moving some families out of poverty, there is a concern that others, especially recipients of income-based jobseeker's allowance and income support without children, are being left behind.[93] The annual benefit uprating in April 2003 saw a mere 70p a week increase for those on income-based jobseeker's allowance – effectively a benefit cut in real terms.[94] Claimants of incapacity benefit and income support also saw meagre benefit rises.[95]

It remains the case that income support levels remain below the Government's own 'headline' indicator of income poverty (households with below 60 per cent of the median income).[96] Table 2.10 shows that benefit rates still fall short of this income poverty level. Here, income support for a couple with two children provides around only 70 per cent of the income poverty level. The failure to keep benefit levels in line with median incomes has meant more people falling behind the rest of the population. Piachaud and Sutherland comment: 'Looking

TABLE 2.10: **Income support and income poverty levels (defined as below 60 per cent of median income after housing costs) 2001/02**

	Income support (IS)	Income poverty level (PL)	IS as % of PL
Couple with one child age 3	132.90	195.00	68.2%
Couple with two children aged 3, 8	166.40	233.00	71.4%
Couple with three children aged 3, 8 11	199.90	282.00	70.9%
Lone parent with one child aged 3	102.20	120.00	85.2%

Source: Author's calculations using income support level 2001/02 and HBAI figures for 2001/02

beyond 2000/01, the tax and benefit changes which have already been announced for 2003/04 do have a major effect – but once again most of this is needed simply to keep up with a moving target.'[97]

While there is some optimism that the Government could just succeed in reaching its first milestone of reducing child poverty by a quarter by 2004/05[98] other calculations by the Institute for Fiscal Studies (IFS), using more recent data, have cast doubt over this possibility.[99] The IFS estimates that to reach the target level, child poverty would have to fall by an average of 200,000 children each year – faster than between 1997 and 2001.[100] If the current rate of decline in child poverty (which was 100,000 children between 2000/01 and 2001/02) continues for three more years, the Government will miss its child poverty target for 2004/05. Indeed, the Government is further behind schedule now than it was based on figures from 2000/01.[101] A 13 per cent increase in the child element of the new child tax credit from April 2004 was announced by Gordon Brown in his 2003 pre-Budget statement; equivalent to an extra £3.50 a week. Although welcome, this is less than the £5 a week called for by CPAG and it remains to be seen if child poverty can be reduced under the current plans.

> 'The overall conclusion concerning poverty since 1997 is that there has been some considerable progress with regard to children, but very little progress with regard to poverty as a whole.'[102]

Raising the incomes of those in the deepest and most persistent poverty will be difficult and will require the transfer of further resources to families. There is much left to do. Even if the 10-year target of halving child poverty by 2010 is reached, levels will still be higher than in 1979.[103]

GOVERNMENT INDICATORS – OPPORTUNITY FOR ALL

In order to monitor progress towards its 20-year target, the Labour Government has published two annual reports that include a range of criteria against which progress is to be judged.[104] *Opportunity for All*, first published in 1999, established a number of indicators which monitor the impact of government policy in tackling poverty and social exclusion.[105] These indicators are arranged according to stages in the life cycle and cover children and young people, people of working age, older people and a set of communities' indicators, examining the progress between the worst performing areas and others. The most recent report is *Opportunity for All, Fifth Annual Report 2003*. A summary of the latest results are reproduced in the Appendix.

Jonathan Bradshaw argues that some of the indicators are too narrow in scope and that some are not, strictly speaking, indicators of poverty.[106] Some concentrate on inputs or causes of poverty (such as worklessness) rather than outcomes, some are based on departmental and service activities rather than outcomes (such as rates of admission to hospital or proportion of 16–18-year-olds in education). The New Policy Institute has also published three reports containing a range of similar indicators shadowing, and in some cases pre-dating, those included in *Opportunity for All*.[107] In view of the wide range of measures, there is a certain lack of clarity about what this combination of indicators actually tells us. The wide range of indicators also leaves it open for the Government to highlight the indicators that show the most favourable results. Nevertheless, an important start has been made in evaluating national progress to eliminate child poverty.

An important element of understanding poverty, and one that has previously been absent from the Government's anti-poverty strategy, is the voice of poor people and their representatives.[108] The need for the 'participation and self-expression of people suffering exclusion'[109] is now included in the European Union's National Action Plans on social exclusion and is recognised as an important part of a successful anti-poverty strategy within the UK's 2003 National Action Plan.[110] In the Government's recent consultation on measuring child poverty, adults and children with experience of poverty were included in the dialogue.[111] Whilst there is still a long way to go to achieve genuine participation, progress is being made towards including the valuable experiences of those in poverty.

OTHER WAYS OF MEASURING POVERTY

Income, the regularity and persistence of poverty as well as ownership of assets, spending and deprivation all need to be taken into account in any reliable poverty indicators. One possible way of measuring poverty would be an index based on a single number making it easier to tell, on balance, whether poverty had risen or fallen over any given period. Such a clear-cut measure might provide clarity and increase public awareness of poverty. The problem with a single composite measure is the danger of 'summarising too much and communicating little'.[112] Alternative proposals suggest a combination of measures, based on income and living standards, that could be made up of a core or headline measure – such as the HBAI figures and the method used in the PSE surveys (to provide a measure of deprivation).[113] Around this core would be supplementary detail of leading trends and indicators such as economic indicators (for example, the Retail Price Index and unemployment figures), evidence on the depth and persistence of poverty and a range of technical assumptions such as housing costs. Similarly, a 'Basic Households Costs' (BHC) approach has also been suggested.[114] This measure establishes a poverty line based on the amount of income needed for an acceptable standard of living. Again, this measure can be supplemented by measures of deprivation, referred to as BHC+.[115]

CONCLUSION

This chapter has looked at facts and figures about poverty in the UK. In the past, the task of estimating the extent of poverty was made much more difficult because governments of all political colours neither established an official poverty line nor attempted to relate rates of benefit to research into people's basic needs. There is still no one official measure or yardstick, although discussions on the measurement of child poverty may promote a clearer definition in the future.

There is no single answer to the question of how many people are poor in the UK today. Poverty is multi-faceted and multi-dimensional.[116] Here, a number of sources have been examined to estimate the extent of poverty, while drawing attention to the pitfalls of each.

The *Family Resources Survey* (FRS) now provides material about the household incomes of families with children, unemployed people, elderly people and sick/disabled people. A breakdown of some of the data by ethnic origin is also given (see Chapter 7). From 2002/03 Northern Ireland will also be included in the analysis. The DWP is committed to producing HBAI each year along with the results of its own indicators in *Opportunity for All*. It also now provides more extensive material modelling the effects of different assumptions.

Poverty grew rapidly between 1979 and 2000. Although there has been a slight fall in numbers since 2000 it remains the case that whichever poverty line is used, just under a quarter of the population were living in poverty in Great Britain in 2001/02. The risk of poverty faced by children is even greater than for society as a whole – with nearly a third of children in Great Britain living in poverty. The *Poverty and Social Exclusion in Northern Ireland* (PSENI) survey shows that the figures are even higher for this part of the UK.[117] About 7.6 million people in Great Britain were living on the 'safety net' benefit of income support/income-based jobseeker's allowance in March 2003. By the mid-1990s, the UK had child poverty rates higher than any other industrialised nation, with the exception of the USA and Russia.[118] Rates rose more dramatically here than in most other countries, rising most steeply in the early 1980s and then again in the early to mid-1990s. Clearly, there have been important changes since 1979, with a decline in the proportion of pensioners and couple families with children in the poorest 10 per cent but a rise in the proportion of single people, couples without children, and lone-parent families among this poorest group. While the average person found her/his income growing very comfortably (by 44 per cent) between 1979 and 1995/96, the poorest 10 per cent saw a fall of 9 per cent in their real income (after housing costs).[119] The latest figures show that the income share of the poorest tenth of the population remained at 2 per cent (after housing costs) between 1994/95 and 2001/02, compared to the richest tenth whose share rose from 27 per cent to 29 per cent over the same period.[120]

Since 1997, a number of policies affecting poor families have been introduced. The controversial cuts in one-parent premium initially reduced the income of some of the poorest families but subsequent increases in child benefit, higher benefits for children on income support and changes to income disregards and new tax credits have improved the situation of many low-income families. The introduction of working tax credit and child tax credit in April 2003, in addition to the pension credit in October 2003, continues to demonstrate a commitment to policies that aim to reduce poverty. Other Government policies attempt to recognise that the risk and persistence of poverty for certain groups require a more dynamic approach. Policies such as the New Deals and the National Childcare Strategy are in part a response to this. However, despite Government commitment to reducing poverty, progress has been disappointingly slow. Unless additional resources are directed at families with children it is doubtful that the target of reducing child poverty by a quarter by 2004/05 will be met.

NOTES

1 M B Katz, *The Undeserving Poor: from the war on poverty to the war on welfare*, Pantheon Books, 1989, p5

2 Department for Work and Pensions, *Households Below Average Income 1994/5–2001/02*, Corporate Document Services, 2003

3 Information provided by HBAI team at Department of Social Security; Department of Social Security, *Households Below Average Income 1979–1996/97*, Corporate Document Services, 1998

4 In order to make comparisons over time, the poverty line used here is households lacking three or more socially perceived necessities taken from the 1983 *Breadline Britain* survey. The 1999 PSE survey uses households lacking two or more items as a poverty line: D Gordon, L Adelman, K Ashworth, J Bradshaw, R Levitas, S Middleton, C Pantazis, D Patsios, S Payne, P Townsend and J Williams, *Poverty and Social Exclusion in Britain*, Joseph Rowntree Foundation, 2000.

5 Office for National Statistics, *Economic Trends Annual Supplement*, No. 26, The Stationery Office, 2000; see note 2; J Matheson and C Summerfield (eds), *Social Trends*, No. 31, Office for National Statistics, The Stationery Office, 2000

6 C Summerfield and P Babb (eds), *Social Trends*, No. 33, Office for National Statistics, The Stationery Office, 2003

7 See note 3. The mean income is the average, found by adding up all the incomes in a population and dividing the result by the number of people.

8 Editorial from *IDS Report 874*, February 2003

9 Office for National Statistics, *Labour Market: work and joblessness*, July 2003; Office for National Statistics, *Labour Market Trends*, Vol. 111, No. 9, September 2003

10 See note 9, *Labour Market Trends*; the figures are for the rate of worklessness for working-age households

11 See note 9, *Labour Market Trends*

12 See note 9, *Labour Market Trends*

13 The Work and Pensions Committee, *Employment for All – Interim Report*, Work and Pensions Committee – Fourth Report, Session 2002/03, House of Commons, April 2003

14 Real terms means the effect of inflation has been removed

15 Department for Work and Pensions, *Statistics on benefit expenditure 1991/92 –2005/06* (real terms – ie, inflation adjusted) (2003/04 prices), Welfare to Work Information Network: www.w2w.org.uk/index.asp, June 2003. Real terms have been calculated using Gross Domestic Product deflators published in the Budget 2003.

16 J Goode, C Callender and R Lister, *Purse or Wallet?: gender inequalities and income distribution within families on benefits*, Policy Studies Institute, 1998; J Pahl, *Money and Marriage*, Macmillan, 1989

17 See note 3, *Households Below Average Income 1979–1996/97*

18 The *Family Resources Survey* definition of a household is a single person or group of people living at the same address as their only or main residence, who either share one meal a day together or share the living accommodation (ie, living room) – see note 2, p227

19 In order to make comparisons between households, HBAI measures are also adjusted or 'equivalised' to take into account family size and the composition of households. (Within HBAI a household is a single person or group of people living at the same address sharing at least one meal a day. A 'benefit unit' or family refers to a single adult or couple living as married and any dependent children.) Equivalisation is based on the assumption that a higher income is needed by a large family than by a single person in order to enjoy the same standard of living. Thus, equivalence scales take a couple as the reference point with a value of one. It is a matter for debate whether the current equivalence scales (the McClement's scales) over- or under-estimate the incomes of certain groups because of the assumptions made about different people's needs.

20 In November 1998, the Statistical Program Committee of the European Union agreed that thresholds of *median* income should be used when making international comparisons of numbers of people on low incomes rather than thresholds of *mean* income

21 P Spicker, 'Child Poverty', in F Bennett, J Ginn, J Grieve Smith, H Land, R Madeley, P Spicker and A West, *Budget 2002: a catalyst response*, April 2002, p24

22 M Desai, 'Drawing the Line', in P Golding, (ed), *Excluding the Poor*, CPAG, 1986

23 Most analyses in *Households Below Average Income 1994/5–2001/02* now include the full-time self-employed. However, there are acknowledged difficulties obtaining accurate information about the incomes of this group and a significant proportion of this group report incomes that do not reflect their living standards, therefore some analyses exclude this group. See note 2, Appendix 2, p233.

24 See note 2

25 Risk 'is the chance of individuals in a group falling below a given threshold (eg, the risk of the unemployed being below the bottom decile median). It is calculated as the number in the group below the given threshold divided by the total number in the group' – see note 2, Appendix 1, p224.

26 See note 2, Table 4.4

27 See note 2

28 See note 2

29 See note 2

30 A child is an individual aged under 16, or an unmarried 16–18-year-old on a course up to and including 'A' level standard (or up to and including 'Highers' in Scotland) – see note 2

31 See note 2

32 However, the Joseph Rowntree Foundation Inquiry looked at changes over a longer period – *Inquiry into Income and Wealth*, Volumes 1 and 2, Joseph Rowntree Foundation, 1995

33 Results prior to 1996/97 derive from the smaller *Family Expenditure Survey*; since 1994/95 the *Family Resources Survey* has been used, with two over-lapping years – 1994/95–1996/97

34 See note 2, Tables D1 and D2 (AHC)

35 A Goodman and A Shephard, *Inequality and Living Standards in Great Britain: some facts*, Institute for Fiscal Studies, December 2002 (updated) p15

36 See note 35, p16

37 The increase in inequality observed since Labour came to power is statistically significant at the 10 per cent level but not at the 5 per cent level; A Shephard, *Inequality Under the Labour Government*, Briefing Note 33, Institute for Fiscal Studies, March 2003, p4

38 See note 2, Table A1; A Shephard, *Inequality Under the Labour Government*, Briefing Note 33, March 2003

39 S Bond and M Wakefield, 'The distributional effects of fiscal reforms since 1997', *IFS Green Budget 2003*, 2003

40 See note 23

41 See note 2, Table A1. The changes in real income of the bottom decile are less certain in accuracy due to sampling error and the choice of equivalence scales.

42 See note 3, *Households Below Average Income 1979–1996/97*, Table A3

43 See note 2, *Households Below Average Income 1994/5–2001/02*, Table A3 (AHC)

44 See note 8

45 See note 8

46 Low Pay Commission, *The National Minimum Wage: fourth report of the Low Pay Commission*, The Stationery Office, March 2003, pxi

47 See note 8

48 S P Jenkins, J A Rigg and F Devicienti, *The Dynamics of Poverty in Britain*, Research Report 157, Department for Work and Pensions, 2001, p7

49 A B Atkinson, *DSS Report on Households Below Average Income 1981–1987*, paper for the Social Services Select Committee, 1990

50 See note 2, p117

51 M S Hill and S P Jenkins, 'Poverty Among British Children: chronic or transitory?', in B Bradbury, S P Jenkins and J Micklewright (eds), *The Dynamics of Child Poverty in Industrialised Countries*, Cambridge University Press, 2001

52 See note 48, p36

53 See note 48, p78

54 L Leisering and S Leibfried, *Time and Poverty in Western Welfare States: United Germany in perspective*, Cambridge University Press, 1999

55 See note 48

56 See note 48

57 See note 51

58 F Devicienti, 'Poverty Persistence in Britain: a multivariate analysis using the BHPS, 1991–1997', Working Paper 2001–02, ISER, University of Essex, 2001

59 Martha S Hill and S P Jenkins 'Poverty Among British Children: chronic or transitory' in B Bradbury, S P Jenkins, J Micklewright (eds) *The Dynamics of Child Poverty in Industrial Countries*, Cambridge University Press, 2001

60 See note 59

61 A person is defined as chronically poor if 'smoothed' income falls below the poverty line. Income is smoothed by averaging income for each year over a six-year period, removing variation between each year.

62 L Adleman, S Middleton and K Ashworth, *Britain's Poorest Children: severe and persistent poverty and social exclusion*, Save the Children/CRSP, 2003

63 See note 62. Child income poverty and deprivation was measured using a combination of three definitions: the child's own deprivation, the deprivation of her/his parents, and the income poverty of their household (households with an income of below 40 per cent of median). Children were defined as being in *severe* poverty if they were poor on all three measures. Children were said to be experiencing *persistent* poverty when in poverty for three out of the five years during the study period.

64 CASE/HM Treasury, 'Lifetime Poverty Dynamics', in *Persistent Poverty and Lifetime Inequality: the evidence*, 1999; Department of Social Security, *Opportunity for All, One Year On: making a difference*, Second Annual Report 2000, Cm 4865, The Stationery Office, 2000; see note 2

65 See note 64, *Opportunity for All, One Year On: making a difference*; see note 2

66 Department for Work and Pensions, *Opportunity for All, Fifth Annual Report 2003*, The Stationery Office, September 2003

67 D Gordon, L Adelman, K Ashworth, J Bradshaw, R Levitas, S Middleton, C Pantazis, D Patsios, S Payne, P Townsend and J Williams, *Poverty and Social Exclusion in Britain*, Joseph Rowntree Foundation, 2000

68 See note 67. The study used three sets of data from surveys carried out by the Office for National Statistics (ONS).

69 See note 68

70 From a list of 54 adult items and activities, 35 were thought necessary for an acceptable standard of living in Britain in 1999 by more than 50 per cent of the population

71 See note 67

72 See note 67

73 See note 67

74 P Hillyard, G Kelly, E McLaughlin, D Patsios and M Tomlinson, *Bare Necessities: Poverty and Social Exclusion in Northern Ireland – key findings*, Democratic Dialogue Report No.16, 2003

75 See note 74

76 See note 74

77 Department of Health and Social Security, *Low Income Families 1985*, HMSO, 1988; Social Security Committee, Second Report, *Low Income Statistics: Low Income Families* (LIF), 1979–1989, HMSO, 1993; Social Security Committee, *First Report, Low Income Statistics: Low Income Families (LIF)*, 1989-1992, HMSO, 1995

78 P Townsend, *Poverty in the United Kingdom*, Penguin, 1979

79 Department for Work and Pensions, *Income-related Benefits: estimates of take-up in 2000/01*, The Stationery Office, 2003

80 Caseload take-up compares the number of benefit recipients – averaged over the year – with the number who would be receiving if everyone took up their entitlement for the full period of their entitlement. Expenditure take-up compares the total amount of benefit received, in the course of a year, with the total amount that would be received if everyone took up their entitlement for the full period of their entitlement. Department for Work and Pensions, *Income-related Benefits: estimates of take-up in 2000/01*, The Stationery Office, 2003

81 National Audit Office, *Tackling Pensioner Poverty: encouraging take-up of entitlements*, 2002

82 H Parker (ed), *Low Cost but Acceptable, A Minimum Income Standard for the UK: families with young children*, The Policy Press/Zacchaeus 2000 Trust, 1998; Family Budget Unit, Memorandum submitted to the Social Security Committee, House of Commons, Session 2000–2001, Social Security Committee: *Second Report, Integrated Child Credit*, The Stationery Office, 14 March 2001

83 See note 82, Memorandum to the Social Security Committee

84 S Middleton, K Ashworth and I Braithwaite, *Small Fortunes: spending on children, childhood poverty and parental sacrifice*, Joseph Rowntree Foundation, 1997

85 D Piachaud and H Sutherland, 'Child Poverty: aims, achievements and prospects for the future', *New Economy*, Volume 8, Issue 2, IPPR/Blackwell, 2001

86 HM Treasury, *Tackling Child Poverty: giving every child the best possible start in life*, Pre-Budget Report Document, 2001:vi. Gordon Brown, the Chancellor of the Exchequer, reiterated this claim at a press conference when he announced that without new policy initiatives child poverty would have risen to 4.7 million by 2001/02, rather than the estimate of 3.5 million, and therefore 'over a million' children were now not living in poverty (13 December 2001).

87 D Piachaud and H Sutherland, *Changing Poverty Post-1997*, CASE paper 63, STICERD, LSE, November 2002

88 See note 85

89 See note 85

90 See note 85, p13; see note 2, Table F2

91 The Families and Children Study (FACS) is an ongoing annual panel survey (following the same people plus new people added each year). It was

initiated in 1999 and is expected to run until 2004. The main aims of FACS are to analyse the effects of work-incentive measures and the effect of policy on family living standards. FACS is commissioned by the Department for Work and Pensions and sponsored by other government departments.

92 S Vegeris and J Perry, *Families and Children 2001: living standards and the children*, Research Report 190, Department for Work and Pensions, 2003. 'Hardship' is used to summarise the extent to which FACS families went without: lacking essential items, living in poor housing and not able to adequately manage their incomes (p83).

93 See note 85

94 *The Guardian*, 26 April 2003. Benefit levels are linked to inflation. Rises in April 2003 were based on inflation rates in September 2002, when the inflation rate was at a low of 1.3 per cent; but it had risen to 3.1 by April 2003.

95 See note 94

96 H Sutherland, T Sefton and D Piachaud, *Poverty in Britain: the impact of government policy since 1997*, Joseph Rowntree Foundation, 2003

97 See note 85, p27

98 See note 96

99 M Brewer, A Goodman, A Shephard, *How has child poverty changed under the Labour government? An update*, Briefing Note 32, Institute of Fiscal Studies, 2003; M Brewer, *What do the child poverty targets mean for the child tax credit? An update*, Briefing note 41, Institute for Fiscal Studies 2003

100 R Chote, C Emmerson and H Simpson, *The IFS Green Budget 2003*, Institute for Fiscal Studies, January 2003

101 See note 100, *How has child poverty changed under the Labour government? An update*, p1

102 See note 86, *Changing Poverty Post-1997*, p27

103 See note 97

104 Department of Social Security, *Opportunity for All: tackling poverty and social exclusion, First Annual Report 1999*, Cm 4445, The Stationery Office, 1999; Department of Social Security, *Opportunity for All, One Year On: making a difference, Second Annual Report 2000*, Cm 4865, The Stationery Office, 2000

105 Indicators are refined and amended each year. For example, one indicator change was to monitor the proportion of 16-year-olds achieving five GCSEs grade (A*-C) instead of the original indicator, the proportion of 16-year-olds achieving one GSCE (A*-G).

106 J Bradshaw, 'Child Poverty Under Labour', in G Fimister (ed), *An End in Sight?*, CPAG, 2001

107 C Howarth, P Kenway, G Palmer and C Street, *Monitoring Poverty and Social Exclusion: Labour's inheritance*, Joseph Rowntree Foundation, 1998; C Howarth, P Kenway, G Palmer and R Miorelli, *Monitoring Poverty and Social Exclusion 1999*, Joseph Rowntree Foundation, 1999; M Rahman,

G Palmer, P Kenway and C Howarth, *Monitoring Poverty and Social Exclusion 2000*, Joseph Rowntree Foundation, 2000

108 F Bennett and C Roche, 'Developing Indicators: The scope for participatory approaches', *New Economy*, March 2000, Volume 7, Issue 1, pp4-28, Blackwell, 2000; Report of the Commission on Poverty, Participation and Power, *Listen Hear: the right to be heard*, The Policy Press/UKCAP, 2000; see also R Lister, *Poverty*, Polity Press, 2004

109 Council of the European Union, *Fight against poverty and social exclusion: common objectives for the second round of National Action Plans*, REV 1 SOC 508, 14164/1/02, Brussels, 25 November 2002

110 Department for Work and Pensions, *United Kingdom National Action Plan on Social Inclusion 2003–05*, DWP, 2003

111 Department for Work and Pensions, *Measuring Child Poverty: preliminary conclusions*, DWP, 2003

112 J Micklewright, 'Should the UK Government measure Poverty and Social Exclusion with a Composite Index?, in DSS/CASE, *Indicators of Progress: a discussion of approaches to monitor the Government's strategy to tackle poverty and social exclusion*, CASE Report 13, 2001, p47

113 J Hills, 'Measurement of Income Poverty and Deprivation: the British approach', in DSS/CASE, *Indicators of Progress: a discussion of approaches to monitor the Government's strategy to tackle poverty and social exclusion*, CASE Report 13, 2001

114 BHC here stands for Basic Household Costs not Before Housing Costs

115 T Startup, *Poor Measures?*, Social Market Foundation, September 2002

116 For a useful discussion of this, see A Goodman, P Johnson and S Webb, *Inequality in the UK*, Oxford University Press, 1997

117 See note 74

118 B Bradbury and M Jantti, *Child Poverty across Industrialized Nations*, Innocenti Occasional Papers, Economic and Social Policy Series No. 71, UNICEF International Child Development Centre, 1999; UNICEF, *A League Table of Child Poverty in Rich Nations*, Innocenti Report Card, Issue No. 1, June 2000, UNICEF, 2000

119 See note 3, *Households Below Average Income 1979–1996/97*

120 See note 2, Table A3 (AHC)

3 Circumstances leading to poverty

Poverty and social exclusion are complex multi-dimensional problems. Childhood deprivation, lack of opportunities in education and employment, poor housing, inequalities in health and other factors act together to create a cycle of disadvantage.

(D White and J Murphy, 'Researching Poverty and Outcomes for Children')[1]

As noted in Chapter 2, people are poor not because of their characteristics (like lone parenthood) but because they lack resources, often from earnings. This chapter highlights how people can become poor because of social and economic processes, such as unemployment and changing family structures. Those who do not have access to paid employment, or who face additional costs (perhaps because of disability) can be poor. Both factors combined can make the experience of poverty particularly acute, and a poor working life can lead to further poverty in old age. Government policies can also perpetuate or contribute to poverty.[2]

Looking at working-age adults with incomes below 60 per cent of the median we can see that some groups are particularly at risk of income poverty:[3]

- head of household or spouse unemployed (70 per cent);
- people on jobseeker's allowance/income support (67 per cent and 62 per cent respectively);
- lone parents of working age (52 per cent);
- local authority tenants (47 per cent) and housing association tenants (51 per cent);

- some ethnic minority groups – Pakistani/Bangladeshi (58 per cent) and Black non-Caribbean (44 per cent);
- working age disabled (30 per cent).

LABOUR MARKET CHANGES

> Unemployment is not caused by individual lack of motivation or willingness to work but is part of a wider structural phenomenon that is closely associated with poverty, discrimination and exclusion.
>
> (European Anti-poverty Network, *Network News*, May 2003)

Changes in the labour market can influence the scale of unemployment, in turn affecting poverty. During times of economic downturn, more people are likely to be without paid work. The number of workless, working-age households (whether counted as unemployed or 'inactive', such as sick or with caring responsibilities)[4] increased from 9 per cent in 1979 to 20 per cent in 1995/96.[5] By May 2003 the proportion of workless households had reduced to 15.9 per cent, although the proportion of workless lone-parent households was much higher at 42.9 per cent.[6] High levels of unemployment were a feature of the 1980s and early 1990s with around 10.6 million people experiencing a spell of unemployment between 1991 and 1995.[7] Since 1997, however, unemployment has been falling and by spring 2003, working-age unemployment had reached levels not seen since the 1970s.[8]

People without paid work are more likely to have low incomes over long periods. During the 1990s, nearly a half of workless households[9] spent three years below the 60 per cent median, compared with around one in fourteen households in paid work.[10] The majority of people in households with an unemployed person were in the lowest fifth of the income distribution (73 per cent on the 'after housing costs' (AHC) measure) in 2001/02. In 2001/02, 61 per cent of workless households were in the bottom 20 per cent of the income distribution. Within this group, benefits and tax credits made up more than half of the total household income.[11]

MACRO RISKS OF UNEMPLOYMENT – THE ECONOMY

The UK economy experienced recessions in the early 1980s and early 1990s; this increased unemployment, especially from redundancies in industries like shipbuilding, mining and steel manufacturing. The proportion of skilled manual workers dropped from 40 per cent in 1971 to 33 per cent in 1996.[12] Collapsing demand for unskilled workers in the 1970s and 1980s accounted for 20 per cent of unemployment over that period.[13]

Longer periods of unemployment accounted for some of the growth in unemployment between the 1970s and 1990s, together with increasing numbers becoming unemployed during the recessions.[14]

Rising unemployment was accompanied by efforts to reduce the head-count of unemployed people by successive changes to the definition of the official count between 1979 and 1995.[15] The claimant count – those classed as unemployed and seeking benefit – is susceptible to changes in benefit rules and administration. The International Labour Organization (ILO) measure – those looking for paid work and available to start, irrespective of benefit status – is more relevant to a focus on worklessness and has been adopted by the Labour Government.

MICRO RISKS OF UNEMPLOYMENT – THE INDIVIDUAL

Some individual characteristics can also be associated with unemployment. Around half of unemployed people were in paid work before they became unemployed and loss of employment came about mainly because of redundancy or a temporary job ending.

Some *occupations* have a higher unemployment rate, such as plant and machine operatives and low-skilled manual work; in contrast, professional occupations have the lowest unemployment rate (see Figure 3.1). Unemployment for men in elementary occupations is almost five times higher than among professional workers.[16]

Individual factors associated with a higher risk of unemployment include lacking qualifications, being male, being single, being older, having dependent children (especially pre-school), being from some ethnic minority groups, and living in rented accommodation.[17] Skills and qualifications are perhaps among the most important factors; the unemployment rate among those with no qualifications in 2002 was 11 per cent, four times that of those with higher qualifications and twice the UK average.[18] People without qualifications were also more likely to experience more 'returns' to benefits after short periods in paid work. Other characteristics associated with unemployment include health problems or lack of access to personal transport.[19]

Where people live can also influence the likelihood of unemployment (see Chapter 9). In June 2003, the UK unemployment rate was 5 per

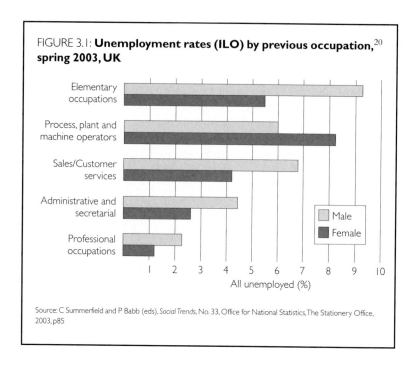

FIGURE 3.1: **Unemployment rates (ILO) by previous occupation,**[20] **spring 2003, UK**

Source: C Summerfield and P Babb (eds), *Social Trends*, No. 33, Office for National Statistics, The Stationery Office, 2003, p85

cent but country and regional rates vary considerably. In Great Britain, London has the highest rate of unemployment at 7.1 per cent, followed by the North East (6 per cent) and the West Midlands (5.6 per cent). Scotland has the highest unemployment of the small nations at 5.5 per cent.[21] Certain localities and communities suffer disproportionately from unemployment. These 'pockets of poverty'[22] exist within prosperous cities and regions – six London boroughs had unemployment levels of more than 10 per cent at the end of 2002.[23]

POLICIES TO TACKLE UNEMPLOYMENT AND WORKLESSNESS

Over the past 20 years, many policies have been intended to reduce the number of claimants, either by placing people on work schemes or by restricting eligibility.[24] The underlying premise of reform since 1997 has reflected New Labour's commitment to a policy strategy of 'work for those who can, security for those who cannot'.[25] The Government views entrance into paid work for people of working age as the best route out of poverty[26] and therefore its promotion is fundamental to current anti-poverty policies. Methods to encourage employment have used a combination of both 'carrot' and 'stick', resulting in an increase in work incentives, such as tax credits and benefit run-ons,[27] as well as mandatory elements of benefit receipt and sanctions for non-compliance.

Since 1997 a series of policies and targets to reduce workless households has been adopted. New Deal programmes have been set up for specific groups, such as young people, those over the age of 50, disabled people and the long-term unemployed. The work-focused nature of benefits has not only centred on the workless/unemployed but also on those previously seen as 'inactive'.[28] The introduction of Jobcentre Plus in 2001, which brings together employment advice and benefit support, has ensured that this 'work-first' approach is also sustained in the delivery of benefits. By 2003, 27.9 million people were in paid work in the UK, an increase of over 1.5 million since 1997 and the highest number in employment since records began.[29]

A Department for Work and Pensions (DWP) evaluation of the New Deal for Young People (NDYP) claims an improvement on youth unemployment – estimating that over the first two years of the programme 60,000 more young people found paid work than would have been the case without NDYP.[30] Similar success is also claimed for the New Deal for Lone Parents (NDLP), which has over half of programme leavers (53.8 per cent) moving into paid employment and off income support.[31]

Although the New Deals appear to be moving people into paid work, return to work jobs, especially temporary or part-time employment, are often low-paid and insecure and therefore paid work, by itself, does not protect against poverty. Research examining the transition from jobseeker's allowance into paid work found that more than half of the return to work jobs were temporary, very few were in the more prestigious sectors and in general people had not accepted the job as a first choice.[32] Also, while the New Deal programmes appear to have helped some people into paid work, several worrying trends have been noted. For example, by the end of June 2003 only around a third of programme leavers on the NDYP had moved into sustained employment, about a quarter of people who entered paid work left within three months and at least one in nine NDYP participants left the programme to move on to another benefit.[33] Similarly, 29 per cent of NDLP leavers returned to income support within 12 months and around 7 per cent of participants were on the programme for the third time.[34] A further problem with the 'work-first' principles of current policy, which prioritises rapid re-entry into employment for those who are unemployed or economically inactive, is that it offers quick-fix solutions and discourages people from engaging in longer-term learning programmes which might lead to qualifications and better employment prospects.[35]

IN-WORK POVERTY

> ... it would be wrong to assume that the absence of a job automatically
> leads to financial poverty or that having a job is a sufficient condition for
> escaping from poverty.
>
> (I Dennis and A C Guio, *Poverty and social exclusion in the EU
> after Laeken – part 2*)[36]

The structure of the labour market, and levels of pay, can affect the risk of poverty for children whose parents are in paid work, especially families with young children, large families, certain minority ethnic groups and lone-parent families.[37] By 1995/96 there were twice as many poor children in working families than in 1979,[38] as a result of greater wage inequality (see Chapter 8) and growing part-time work.[39] In 2001/02 a large proportion of poor children (52 per cent of those children in income poverty) lived in a household in which at least one member worked. Part-time incomes are often insufficient to lift a family out of poverty, with almost a third of households with one (or more) of its members working part time being in the bottom fifth of incomes.[40] A recent report by the Low Pay Commission showed that 70 per cent of low-paid jobs were part-time; of these low-paid jobs 53 per cent were undertaken by women.[41] Lone parents' employment options, and those of mothers generally, are restricted by the availability and cost of childcare (even with the childcare element available through child tax credit).[42] This may explain, to some extent, why part-time work is sought despite its low pay.

'FLEXIBLE' WORK AND LOW PAY

The number of those in part-time and temporary work has increased by over a third since 1987. In June 2003, 6 per cent of all employees were in temporary work – 1.5 million workers. A further 7.17 million people were working part time. Of this total, 5.66 million were women – around 42 per cent of all women in paid work. Male part-time workers accounted for 9 per cent of all male employees of working-age (1.53 million).[43] People entering employment after a period out of paid work tend to be more likely to get a low-paid, insecure job. 'Entry jobs' – those taken by the previously unemployed – tend to be in high turnover sectors such as retail and clerical, and in less skilled manual and non-manual occupations, often part-time or temporary.[44] In one study, three-quarters of the jobs obtained by people previously out of employment were 'flexible' jobs, resulting in little upward mobility during the course of four years.[45]

THE LOW PAY, NO PAY CYCLE

People who are low paid can also be vulnerable to unemployment, and are often lower paid if subsequently returning to paid work, hence a 'low pay, no pay' cycle.[46] A worker re-entering paid work after involuntary job loss will earn on average 9 per cent less than in her/his previous job.[47] The longer someone stays in paid work once s/he has left benefit, the better her/his chances of keeping off benefit.[48] Similarly, the more often someone claims benefit, and the longer s/he does so, the shorter the time subsequently spent in paid work.[49]

Low-paid work has lifelong consequences. Research carried out on behalf of the Equal Opportunities Commission revealed that low-paid employees are seeking to keep costs down by not paying their national insurance contributions, in effect leading to exclusion from social security benefits such as unemployment and sickness benefits as well as pensions, and so putting such workers at greater risk of poverty during their working life and in old age.[50]

WHO ARE THE LOW PAID?

Low pay has been more common for less skilled, poorly educated workers, women, part-timers, home workers and ethnic minority workers, often in the service and retail industries.[51] Women, and older and less educated workers, are more likely to remain low paid than younger workers, and the longer someone has been low paid, the more likely s/he is to remain so.

- About one-half of people who are low paid will increase their earnings over two years, but three-quarters of those who have been low paid for two years will be low paid in the third year.[52]

Young people are disproportionately affected by low wages, particularly those with limited education. Those without any educational qualifications are three times less likely to get work-related training as those with qualifications, putting their longer-term employment and income prospects in jeopardy.[53]

IN-WORK SUPPORT

The introduction of a national minimum wage in April 1999 and uprating in 2001 raised the earnings of around 1.2 million low-paid workers.[54] A further uprating in 2002 benefited fewer workers as it had fallen behind the increase in the earnings of the lowest paid over the period. The minimum wage was again increased in October 2003, with provisional rises due in 2004.[55] In-work benefits for families with children (family credit) and disabled people (disability working allowance) were replaced by tax credits (working families' tax credit and disabled person's tax credit respectively) in October 1999. By the end of February 2002, 1.3 million families were in receipt of working families' tax credit.[56]

Families receiving working families' tax credit in 2001 were on average better off by £64 a week than if they had remained on income support.[57] There is also some evidence that working families' tax credit was more beneficial, in terms of reducing hardship, than the family credit it replaced.[58] Research has found that working families' tax credit was seen as an essential component of family income; more than half of recipients said they 'couldn't manage at all' without it and a further quarter said they could only manage by making severe cutbacks.[59] The estimated take-up rate of working families' tax credit, 2000 to 2001, among lone parents was 77 per cent to 83 per cent, relatively high compared to a 49 per cent to 53 per cent take-up among couple families.[60] Lone parents tended to stay on working families' tax credit for longer than couple families, who were more likely to move out of eligibility due to increased incomes.[61] The working tax credit replaced working families' tax credit and disabled person's tax credit in April 2003 and extends in-work support by providing for some of those without children or disabilities. The working tax credit combined with the child tax credit also provides support for families with children. By July 2003, 4.3 million families had child tax credit or working tax credit awards.[62]

Other in-work benefits can be payable (such as housing benefit and council tax benefit), though gains in tax credits can sometimes be offset by losses in housing benefit. The 'poverty trap' arises where a modest increase in gross earnings rarely leads to higher net disposable income as only very low levels of earnings above income support level are permitted before entitlement to housing benefit is reduced.[63] Fear of experiencing financial difficulties due to loss of benefits may act as a disincentive to enter employment, even with tax credits.[64] A recent study of low-income families found that, for some families, entering the labour market after a period on benefits resulted in a lower standard of living than when on benefits; the high costs of childcare and the strain of paying back large pre-work debts meant the family were financially worse off in paid work, especially if their work was low paid.[65] However, other research has found that in-work support such as benefit run-ons for housing benefit and council tax benefit have an enabling effect on peoples' move into paid work,[66] although another study found awareness of such benefits to be extremely low.[67] A further issue for many families is the lack of entitlement to free school meals once the parent leaves income support or income-based jobseeker's allowance, though tax credit rates are intended to take this into account.

CHANGES IN FAMILY LIFE

Changes in family structure are associated with increased risk of poverty for some families. Divorce increased by 42 per cent between 1973 and 1997; divorced and separated people now account for over 10 per cent of the adult population.[68] Births outside marriage grew from 8 per cent in 1973 to 40 per cent by 2001.[69] Some families, such as lone parents, are particularly at risk of poverty (see Chapter 5), and poverty itself can place strains on family roles and relationships (see Chapter 4).[70] Families with children can also incur additional costs (see Chapter 5).

Labour market changes have also affected families; the female labour participation rate went from 29 per cent in 1970 to 72 per cent by 2002,[71] with more mothers returning to paid work within a year of giving birth. However, while many more women are entering paid work the employment position for female lone parents is considerably worse relative to that of mothers in couple families. The employment rate for lone parents in Great Britain was 53 per cent in 2003,[72] in contrast to over 70 per cent for mothers in couple families. When in paid work lone parents are usually in low-paid jobs with little opportunity for career progression or training.[73]

Childbirth, as well as other family changes like divorce, is associated with poverty:

- For one in three people, the birth of a child results in a drop down the income distribution by a fifth or more, and for 10 per cent to 15 per cent, it results in poverty.
- A tenth of all entries into low income for women are associated with separation or divorce, the chances of poverty being four times higher if the mother is not in paid work.[74]

Each year about one in ten individuals change family type, and about a quarter change economic status. Research examining the dynamics of poverty found changes in earnings to be the most important factor associated with movements into and out of poverty; increases in earnings were associated with 62 per cent of poverty exits and decreases in earnings were associated with 44 per cent of poverty entries. But *demographic* events (changes in household composition, such as childbirth) are also highly significant, especially in accounting for movements into low income more than movements out, compared with any one *income* event (such as a drop in wages, job loss or gain for household members), as shown in Table 3.1.[75]

TABLE 3.1: **Main events associated with moving into or out of income poverty***

Event	Into low income (%)	Out of low income (%)
Demographic event	39	19
Household head earnings change	26	33
Spouse or other earnings change	18	29
Non-labour income change	17	20

*The poverty line used was 60 per cent of median contemporary national income

Source: Adapted from S P Jenkins, J A Rigg, F Devicienti, *Dynamics of Poverty in Britain*, Department for Work and Pensions Research Report 157, 2001

LONE PARENTS

The number of lone parents tripled to 1.5 million between 1971 and 2002.[76] Such an increase in lone parenthood reflects changing family patterns; around three in five lone parents are ex-married (divorced, separated or widowed).[77] By 2002, nearly a quarter (22 per cent) of all households with dependent children were headed by a lone parent, compared with only 8 per cent in 1971.[78] At present, Great Britain has the largest lone parent population and the highest proportion of non-working lone parents than any other OECD13 country.[79]

The majority – 90.5 per cent – of lone parents are women.[80] Half of women separating from their partners experience a drop in income, whilst men are more likely to have an increased income.[81] Indeed, men's chances of leaving poverty greatly increase with separation from a partner.[82]

The fastest growing component of lone parenthood since the 1980s has been *single or never-married lone parents* – 43 per cent of lone parents in 2002 – although many in this group are in fact ex-cohabitees.[83] The increase in single and never-married lone parents has been thought to reflect disadvantages among the family of origin, such as having lived in the social rented sector, and changing employment opportunities. Family change can be analysed as an *effect* of labour market change, such as male unemployment, rather than only as a cause.[84]

Single never-married lone parents have the highest rate of non-employment of all groups. Time spent caring for children and a lack of work skills and experience affect their ability to take on paid work.[85] In spring 2003 the proportion of lone-parent households that were workless was 43 per cent.[86] Even in paid work, lone parents are likely to be in low-paid jobs or work part time and are almost always financially worse off than couple families.[87] In 2001, lone parents were three times more likely to qualify for in-work support than working couples because of their lower incomes.[88] As well as lower incomes, lone-parent families also suffer a higher level of deprivation and poorer health, and are half as likely to own their home as couple families (see Table 3.2).[89] A recent survey among lone parents found that more than half (53 per cent) said they skipped meals to save money, with 28 per cent doing so regularly.[90]

Couples at greatest risk of *marital breakdown* tended to be those who had conceived before marriage and those who were younger when they married.[91] Signs of affluence, such as marrying later and owner-occupation, were associated with marriage stability, whereas early marriage, living in rented accommodation or remaining in the parental

TABLE 3.2: **Indicators of disadvantage: a comparison between lone-parent and couple-family households**

	Couples	Lone parents
Percentage of households who:		
are home owners	78	34
have a car	93	50
have a computer	73	45
say their health is good	71	57

Source: W Sykes and A Walker, *Results from the 2000 General Household Survey*, Office for National Statistics, 2002

home were linked to breakdown.[92] Relationship breakdown seems to be more important than job loss as a route into non-working lone parenthood.[93] Changes in domestic arrangements were also more important as a route *out* of poverty for lone-parent households, compared to other poor households, than labour market changes.[94]

Lone-parent families have high entrance rates into poverty and a lower chance of exiting poverty:

> ...poor people living in lone parent households were about one-quarter less likely to leave poverty than the average poor person, and non-poor individuals from lone parent households were about three times more likely than the average non-poor person to fall into poverty.[95]

An increasing number of lone parents have relied on income support, rising from 213,000 in 1971 to 861,000 in 2002, although since 1996 the number of lone parents receiving income support has been falling. Currently, lone parents represent 22 per cent of the income support caseload and 63 per cent of those with a claim of two years or more.[96] In 2002 more than a third to two-thirds of the income of lone parents came from social security benefits, though for lone parents with just one child income from paid work was as important as benefits and tax credits.[97]

POLICIES FOR FAMILY SUPPORT

Child benefit was introduced in the late 1970s as a new means of off-setting some of the costs of a child (see Chapter 5). An additional sum for lone parents was payable with child benefit (one parent benefit), though concerns about the growing numbers of lone parents led to plans for its abolition and the corresponding means-tested premium in 1996, and this was subsequently carried out in 1998 for new lone parents. However, a real increase in child benefit in 1999 meant that the benefit was 25 per cent higher (about £3.20 in real terms) by the end of 2002 than it would otherwise have been.[98] This increase, together with a substantial rise in means-tested payments for children, has largely compensated for the reduction. These increases, together with the child tax credit and working tax credit, introduced in 2003, are the basis of the Government's 'seamless system of income related support for families with children'.[99]

SICKNESS AND DISABILITY

Sick and disabled people experience disadvantage in education, the labour market, and have a greater reliance on benefits. Although there are questions of how to define 'disability' the trends show that, for example, between 1984 and 1996, there was a doubling of households containing at least one sick or disabled person.[100] Disabled people are more likely to have no formal educational qualifications, live in social housing, be unemployed and have lower earnings than non-disabled people.[101] Sick or disabled people are at much greater risk of facing poverty and deprivation than non-disabled people.[102]

In 2002, one in five of the working-age population – 6.8 million people – were estimated to have a disability; almost three-fifths report three or more impairments.[103] The risks of becoming disabled were higher for older people, and for those on low incomes, in social rented housing and in particular areas (highest in Wales, the North West and North East). In June 2003, 2.7 million people of working age were dependent on benefits because of their sickness or disability.[104]

SICKNESS

Sickness differs from disability, though there are sometimes overlaps; disabled people are not necessarily sick, and ill-health may not lead to disability.[105] However, there is an association between poor health and poverty, explored in the next chapter. The Acheson Inquiry into inequalities in health indicated that, whilst some people in poor health may become unemployed, this does not fully explain the links between unemployment and ill-health.[106] It does, however, illustrate that ill-health can increase the risk of unemployment, and that unemployment can in turn damage health.

Labour market change may also affect illness; for instance, to be in work, men aged 20–59 had to be in better health in 1993 than 20 years earlier. In 1979, 72 per cent of men in the lowest socio-economic group were in paid work despite long-term health problems, but by 1993 only 43 per cent in the same category were employed.[107] Sickness and disability are major reasons for economic inactivity among men. In 2002, 43 per cent of 'inactive' men aged 25–34 were long-term sick or disabled. This increased to 64 per cent for men aged 35–49.[108]

DISABILITY

Disabled people are at particular risk of poverty because of lower incomes worsened by additional disability-related costs.

HIGHER COSTS

The additional costs faced by disabled people can be considered as two types:

- personal support – ie, the goods and services needed to help with tasks that non-disabled people can do by themselves, like housework and intimate tasks such as dressing and bathing; *and*
- higher spending on everyday items like heating, laundry and transport, as well as expenditure on special equipment.[109]

The 2002 Leonard Cheshire report on social exclusion and disability found that one-third of disabled people surveyed could not afford the extra heating costs arising from their disability. One in five could not afford necessary personal support when training or at their workplace.[110]

Those with the most severe impairments are more likely to have additional costs. An analysis of the extra expenditure associated with disability found:

- extra costs associated with low severity of impairment ranged from £20 to £97 per week (2001 prices);
- extra costs associated with a high level of severity ranged from £113 to £551 per week[111] (2001 prices);
- in couples where both adults are disabled, costs rise to four times the extra costs for a single disabled adult.[112]

If income is adjusted to take into account extra costs incurred because of disabilities, the poverty rate for the disabled population rises dramatically to 61 per cent.[113] The research concludes that failure to take into account the additional costs of disability 'has a substantial impact not only on the relative position of disabled and non-disabled people in the income distribution, but also on estimated poverty rates in the population as a whole'.[114] In other words, more disabled people are in poverty than official (HBAI) figures show, which in turn means that overall poverty rates (after housing costs) are also higher, by an estimated 3 percentage points.[115]

Comparing disabled and non-disabled people's perceptions of their financial situation, disabled people who were not poor were three times more likely than 'non-poor, non-disabled' people to report financial difficulty, which could mean that the extra costs reduced living standards.[116]

TABLE 3.3: **Perception of financial situation by poverty and disability**

	'Poor' disabled %	'Poor' non-disabled %	'Non-poor' disabled %	'Non-poor' non-disabled %
Very difficult	18.3	14.0	9.1	3.0
Quite difficult	24.1	20.1	13.5	6.9
Getting by	42.9	37.8	36.1	27.6
Doing all right	7.9	19.2	20.0	33.1
Comfortable	6.8	8.8	21.3	29.4

Source: H Barnes, *Working for a Living? Employment, benefits and the living standards of disabled people*, The Policy Press, 2000

Rising extra costs have partly come about because of the expanding numbers of local authorities charging for their community care services.[117] An Audit Commission survey found that most authorities charged for items like personal care and mobile meals, with increasing maximum weekly amounts. The numbers of people claiming benefits for extra disability-related costs (such as disability living allowance) have grown considerably since their introduction.

LOWER INCOMES

- Two-fifths (43 per cent) of sick and disabled people are in receipt of means-tested benefit and constitute a quarter of long-term claimants.[118]
- Between 1995 and 2002 the average weekly payment of incapacity benefit fell from £83.48 a week to £82.47 and currently amounts to less than 17 per cent of average earnings.[119]
- People receiving disability benefits tend to be just above the bottom of the income distribution. In 2001/02, 39 per cent of households with one or more disabled children and 75 per cent of households with a disabled child and adult were in the bottom two-fifths of the income distribution.[120]

However, given additional costs, incomes alone may not be a good reflection of living standards. The numbers of disabled people experiencing financial hardship may be much higher than income figures alone indicate.

Labour market changes described above, such as the increase in workless households, have had a significant impact on disabled people:

- Only 46 per cent of disabled women and 51.4 per cent of disabled men of working age are employed compared to 75.3 per cent of non-disabled women and 85.8 per cent of non-disabled men.[121]
- Unemployment rates are twice as high for disabled people overall and highest for people with mental illness (74 per cent) and learning disabilities (66 per cent).
- Over 1 million disabled people out of paid work and on benefits would like to have paid employment.[122]
- Fewer disabled people are in two-earner households.
- A third of disabled people who move into paid work have lost their job by the following year, compared with a fifth of non-disabled people.[123]

When employed, disabled people are more likely to be in manual occupations than non-disabled people and more likely to be lower paid.

POLICIES FOR SICK AND DISABLED PEOPLE

Benefits for disabled people were introduced in the 1970s for income maintenance (for inability to work, such as invalidity benefit), or as a contribution towards extra costs (such as attendance allowance). During the 1980s and 1990s, some entitlement was restricted, including earnings-related additions. In response to the tripling of invalidity benefit awards, tighter eligibility criteria and reduced payments were introduced in 1995, as well as a change of name (to incapacity benefit). However, few who were disallowed benefit returned to paid work, and a significant proportion (35 per cent) subsequently re-claimed incapacity benefit.[124] Since 1993, the number of people on incapacity benefit has continued to rise; in July 2003, 1.5 million were receiving this benefit. At the same time, the caseload of people on income support with a disability premium has also continued to grow.[125] The number of people on sickness and disability benefits has increased by 84,000 over the last three years.

On taking office in 1997, the Labour Government set up a Disability Rights Task Force to recommend action on discrimination against disabled people, and a Disability Rights Commission was established in April 2000. A New Deal for Disabled People, a personal adviser service, access to work (AtW) programme and tax credits have been developed to support disabled people's entry into paid work. As well as further limits on eligibility for incapacity benefits and a more 'active' approach to disability benefits generally, the government also introduced a disability income guarantee in 2001. This provides a guaranteed minimum income to adults with severe disabilities and to families with disabled children. Legislative change, such as disability discrimination legislation (Adjustment of Premises), due to be implemented in October 2004, is part of a longer-term programme designed to improve access and equality in the workplace for disabled employees.

Working tax credit replaced disabled person's tax credit in 2003. The guaranteed minimum income of a full-time worker receiving disabled person's tax credit rose from £172 per week in 2002/03 to an estimated £194 a week in 2003/04 after the introduction of working tax credit.[126]

PROVIDING CARE

Although saving the state an estimated £57 billion per year,[127] many people who provide unpaid care to an elderly or disabled person can themselves be vulnerable to poverty, often as a result of giving up paid work or through incurring additional expense, or both. (For caring for children, see Chapter 5.)

In 2002, an estimated 6.8 million adults in Great Britain were carers.[128] One in five (21 per cent) had been carers for at least ten years and nearly half (45 per cent) had been carers for five years or more.[129] A third of carers cared for someone within the household, and one in three spent 20 hours or more each week in caring activities.[130] The proportion spending long hours caring increased after 1993, apparently coinciding with the implementation of 'community care'.

LOW INCOMES AND HIGHER COSTS

On becoming a carer the loss of wages, the low level and restricted eligibility for social security benefits, and additional costs combine to increase the likelihood of hardship.

Research by Carers UK and CPAG found that many carers were unable to afford necessities like paying fuel bills, one in five cut back on food, and one in three were in debt.[131] The longer the time spent caring, the greater the financial difficulties encountered. One reason for carers' low incomes is that they are less likely to undertake paid work. The Family Resources Survey 2001–2002 found that 42 per cent of male carers and 25 per cent of female carers worked full time, compared with 52 per cent of all men and 29 per cent of all women in the survey.[132] For 29 per cent of carers, social security benefits were the main source of household income.[133] A Women's Unit study showed that caring may have a greater impact on men's employment, as men who were unemployed when caring began were twice as likely to remain unemployed; women seemed more likely to reduce their hours.[134] The Carers National Association survey showed that over seven in ten carers had given up paid work, and believed they were worse off since caring began.[135] A third of carers surveyed received income support, notably younger carers and those from minority ethnic groups.[136] They were also more likely to have given up paid work to care (70 per cent, compared with 55 per cent of non-recipients of income support). Both groups faced financial hardship, especially those receiving income support.

When employed, carers tend to work for fewer hours and lower pay:

- In one survey, almost three-quarters of carers had suffered an average annual loss of £5,000.[137]
- Caring can reduce wages by an estimated 12 per cent.[138]

As well as low incomes, carers often have extra outgoings; over two-thirds of carers in the above survey incurred costs because of the additional expense associated with disability, such as transport to the disabled person's home.[139] Carers also paid in terms of health costs – 39 per cent reporting that their physical or mental health had suffered as a result of caring.[140]

POLICIES FOR CARERS

Since the late 1970s, invalid care allowance has been payable to carers who care for people on certain benefits and who do not undertake any substantial paid employment. Invalid care allowance, renamed carer's allowance in April 2003, has tended to go to people on low incomes, largely because of the lower likelihood of employment.[141] In 1990, a carer's premium was added to means-tested benefits. Entitlement to benefits for caring has been tied to the disabled person's benefit, so that only those looking after someone receiving the highest rates of disability living allowance or attendance allowance were eligible for the carer's allowance. These benefits are withdrawn, as is the carer's allowance, if the person being cared for spends four weeks in hospital, effectively causing financial hardship for both parties.

The Labour Government launched a National Carers Strategy in 1998 and has subsequently extended respite care, increased the carer's premium and extended and improved the carer's allowance. The earnings limit on invalid care allowance was increased to £75 a week in 2002. Older carers (over 65) were entitled to carer's allowance (formerly invalid care allowance) from October 2002, although eligibility is restricted to carers whose pension is less than £42.45 a week (2003 prices) so this may be of little benefit to many older carers.

GROWING OLD

> Our aim is to end pensioner poverty in our country.
> (Labour party conference speech by Gordon Brown, September 2002)

In 2001 there were 9.4 million people aged 65 and over, more than double the older population in 1961; of this number, 1.1 million people were aged 85 and over.[142] Almost a quarter of all households in the UK consisted of pensioners only.[143] Life expectancy has increased and for those aged 65 is 15 years for men and nearly 20 years for women.[144] Population projections suggest that the number of people aged 65 and over will exceed those aged under 16 by 2014.[145]

INEQUALITY IN PENSIONER INCOMES

Between 1979 and 1996/97 the average net income of all pensioners grew faster than average earnings over the same period; pensioner incomes continued to increase between 1994/95 and 2001/02, by around an estimated 23 per cent.[146] Such growth reflects the increases in incomes from benefits, occupational pensions and private investments.[147] However, there is considerable inequality in pensioner incomes, with those in the top fifth of the income distribution seeing a much larger rise in their income since 1979, compared with those pensioners in the bottom fifth (see Figure 3.2 below).

- The gap between rich and poor pensioners has grown from 50 per cent of national average earnings since 1979 to 66 per cent in 2000/01.[148]
- For both pensioner couples and single pensioners, the median net income (after housing costs – AHC) of the top fifth in 2001/02 was more than three times that of the bottom fifth.
- Pensioner couples in the bottom fifth received £136 a week in 2001/02 (AHC), compared with £498 for the top fifth; among single pensioners, the bottom fifth received £71 and the top fifth £238.
- 32 per cent of pensioner units in 2001/02 received one or more income-related benefits (such as minimum income guarantee, housing benefit or council tax benefit).[149]
- In 2001–02 retired households mainly dependent on state pensions had half the gross weekly income of retired households with other forms of income.[150]

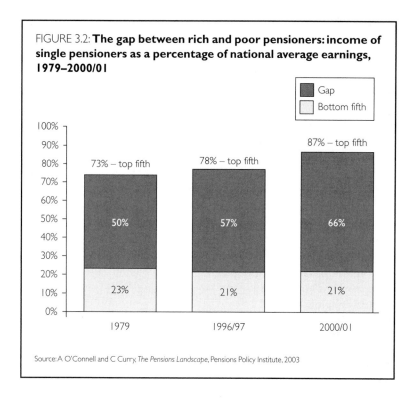

FIGURE 3.2: **The gap between rich and poor pensioners: income of single pensioners as a percentage of national average earnings, 1979–2000/01**

Source: A O'Connell and C Curry, *The Pensions Landscape*, Pensions Policy Institute, 2003

Reported income from occupational pensions rose from 40 per cent in 1979 to 57 per cent in 1996/97 – an increase of 162 per cent in real terms over this period.[151] In general, the higher someone's weekly income, the increased likelihood of belonging to a private pension scheme and vice versa.[152] In 2001, of those people earning over £600 a week, 73 per cent of men and 80 per cent of women contributed to an occupational pension scheme, compared with 20 per cent of men and 26 per cent of women earning between £100 and £200 per week.[153] In 2001/02, 43 per cent of pensioners in the bottom fifth of the income distribution received income from an occupational pension, half the proportion of pensioners in the top fifth (85 per cent).[154]

Inability to pay for pension provision can lead to a low income in old age. Over half of those in the bottom fifth of the income distribution in 2001/02 did not receive any occupational pension, representing 43 per cent of all pensioner couples and 27 per cent of all single pensioners.[155] Tax relief remains weighted in favour of the already wealthy. Of the £9 billion spent on tax relief for pensions, over half is received by the wealthiest 10 per cent of the population.[156]

PENSIONER POVERTY

Pensioners are more likely to be at risk of being persistently poor – defined as spending at least three years in the bottom three-tenths of incomes – than working age people. Between 1998 and 2001, 18 per cent of pensioners were experiencing persistent poverty, compared with around 7 per cent of the working population.[157]

The poorest pensioners now tend to be:

- older;
- women;
- carers;
- from minority ethnic groups;
- in workless households;
- persistent low earners;
- people with a long-term illness or disability.[158]

These groups are poorer as a result of being low paid during working life (and so with limited second-tier pensions) and/or because of reduced benefit entitlement. Women are particularly vulnerable to loss of entitlement since they are more likely than men to take time out of the labour market because of caring responsibilities and consequently lose out on building up a decent pension. Currently just 49 per cent of women receive the full state pension in their own right, compared with 92 per cent of men.[159]

Older pensioners have lower incomes than the more recently retired. In 2001/02 pensioner couples where the man was aged 75 or over received £275 net income per week, compared with £347 for those aged under 75.[160] Twice as many people aged over 80 were in the bottom fifth of pensioner incomes in 2000 than people in their 60s.[161] This may be due to more newly retired people having private pensions, more women in the older age groups, and the more generous indexing of pensions and earnings-related second tier pensions of the newly retired. Many ethnic minority pensioners may have arrived in the UK in the middle of their working lives and therefore be less likely to have basic entitlement, or if unemployed or low paid, may be missing out on occupational pensions (see Chapter 7).[162] The number of disabled pensioners rose by a quarter between the 1970s and 1990s,[163] having lower incomes than those without a disability, being more likely to have worked in manual trades, with few qualifications, and living in local authority accommodation.[164]

The process of becoming retired seems to be associated with subsequent low income. Retirement represents a marked change for someone formerly in full-time work, but less so for someone previously unemployed, disabled, or a carer:

- For men, being in full-time work reduces the chances of being in the poorest third on retirement.
- For women, work status is less relevant. Factors associated with a greater likelihood of being poor include living in social housing, not being in an occupational pension scheme, and retiring before state pension age.
- People with a working partner are three times less likely to be poor; those without a partner at all were the poorest.[165]

POLICIES FOR PENSIONERS

Between 1975 and 1980 significant reform of the pension scheme formally indexed the basic state pension to rises in national earning or prices, whichever was the higher. A new State Earnings-Related Pension Scheme (SERPS) was introduced which, if allowed to mature, would have been redistributive towards the low-paid and women.[166] The pension reforms following a Conservative election win in 1980, however, cut state pensions and favoured individuals' private provision. Successive governments have encouraged second-tier provision rather than increasing the basic pension.

In April 2002 the Labour Government introduced the State Second Pension to replace SERPS, designed to help low and modest earners by providing a higher pension. The State Second Pension will also provide contribution credits for some carers and people with a long-term illness or disability. Although the basic state pension has been increased each year since 2001 it is still only worth 15 per cent of average male earnings.[167] The Government published its Green Paper on the reform of occupational and private pensions in 2002, which proposes:

- the simplification of the pensions system;
- flexibility in moving from work to retirement;
- creating opportunities that encourage continuing participation in paid work for older people, rather than early retirement.

The minimum income guarantee – income support for over-60s – was introduced in April 1999 but take-up has been poor, with between a quarter and one-third of eligible pensioners not claiming their entitlement.[168] The Government has also introduced a winter fuel allowance for pensioner households and free TV licences for the over-75s. The additional cost of policies between 1997 and 2004 designed to benefit pensioners financially, and therefore tackle pensioner poverty, will amount to £7.3 billion.[169] Even so, the proportion of pensioners on incomes below 60 per cent of the median in 2001–02 was high, 22 per cent – 2.2 million pensioners – a fall of just 400,000 since 1997.[170] This is because while the poorest pensioners have seen income gains, these have simply maintained pensioner incomes in line with those of the overall population.

In October 2003 the pension credit replaced the minimum income guarantee as the main form of means-tested support for pensioners. More pensioners now qualify for pension credit than under the previous minimum income guarantee; an estimated 58 per cent of families with an individual aged 60 or over, up from 51.4 per cent of families before the reform.[171] The pension credit also increases the number of people who are eligible for housing benefit and council tax benefit.[172] Pension credit has two parts: the 'guarantee credit' and the 'savings credit'. The guarantee credit element provides a contribution towards a guaranteed income of a least £102.10 a week for single pensioners or £155.80 if in a couple. The 'savings credit' component of the pension credit offers additional income and is said by the Government to 'reward' less well-off pensioners who have accumulated moderate savings, although only those aged 65 and over and who qualify for a full state pension are entitled to the savings element of the pension credit. The rules for assessing savings over £6,000 are more generous than those for past schemes, and more pensioners are expected to benefit. While it is estimated that the pension credit will raise the income of half of all pensioners, this largely depends upon full take-up of benefit entitlements.[173] The Department for Work and Pensions target of a 75 per cent take-up rate will still leave one million pensioners not receiving pension credit by 2006.

CONCLUSION

Factors influencing poverty during the past 20 years include labour market change, reflecting trends in the wider economy and pushing up unemployment during recessions. Flexible and low-paid work has grown, resulting in a 'low pay, no pay cycle' for some people on low incomes. At the same time, changes in family life have contributed to the growth in lone parenthood. Rising numbers of people with a sickness or disability, often facing additional costs, have been excluded from paid work. A growing older population, with inadequate financial provision, either from state or occupational pension schemes, has reinforced pensioner inequality and poverty.

Policies during the 1980s and early 1990s tended to exacerbate poverty by restricting benefit entitlement. More recently, the Labour Government has sought to reduce the proportions of households without paid work through policies such as the New Deals, and to increase the returns of paid work via the national minimum wage and tax credits. Additional financial support has been targeted at families with children, largely through increases in means-tested support and in-work incentives. The emphasis on tackling poverty relies heavily on getting people into paid work. Reliance on such 'work-first' principles alone may not be enough.

NOTES

1 D White and J Murphy, 'Researching Poverty and Outcomes for Children', in A Fleiss, *The Department for Work and Pensions Research Yearbook 2000/2001*, Corporate Document Services, 2002, p9

2 See examples in Social Exclusion Unit, *Bringing Britain Together: a national strategy for neighbourhood renewal*, Cabinet Office, 1998

3 Department for Work and Pensions, *Households Below Average Income 1994/5–2001/02*, Corporate Document Services, 2003 – Tables 5.7, 5.8 and 5.9 (all AHC)

4 The International Labour Organization (ILO) definition of unemployment includes: those aged 16 and over who are without a job and who are available to start work in the next two weeks, who have been seeking a job in the last four weeks or are waiting to start a job already obtained. Economically active – those in employment plus those unemployed. Unemployment rate – the percentage of the economically active who are unemployed. Economically inactive – people who are neither in employment nor unemployed eg, all people under 16, those looking after a home or retired, or those permanently unable to work.

5 HM Treasury, *Tackling Poverty and Extending Opportunity: the modernisation of Britain's tax and benefit system*, Number 4, 1999

6 Office for National Statistics, *Work and worklessness among households Spring 2003*, July 2003 (amended version September 2003)

7 HM Treasury, *Employment Opportunity in a Changing Labour Market: the modernisation of Britain's tax and benefit system*, Number 1, 1997

8 The claimant count rate (the number of people claiming unemployment-related benefits), at 3.1 per cent, is the lowest since August 1975. The ILO working-age unemployment level is also the lowest since the series began. Office for National Statistics, *Labour Market Trends*, Vol. 111, No. 9, September 2003.

9 A workless household is a household that includes at least one person of working age (that is a woman aged between 16 and 59 or a man aged between 16 and 64) where no one is in employment.

10 See note 3

11 See note 3

12 R Walker with M Howard, *The Making of a Welfare Class? Benefit receipt in Britain*, The Policy Press, 2000

13 M Campbell with I Sanderson and F Walton, *Local Responses to Long-Term Unemployment*, Joseph Rowntree Foundation, 1998

14 See note 7

15 P Bivand, *Economic Inactivity and Social Exclusion*, Centre for Economic and Social Inclusion: http://www.cesi.org.uk, 2002

16 'Elementary work' is that which mainly involves routine tasks and does not require formal qualifications, C Summerfield and P Babb (eds), *Social Trends*, No. 33, Office for National Statistics, The Stationery Office, 2003, p85

17 See note 13

18 C Summerfield and P Babb (eds), *Social Trends*, No. 33, Office for National Statistics, The Stationery Office, 2003

19 H Trickey, K Kellard, R Walker, K Ashworth and A Smith, *Unemployment and Jobseeking: two years on*, DSS Research Report 87, 1998

20 See note 4

21 See note 8, *Labour Market Trends*

22 TUC, *Pockets of Poverty Report*, www.tuc.org, June 2002

23 Office for National Statistics, *Labour Market Statistics November 2002*, 2002; see note 22

24 J Pullinger and C Summerfield, *Social Focus on the Unemployed*, The Stationery Office, 1998

25 Department of Social Security, *New Ambitions for Our Country: A new contract for welfare*, The Stationery Office, 1998

26 Department for Work and Pensions, *UK National Action Plan on Social Exclusion 2003–05*, DWP, 2003, p4

27 Benefit run-ons are periods of continuation of benefit payments after someone claiming benefits has started paid work, designed to ease the transition from welfare to work. Examples of benefit run-ons include: lone parent run-on, housing benefit run-on and council tax benefit run-on.

28 Department for Work and Pensions, *Opportunity For All: fourth annual report*, The Stationery Office, 2002. 'Inactive' means those who are workless but not classified as unemployed; this group includes the long-term sick, disabled people and non-working single parents.

29 See note 21

30 M White and R Riley, *Findings from the Macro-evaluation of the New Deal for Young People,* Research Report 168, Department for Work and Pensions, 2002

31 M Evans, J Millar and S Sarre, *New Deal for Lone Parents: second synthesis report of the national evaluation,* Department for Work and Pensions, 2003

32 K Ashworth and W C Liu, *Jobseeker's Allowance: transitions to work and early returns to JSA,* Department for Work and Pensions In-house Report, 2001, p18

33 Trade Union Congress (TUC) briefing document, *Labour Market Programmes,* Number 46, in the TUC Welfare Reform Series, January 2003; TUC, Briefing document, *New Deal 18–24: latest results,* September 2003

34 See note 21

35 Learning and Skills Development Agency, *Work First or Learning First?: welfare policies must break down barriers to learning,* September 2003, p2

36 I Dennis and A C Guio, *Poverty and social exclusion in the EU after Laeken – part 2,* Statistics in focus, population and social conditions, THEME 3, September 2003

37 HM Treasury, *Tackling Poverty and Making Work Pay – Tax Credits for the 21st Century: the modernisation of Britain's tax and benefit system,* Number 6, HM Treasury, March 2000

38 P Gregg, S Harkness and S Machin, *Child Development and Family Income,* Joseph Rowntree Foundation, 1999

39 HM Treasury, *Supporting Children Through the Tax and Benefit System: the modernisation of Britain's tax and benefit system,* Number 5, HM Treasury, November 1999

40 See note 3, Table 3.1 (AHC)

41 Low-paid jobs were those paying less than £4.05ph (age 22+) or £3.45ph (18–21), Low Pay Commission, *The National Minimum Wage: fourth report of the low pay commission, Building on Success,* The Stationery Office, March 2003

42 W O'Connor and R Boreham, *Investigating Low Market Participation Among Lone Parents in London: a review of the methods,* In-House Report • 104, Department for Work and Pensions, November 2002

43 See note 21

44 P Gregg and J Wadsworth, 'The Changing Nature of Entry Jobs in Britain', in P Gregg (ed), *Jobs, Wages and Poverty: patterns of persistence and mobility in the new flexible labour market,* Centre for Economic Performance, 1997

45 M White and J Forth, *Pathways Through Unemployment: the effects of a flexible labour market,* Joseph Rowntree Foundation, 1998

46 M Stewart, 'Low Pay, No Pay Dynamics', in *Persistent Poverty and Lifetime Inequality: the evidence*, HM Treasury Occasional Paper No.10, 1999

47 P Gregg, 'Scarring Effects of Unemployment', in *Persistent Poverty and Lifetime Inequality: the evidence*, HM Treasury Occasional Paper No.10, 1999

48 See note 32

49 See note 32

50 K Purcell, A McKnight and C Simm, *Lower Earnings Limit in Practice: part-time employment in hotels and catering*, Research Discussion Series, Equal Opportunities Commission, 1999

51 J Seymour (ed), *Poverty in Plenty: a human development report for the UK*, UNED-UK, 2000; Low Pay Commission, *The National Minimum Wage: fourth report of the Low Pay Commission, Building on Success*, The Stationery Office, 2003

52 M Stewart, 'Low Pay, No Pay Dynamics', in *Persistent Poverty and Lifetime Inequality: the evidence*, HM Treasury Occasional Paper No.10, 1999

53 G Palmer, M Rahman and P Kenway, *Monitoring Poverty and Social Exclusion*, Joseph Rowntree Foundation, 2002

54 See note 41; Low Pay Commission, *The National Minimum Wage: fourth report of the Low Pay Commission, Building Success*, The Stationery Office, 2003

55 The national minimum wage rate in October 2003: £4.50ph for adults and £3.80ph for 18–21-year-olds

56 See note 29

57 S McKay, *Working Families' Tax Credit in 2001*, Department for Work and Pensions, Corporate Document Services, 2003

58 See note 57

59 See note 57

60 Inland Revenue, *Working Families' Tax Credit: estimates of take-up rates in 2000–01*, 2002

61 See note 57

62 Inland Revenue, *Analysis and Research, Child Tax Credit and Working Tax Credit Quarterly Statistics*, July 2003

63 House of Commons Social Security Select Committee, *Housing Benefit*, Volume 1, Annex 2, HC 385-I, July 2000

64 S Woodland, W Mandy and M Miller, *Easing the transition into work (Part 2 – client survey)*, Research Report 186, Research Summary, Department for Work and Pensions, April 2003

65 C Farrell and W O'Connor, *Low-income Families and Household Spending*, Research Report 192, Department for Work and Pensions, July 2003

66 T Harries and K Woodfield, *Easing the Transition into Work: a qualitative evaluation of transitional support for clients returning to employment*, Research Report 175, Department for Work and Pensions, October 2002

67 See note 66. Three-quarters of respondents in the study did not know about key work-incentive benefits (job grant and benefit run-ons).

68 Divorced and separated people are concentrated in the younger or middle-aged adult population.

69 See note 19

70 S Yeandle, K Escott, L Grant and E Batty, *Women and Men Talking about Poverty*, Working Paper Series No.7, Equal Oportunities Commission, 2003; see note 7

71 Office for National Statistics, *Labour Market Trends*, Vol. 111, No. 6, June 2003

72 Department for Work and Pensions, *Opportunity for All: Fifth Annual Report 2003*, The Stationery Office, 2003

73 J Casebourne, 'Work-life Balance and Lone Parents', *A Quality Life for Lone Parents and their Children*, Report of Gingerbreads Annual Conference, April 2002

74 See note 7

75 S P Jenkins, J Rigg, *Dynamics of Poverty in Britain*, Department for Work and Pensions, Research Report 157, 2001

76 ONS, *Census 2001 – the Big Picture*, Office for National Statistics, 2002

77 One Parent Families, *One Parent Families Today: the facts*, 2003, p2

78 ONS, *Living in Britain: results from the 1998 General Household Survey*, Office for National Statistics, 2000; ONS, *Census 2001 – the Big Picture*, Office for National Statistics, 2002

79 OECD – Organisation for Economic Co-operation and Development. D Kasparova, A Marsh, S Vegeris and J Perry, *Families and Children 2001: work and childcare*, Research Report 191, Department for Work and Pensions, 2003, p44

80 See note 18

81 See note 77

82 C Bourreau-Dubois, B Jeandidier and F Berger, *Poverty Dynamics, Family Events and Labour Market Events: are there any differences between men and women?*, Conference paper presented at EPUNet 2003 conference, Institute for Social and Economic Research, July 2003

83 See note 77

84 S McKay, 'Exploring the Dynamics of Family Change: lone parenthood in Britain', in L Leisering and R Walker (eds), *The Dynamics of Modern Society*, Policy Press, 1998; D Webster, *Memorandum to the Select Committee on Social Security, Tax and Benefits: interim report*, House of Commons, November 1997

85 J Millar and T Ridge, Families, *Poverty, Work and Care: a review of literature on lone parent and low income couple families*, Research Report 153, Department for Work and Pensions, 2001

86 Office for National Statistics, *Work and Worklessness among Households*, Spring 2003, July 2003 (amended September 2003)

87 See note 85; see also Trades Union Council, *Women and Poverty*, TUC, 2002

88 S Vegeris and J Perry, *Families and Children 2001: living standards and the children* Research Report 190, Department for Work and Pensions, 2003

89 W Sykes and A Walker, *Results from the 2000 General Household Survey*, 2002. Couple families are households comprising a couple with dependent children.

90 Results from One Parent Families Members Survey, http://www.oneparentfamilies.org.uk, May 2003. Eight hundred and twelve lone parents (who were members of One Parent Families) took part in the survey.

91 See note 84

92 See note 84

93 M Iacovou and R Berthoud, *Parents and Employment*, Research Report 107, Department of Social Security, 2000

94 S P Jenkins, J A Rigg and F Devicienti, *The Dynamics of Poverty in Britain*, Research Report 157, Department for Work and Pensions, 2001, p53

95 See note 94, p52

96 Figures at September 2002, income support figure excludes disabled lone parents; Office for National Statistics, Information and Analysis Directorate, January 2003; Department for Work and Pensions, *Work and Pensions Statistics – 2002*, 2002

97 Department for Work and Pensions, *Family Resources Survey 2001–2002*, 2003

98 M Brewer, T Clark and M Wakefield, *Five Years of Social Security in the UK*, Institute for Fiscal Studies, WP02/12, 2002, p11. The rise in child benefit was restricted to the first child only.

99 See note 28

100 Office for National Statistics, *Labour Market Trends*, Vol. 105, No. 9, September 1997. For a discussion of definitions, see R Walker with M Howard, *The Making of a Welfare Class: benefit receipt in Britain*, The Policy Press, 2000; T Burchardt, *Enduring Economic Exclusion: disabled people, income and work*, Joseph Rowntree Foundation, 2000; I Bell, N Houston and R Heyes, 'Workless Households, Unemployment and economic inactivity', in Office for National Statistics, *Labour Market Trends*, Vol. 105, No. 9, September 1997

101 Department of Health, *Health Survey for England 2001*, 2001

102 C Heady, 'Sickness and Disability', in M Barnes, C Heady, S Middleton, J Millar, F Papadopoulos, P Tsakloglou, *Poverty and Social Exclusion in Europe*, Edward Elgar, 2002

103 See note 101

104 Department for Work and Pensions, *DWP Statistical Summary – September 2003*, First Release

105 Further discussed in R Berthoud, J Lakey, S McKay, *The Economic Problems of Disabled People*, Policy Studies Institute, 1993

106 D Acheson, *Independent Inquiry into Inequalities in Health Report*, The Stationery Office, 1998

107 M Bartley and C Owen, 'Relation Between Socio-economic Status, Employment and Health During Economic Change, 1973–1993', *British Medical Journal*, Vol. 313, 24 August 1996

108 C Barham, *Economic Inactivity and the Labour Market*, Office for National Statistics, February 2002

109 Leonard Cheshire Foundation, *Inclusive Citizenship: the Leonard Cheshire social exclusion report 2002*, 2002

110 See note 109

111 A Zaidi and T Burchardt, *Comparing Incomes When Needs Differ: equivalisation for the extra costs of disability in the UK*, CASE paper 64, February 2003, p17. The ranges given are: pensioner couple households, both disabled (£20 and £113) and non-pensioner couple both disabled (£97 and £551)

112 A Zaidi and T Burchardt, *Equivalisation for the Extra Costs Of Disability: comparing incomes when needs differ*, Paper for Income Distribution and Welfare International Workshop for the Bocconi University Centre, June 2002

113 Using the threshold of 60 per cent of median income; see note 111

114 See note 111

115 See note 111

116 H Barnes, *Working for a Living? Employment, benefits and the living standards of disabled people*, The Policy Press, 2000

117 Audit Commission, *Charging with Care: how councils charge for home care*, 2000

118 DWP statistics cited in G Palmer, M Rahman and P Kenway, *Monitoring Poverty and Social Exclusion 2002*, Joseph Rowntree Foundation, 2002. Long-term recipients are those people in receipt of benefit for over two years.

119 G Preston, 'Measuring Poverty', *Disability Rights Bulletin – Summer 2002*, Disability Alliance, p5

120 See note 3

121 See note 21

122 Office for National Statistics, Labour Force Survey, Spring 2002

123 T Burchardt, *Enduring Economic Exclusion*, Joseph Rowntree Foundation, 2000

124 R Dorsett, L Finlayson, R Ford, A Marsh, M White and G Zarb, *Leaving Incapacity Benefit*, DSS Research Report 86, Corporate Document Services, 1998

125 Department for Work and Pensions, *Income Support Statistics: November 2002* Quarterly Statistical Enquiry, 2003

126 See note 28, p67

127 Carers UK, *Without Us…?: Calculating the cost of carers' support*, 2002

128 Statistics from Carers UK, www.carersonline.org.uk

129 J Mayer and H Green, *Carers 2000*, The Stationery Office, 2002

130 Department for Work and Pensions, *Family Resources Survey 2001–2002*, 2003

131 M Howard, *Paying the Price: carers, poverty and social exclusion*, CPAG, 2001

132 See note 130

133 See note 130

134 K Rake (ed), *Women's Incomes Over the Lifetime: a report to the Women's Unit*, Cabinet Office, 2000

135 E Holzhausen and V Pearlman, *Caring on the Breadline: the financial implications of caring*, Carers National Association, 2000

136 See note 135

137 Carers National Association, *The True Cost of Caring: a survey of carers' lost income*, 1996

138 D Madden and I Walker, *Labour Supply, Health and Caring: evidence from the UK*, University College, Dublin

139 See note 135

140 See note 135

142 E McLaughlin, *Social Security and Community Care*, Research Report 4, Department of Social Services, 1991

142 See note 18, p30

143 See note 18

144 See note 18

145 See note 18

146 Office for National Statistics, *The Pensioners' Income Series 2001/02*, Office for National Statistics, 2003. Recent growth estimates are subject to particular uncertainty, but the average almost certainly grew faster than average earnings (up 12 per cent between 1994/95 and 2001/02).

147 See note 146

148 A O'Connell and C Curry, *The Pensions Landscape*, Pensions Policy Institute, February 2003

149 See note 146

150 B Botting (ed), *Family Spending: a report on the 2001–2002 expenditure and food survey*, Office for National Statistics, The Stationery Office, 2003

151 See note 146. Real terms means the effect of inflation has been removed.

152 J Ginn, Gender, *Pensions and the Lifecourse: how pensions need to adapt to changing family forms*, The Policy Press, 2003

153 Office for National Statistics, 'Current pension scheme membership by sex and usual gross weekly earnings', *Living in Britain*, 2002

154 See note 146

155 See note 3

156 *The Guardian*, 7 May 2003

157 See note 73

158 See notes 19 and 152

159 Help the Aged, www.helptheaged.org.uk, March 2003

160 See note 146

161 Department of Social Security, *The Changing Welfare State: pensioner incomes*, Department of Social Security, Paper 2, 2000

162 R Berthoud, *The Incomes of Ethnic Minorities*, Joseph Rowntree Foundation, 1998; L Platt, *Parallel Lives?: Poverty among ethnic minority groups in Britain*, CPAG, 2002

163 R Berthoud, *Disability Benefits: a review of the issues and options for reform*, Joseph Rowntree Foundation, 1998

164 R Disney, E Grundy and P Johnson, *The Dynamics of Retirement*, DSS Research Report 72, Corporate Document Services, 1997

165 E Bardasi, S Jenkins and J Rigg, *Retirement and the Economic Well-being of the Elderly: a British perspective*, ISER working paper, 2000; see also note 148

166 Under SERPS, benefits based on the best 20 years of earnings (revalued at state pension age) would accrue at 1.25 per cent per annum and entitlements were transferable across jobs or across gaps in employment – see note 153, p15

167 See note 153

168 Comptroller and Auditor General, *Tackling Pensioner Poverty: encouraging take-up of entitlements*, The Stationery Office, HC 37 Session 2002–2003, November 2002

169 A Goodman, M Myck, A Shephard, *Sharing in the Nation's Prosperity?: pensioner poverty in Britain*, Institute for Fiscal Studies, March 2003

170 See note 3 – *Households Below Average Income, 1994/5–2001/02*

171 M Brewer and C Emmerson, *Two Cheers for the Pension Credit?*, Briefing Note No.39, Institute for Fiscal Studies, October 2003

172 See note 171

173 See note 171

4 Effects of poverty and deprivation

The effects of poverty and social exclusion are plain to see. The loss of human dignity, low self-esteem and the inability to take part fully in society can wreck lives ... Poverty is more than a lack of income and social exclusion more than a lack of personal possessions.

(Department for Work and Pensions, *Opportunity for All: fourth annual report*)[1]

The last chapter looked at some of the circumstances which can lead to poverty. This chapter highlights some of the effects of poverty and deprivation, which can be practical, psychological, physical and relational.[2] The specific impact on children is considered in Chapter 5.

This chapter includes evidence from the *British Household Panel Survey* (BHPS), a comprehensive longitudinal survey, as well as smaller-scale studies. It also includes results from the large-scale *Poverty and Social Exclusion in Britain* (PSE) survey and a similar *Poverty and Social Exclusion in Northern Ireland* (PSENI) survey, which reveals the extent to which people lacked items that the majority of the population perceive as essential, and whether their incomes were too low to afford them. These surveys also investigated exclusion (from services, social activities and social relationships).[3]

LIVING ON A LOW INCOME

Life on a low income means going without, which in turn can lead to longer-term problems such as poor health, debt, poor housing and homelessness.[4] These effects will be considered later in the chapter; here we examine the extent to which people go without basic essentials.

THE BARE NECESSITIES

One approach to poverty is to adopt the 'consensual' approach, along the lines of the *Breadline Britain* surveys.[5] This entailed asking a representative sample of the population which items they regarded as necessities, with those items attracting 50 per cent or more support being considered 'essential'. Using this approach, the PSE survey found that 35 out of 54 items were viewed as 'essential' in 1999.[6] People were then classified as 'poor' if they lacked two or more essentials *because they could not afford them*. A similar consensual measure of poverty has also been recently used in a PSENI survey conducted in 2002 and early 2003. The PSENI survey defined people as 'poor' if they lacked three or more 'necessary' items and had, on average, an equivalised income of £156.27 a week.[7] Some people might lack items but have a relatively high income (eg, having obtained a job), so were classified as having 'recently risen out of poverty'; conversely, those who did not lack items but had a low income (eg, having recently lost a job) were 'vulnerable to poverty'. Using these definitions the PSE survey found that in 1999:

- 25.6 per cent were poor;
- 10.3 per cent were vulnerable to poverty;
- 1.8 per cent had risen out of poverty.

Similarly, in the PSENI 2002/03 survey:

- 29.6 per cent were poor;
- 12.1 per cent were vulnerable to poverty;
- 2.1 per cent had recently risen out of poverty.

GOING WITHOUT HOUSEHOLD ITEMS

Many people on a low income will go without essential items because they do not have the money to purchase them. According to the PSE survey, 14 per cent of adults could not afford to keep their home decorated, 12 per cent could not afford to replace electrical goods and 12 per cent could not afford to replace worn out furniture.[8]

CUTTING BACK ON FOOD

> I normally just fill myself up on bread or crisps and chocolate because it's cheap…
>
> (16-year-old, 7–9 months pregnant, H Burchett and A Seeley, *Good Enough to Eat?*)[9]

Money for food can be used as a reserve to iron out fluctuations in income and to meet emergencies. Hence people on low incomes often go without food, eat less, or buy cheaper foods than people who are better off. A poor diet can cause cognitive defects, and even short-term nutritional deficiencies can influence children's behaviour, ability to concentrate and perform complex tasks.[10]

- Four per cent of adults in the PSE survey (1999), and 5 per cent of adults in the PSENI survey (2002/03), could not afford fresh fruit and vegetables daily.[11]
- Another survey found that 1 in 20 mothers sometimes went without food to meet the needs of their children, with lone mothers on income support 14 times more likely to go without than mothers in two-parent families not on benefit.[12]
- Many pregnant teenagers are missing meals frequently and eating unhealthily because of a lack of money.[13]
- A 2002 study noted that low-income diets were very limited, especially for lone mothers, as varying meals involved the risk of wasted food and money.[14]
- A survey of carers carried out by the Carers National Association during 2000 showed more than one in five (22 per cent) were cutting back on food.[15]
- Many young people living in poverty go without food.[16]

As well as cutting back, people on low incomes may not be getting a nutritious diet.

- Working households ate 85 per cent more vegetables than workless households; only a third of unemployed men ate fruit on five or six days a week, compared with half of employed men.[17]
- A recent study found the diets of those on a low income to be nutritionally poor, relying on 'cheap calories' from processed low-cost food. Food diaries used in the study revealed that during the research period fruit was rarely, if ever, eaten.
- The same study found that 'eating out' was considered a treat by low-income respondents, one that generally involved fast-food chains or local chip/kebab shops.[18]

Supermarkets are often located in out-of-town premises. People without a car are more dependent on small local shops, often where prices are higher and the range of fruit and vegetables is smaller and of lower quality. Poor people also pay proportionately more for their food; low-income families tended to shop 'little and often' at local discount supermarkets. If people have limited storage space and no transport, they do not have access to the savings offered by bulk purchase.[19]

Interviews with low-income families have shown that when income increased, often as a result of moving into better-paid work or through re-partnering in the case of lone parents, the family's diet improved in both quantity and quality.[20]

CUTTING BACK ON FUEL

Research also shows the caution of many low-income families in the use of heating, particularly if they are at home all day, or for those who need to stay warm for health reasons or because of young children.

> Individual rooms were heated as needed – normally during the coldest part of the late evening. Central heating, even where it was available, was not used.
>
> (E Kempson, *Life on a Low Income*)[21]

The poorest spend much less than the better-off on fuel, but what they do spend represents a higher proportion of their income. The *Expenditure and Food Survey* (EFS) 2001–2002 showed that households in the lowest 20 per cent of income distribution spent 21 per cent of total weekly outcome on housing, fuel and power, compared with 7 per cent in the top 20 per cent.[22]

When households need to spend more than 10 per cent of their income to provide adequate heat and energy, they are commonly considered by the Government to be in 'fuel poverty'.[23] On this basis, three million UK households are currently in fuel poverty, with those aged over 60 most at risk.[24] The Government initiated a UK Fuel Poverty Strategy in November 2001, with a commitment to end fuel poverty for vulnerable households by 2010.[25] The Warm Front Scheme, providing packages of insulation and heating measures, is the Government's key policy for tackling fuel poverty and claims to have helped 500,000 low-income households so far.[26]

CUTTING YOUR CLOTH – GOING WITHOUT CLOTHING

The PSE survey showed that, in 1999:

- 4 per cent of adults could not afford a warm, waterproof coat, and 5 per cent could not afford two pairs of all-weather shoes;
- 12 per cent of children defined as 'necessity deprived' (lacking at least two necessary items) did not have a warm coat, and 11 per cent lacked properly fitting shoes because their parents could not afford to buy them.[27]

Many low-income families buy second-hand clothes for themselves, and sometimes for their children, although parents would often try to ensure that children had new clothes as far as possible.[28] Recent research investigating children's perceptions of poverty found that many children identified clothes as an essential part of 'fitting in'. 'Suitable' clothing had significant implications for self-esteem and peer-group inclusion:

> I just want to fit in the group, 'cos it's like I get…, people take the mick out of me because I can't afford things. Like my trainers are messy…and I need new trainers and clothes…I can't get decent clothes like everyone else does.
>
> (Bella, 12 years old)[29]

BUDGETING

Whilst many people on low incomes manage their finances with skill and resourcefulness, living on a limited income can lead to difficulties with money management, simply because there is not enough money to 'get by'.

> You have to think about what you buy and set a budget first. The bills come first, and then food. We can just about maintain our basic needs – we cannot afford leisure costs.
>
> (*Women and Men Talking about Poverty*)[30]

People may experience acute worry about finances when initially falling into a low income – for example, due to the loss of paid work or family change, such as becoming a lone parent. In the early stages there may be a high risk of arrears as existing commitments become unmanageable or savings are eroded. Managing a limited budget becomes central to everyday life and can be a source of extreme anxiety and stress, especially for women, who often carry the burden of budgeting in low-income families.[31] Many people live on low incomes for long periods, but in some cases the more practice at money management, the more experienced budgeters they become.[32]

> I had to learn to budget, I couldn't budget at first.
> (*Women and Men Talking about Poverty*)[33]

People adopt various strategies such as cutting back or going without necessities, when coping on a low income; but this alone may not be enough. Many people on low incomes have to borrow money regularly, in order to pay for essential items and just to 'get by'.[34] One effect of persistent low income may be falling into debt, not because of an inability of people in poverty to manage their financial situation but because their income is insufficient to meet basic daily needs.[35]

DEBT

It is very hard to avoid debt. Debt is part of our lives most of the time.

> To avoid debt you even have to cut down on essentials.
> (Bangladeshi woman, *Women and Men Talking about Poverty*)[36]

From 1997 to 2002, debt problems handled by the Citizens Advice Bureaux (CAB) increased by 47 per cent.[37] Many of those seeking help with debt are living in poverty.[38] The CAB took on 1.5 million new debt cases in 2001/02 alone and debt is the second largest area dealt with by the organisation. Recent research found that a quarter of households had been in arrears on one or more of their financial commitments in the past year.[39] This may not even be indicative of the number of people experiencing problem debt as seeking advice is often a last resort; instead many people take on further borrowing to cope with existing debt problems.[40]

The UK has the lowest standard of consumer protection for poor people in northern Europe and is one of the few countries to have no statutory ceiling on the amount of interest charged on a loan.[41] Those on low incomes are often excluded from mainstream credit and may turn to alternative sources, including 'doorstep' lending companies, where excessively high interest rates of 160 to 1,000 per cent APR may be charged.[42]

FINANCIAL EXCLUSION, DEBT AND POVERTY

A national policy forum organised in 2002 by Church Action on Poverty (CAP) identified some key barriers to financial inclusion:[43]

- unemployment and lack of income;
- a lack of creditworthiness;
- postcode stigma – higher than normal prices because of location;
- inappropriate requirements for proof of identity;
- strict payment deadlines.

Around 10 per cent of adults, including nearly a quarter (24 per cent) of lone parents, have no bank account and as a result have limited access to financial services and lose out on discounts available to people who pay by direct debit.[44] In 2002 an estimated 7.8 million adults were denied access to mainstream credit sources, such as banks and finance houses.[45] Financial exclusion means that people must go without credit – which for many in poverty is not possible if basic needs are to be met – or rely on alternatives: borrowing from friends and family, mail-order catalogues, pawn shops and 'doorstep' credit companies. Some groups, such as lone parents on benefit and the long-term unemployed, may be excluded even from the alternative licensed credit market and are therefore vulnerable to exploitation by unlicensed money-lenders.[46]

A 2002 survey of three streets on a disadvantaged estate in Tyneside found that the average repayment being made to credit lenders was £60 per household per week. Interest repayments were taking away a third on average of an already limited household income.[47] Extortionate repayments can lead to a continual cycle of debt and poverty for those 'caught between low income and high cost credit'.[48] However, some people with low incomes choose to borrow from alternative credit providers, despite the high costs, because their needs are not met by mainstream credit services. Many people on low incomes need to borrow and repay small amounts of money over short periods of time; something seen as uneconomical by mainstream financial companies.[49]

The Department of Trade and Industry is currently reviewing changes to the 1974 Consumer Credit Act, and legislation against extortionate credit is expected to be introduced in 2004. Although such initiatives may help to tackle over-indebtedness, what is also required is a wider range of financial services tailored to the needs of people on low incomes, both to prevent financial exclusion and to protect against the consequences of debt.

The Government is also attempting to tackle financial exclusion via two key schemes for low-income households: universal banking services and the 'savings gateway'. Both initiatives aim to increase financial inclusion and encourage saving among people on a low income. In addition, the universal banking is central to the Government's shift towards the direct payment of benefits into a bank account, replacing payment via order books or girocheque. The universal banking services consists of two elements: access to a basic bank account at Post Office branches and a Post Office card account – an account solely for benefit recipients who do not want to, or are unable to, open a basic bank account.[50] The savings gateway, currently being piloted in five areas of the UK, is a 'means-tested' savings account for those on lower incomes. It aims to provide an inducement to begin or continue saving through a government-funded matching of savings, pound for pound, providing up to a total of £375, or the highest balance in the account during the savings period (of 18 months) if below this ceiling amount. Policy, however, has not been constructed around the needs of disadvantaged consumers; basic bank services, for example, may not be able to provide the products needed for people on a low income.[51] In addition, saving may avoid future debt problems but for those in poverty 'the need for a higher income, or affordable credit, can be a higher priority than their need for savings products'.[52]

VULNERABLE TO DEBT

- A third of households with incomes of less than £9,000 a year have problems with debt.[53]
- Financial difficulties are largely due to arrears in household bills, such as those for basic utilities, rent or mortgages, rather than consumer credit commitments.[54]
- Thirty-three per cent of social housing/housing association tenants were in rent arrears in 2001 compared to 8 per cent of homeowners with mortgage debt.[55]
- Multiple debts: two-thirds of social housing tenants in serious arrears owed money to other creditors.[56]

Some claimants can be living below the basic income support level because their benefit is reduced at source. Benefit deductions can be made for social fund loans, overpayment of benefit, debt or fines. Whilst deductions can help with budgeting, they can be problematic because benefit levels are low.[57] Many families in poverty are already in severe debt and repayments taken by utilities companies or the social fund further reduces their already low income.[58]

WHO FALLS INTO DEBT?

Financial difficulties and arrears are strongly associated with low incomes.

A recent survey asked 1,647 householders questions about their credit use and that of their partner, if they had one. This study into 'over-indebtedness' found:

- one in seven households reported experiencing debt because their income was low;
- financial difficulties were associated with starting a family or with relationship breakdown;
- nearly half of all lone parents had been in arrears in the past year;
- loss of income placed people at risk from debt – half of all households having financial problems said this was due to loss of income;
- unemployed households were more than twice as likely (43 per cent) to have experienced arrears than those with one or more members in full-time employment (18 per cent).[59]

Recent research by Citizens Advice found that women, social landlord tenants and the unwaged were most likely to have debts associated with poverty.[60]

A combination of low income and high costs can also cause debt. Disabled people can incur expenses, such as special diets, extra heating and hot water, higher transport costs, and so are often at risk of falling into debt.[61] The 'over-indebtedness' study found that those people who were unable to undertake paid work through long-term sickness or disability were twice as likely to experience financial difficulties.[62]

IMPACT OF DEBT

Debt has significant effects for those with a low income. The financial costs of repayments reduce an already low budget, resulting in families going without essential items. Other costs of debt are those incurred on health, relationships and opportunities.

- In a Citizens Advice survey, a quarter of people with debt problems were receiving treatment for stress, anxiety and depression.[63]
- People in poverty reported that debt damaged friendships and strained family relationships.

- Problem debt has a draining and demoralising effect on people's quality of life. Debt was described as something that is 'always there' by those in poverty.[64]
- Debt can be a barrier to paid work; lone parents without problem debts were more likely to enter employment than those who reported debts (31 per cent compared to 17 per cent).[65]
- Another effect is fear of further family disruption: people with mortgage arrears feared that their home could be repossessed and their children taken into care.[66]

> Those who juggled bills and got into debt often did so by adopting social conventions about what to buy in an attempt not to appear different from others. The second group, whose approach was to cut back, tried to conceal their poverty by cutting themselves off from social interaction and avoiding, at all costs, stigmatising debt. In their own way, both groups were adopting social conventions; either they kept up appearances or they avoided debt. Living on a low income meant they could not do both.
>
> (E Kempson *et al*, *Hard Times?*)[67]

As we have seen, debt can create further problems, such as more debts and homelessness. Hence another effect of poverty can be living in poor housing, perhaps with high costs or arrears, in some cases being vulnerable to homelessness. This is considered in the next section.

HOUSING AND HOMELESSNESS

POOR-QUALITY HOUSING

Despite improvements to housing conditions, seven million English households – 33 per cent of all dwellings – are 'non-decent '(ie, not in good repair, not adequately heated, or in need of modernisation). Of these dwellings, 4.2 per cent are 'unfit' (structurally unsound, damp, with poor heating/ventilation or inadequate essential utilities).[68] Lone parents and people from minority ethnic communities are more likely to live in poor-quality, non-decent, accommodation,[69] as are those living in the poorest fifth of all households and households in receipt of income- or disability-related benefits.[70] Research looking at severe child poverty found that deficiencies associated with housing, such as overcrowding, damp, and not having enough money to replace worn-out furniture, are aspects of poverty and deprivation that parents were unable to protect their children from.[71] In a 2003 survey of 800 low-income households, 75 per cent of survey respondents said their homes were cold and damp and 39 per cent reported overcrowding.[72] The widespread existence of poor-quality housing has been shown to have a significant impact on health.[73]

- Private tenants are the most likely to live in poor housing. Nearly a third of private tenants live in housing that is unfit, including 45 per cent of elderly tenants and 30 per cent of families with children.
- Many inhabit cold, damp, mouldy and overcrowded homes – conditions linked to gastroenteritis and asthma.
- A recent study of low-income households found that half of all parents blamed their damp, cold and draughty homes for their children's ill-health.[74]
- Overcrowding and living in high-rise flats are associated with psychological symptoms, such as depression.
- Experience of multiple housing deprivations increased the risk of severe ill-health or disability across the life course by 25 per cent on average.[75]

Recent analysis of the PSE survey revealed that many people in poverty are homeowners. Although the overall poverty rate for homeowners is lower than that for other housing sectors, because it is the largest housing sector (68 per cent of all households) homeowners account for around half of all those in poverty. The research also found that while tenants experienced poorer physical health and social exclusion, poor homeowners tended to suffer mental health problems and difficulties with the condition of their accommodation.[76]

HIGH HOUSING COSTS AND ARREARS

Changes in the housing market over the past 20 years have made it more difficult for people on low incomes to find and keep affordable accommodation.[77] Rents have risen ahead of inflation as a result of subsidy reduction in the social housing sector and the effects of deregulation in the private sector. Very high house prices, a rise of 10 per cent in 2003,[78] have meant that many people cannot meet the expense of buying their own home.[79] Such a scarcity of affordable housing puts pressure on the social housing sector. However, despite an increase in demand, there are over one million fewer homes available in the social housing sector than 25 years ago.[80]

The structure and administration of housing benefit have been key factors in rent arrears and homelessness. In 2002 nearly three-quarters (71 per cent) of Citizens Advice clients facing court action over rent arrears had unresolved problems with their housing benefit.[81]

HOMELESSNESS

Official statistics can underestimate the extent of homelessness. The *Households Below Average Income* (HBAI) statistics cover only private households, excluding people sleeping rough or in bed and breakfast (B&B) accommodation. Homelessness statistics also exclude those who have not been accepted by local authorities as homeless according to the criteria of being 'unintentionally homeless' or in priority need (eg, families with dependent children or a pregnant woman, households that are considered 'vulnerable', perhaps because of mental illness or physical disability). From July 2002, priority need was extended to include more people defined as 'vulnerable', such as applicants aged 16 or 17 or those vulnerable because of being in care, custody or the armed forces.[82] In 2002, 125,750 households in England were found to be homeless and in priority need by local authorities; a further 69,860 homeless households were entitled only to advice and assistance.[83] This number is a dramatic increase when compared to the 55,530 households accepted as homeless in 1979.[84] Homelessness numbers have risen in all parts of the UK since 1997, most dramatically in Northern Ireland, which saw an increase of 25 per cent between 2000 and 2001.[85]

- Over one million households in England were homeless at some time during the ten years ending 1998–99; those from minority ethnic communities, lone-parent families and under 45-year-olds were especially vulnerable.[86]
- 93,480 households were living in temporary accommodation at the end of June 2003, more than double the number in 1997 (see Figure 4.1).
- The number of these households in B&B accommodation increased by 180 per cent between 1997 and the end of 2002.[87]
- One study of B&B accommodation in London found inadequate facilities for families with children: 96 per cent of B&B dwellings had shared cooking amenities, 80 per cent had shared toilets and bathrooms and 58 per cent had no access to a washing machine.[88]
- The number of people sleeping rough in England has decreased from 2,000 in 1998 to an estimated 596 people in 2002.[89] However,

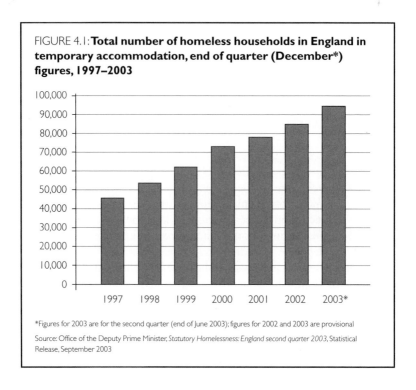

FIGURE 4.1: **Total number of homeless households in England in temporary accommodation, end of quarter (December*) figures, 1997–2003**

*Figures for 2003 are for the second quarter (end of June 2003); figures for 2002 and 2003 are provisional

Source: Office of the Deputy Prime Minister, *Statutory Homelessness: England second quarter 2003*, Statistical Release, September 2003

there are around 400,000 single 'hidden' homeless people, staying on friends' floors, in squats or hostels.[90]

In 2002, the Government set an ambitious target that, by March 2004, no homeless family with children should be placed in B&B accommodation, except in an emergency, and even then, for no more than six weeks. In June 2003, households with children or expectant mothers accounted for 32 per cent of all those homeless households in B&B accommodation, a substantial fall when compared with 54 per cent the previous year, in June 2002. However, the figures for homelessness overall have increased by 14 per cent over the same period, with the number of those in hostel accommodation rising by 12 per cent and those 'homeless at home' (while awaiting housing) by 38 per cent.[91] Since July 2003 legislation (the Homelessness Act 2002) has required every housing authority in England to adopt and publish a homelessness strategy, with the aim of preventing homelessness and ensuring the provision of suitable accommodation and support for people who are homeless or at risk of becoming homeless.[92]

CAUSES OF HOMELESSNESS

A principal cause of homelessness is a shortage of affordable housing, primarily affecting people on low incomes.[93] However, the immediate triggers for becoming homeless included the following:

- In 2002, 35 per cent of homeless people in England lost their last home because friends or relatives could no longer accommodate them; 22 per cent because of relationship breakdown, 16 per cent involving violent breakdown; and 3 per cent because of housing arrears.[94]
- In 1999, 63 per cent of women aged 30 to 49 cited domestic violence as the key reason for their homelessness.[95]
- Eviction for rent arrears is also an important cause of homelessness. Court Service data show that 30,350 outright possession orders and a further 70,293 suspended possession orders were granted to social landlords in England and Wales in 2001, an increase of 102 per cent since 1994.[96]

IMPACT OF HOMELESSNESS

Homelessness can have a negative impact on health and on a child's education.

- Child development is impaired through lack of space for safe play and exploration. Homeless children are educationally disadvantaged by mobility, frequent change of schools and the stigma of homelessness.[97]
- Homeless children are twice as likely to be admitted to hospital, with high admission rates for accidents and infectious diseases.[98]
- Twice as many people living in B&Bs experience psychological distress than in the general population, and they are more likely to have infections and skin conditions.[99]
- Homeless people, especially rough sleepers and hostel dwellers, have very high mortality rates and low life expectancy – one study estimated the average age of death is 42 years for rough sleepers.[100]
- Although more likely to suffer from poor health, single homeless people were 40 times less likely than the general population to be registered with a GP in 2001.[101]

The association between housing situation and illness highlights another effect of poverty – poor health, which is considered next.

POOR HEALTH

> Poor health is both a symptom of living in a poorer neighbourhood and a cause of its continuing decline...problems can be compounded by poor access to health services, but also by poor day-to-day access to healthy, affordable food, safe leisure and recreation.
> (Neighbourhood Renewal Unit, *Health and Neighbourhood Renewal*)[102]

The widening income inequality in the past two decades has been accompanied by a parallel trend in health inequalities, although the precise causal relationship is still being debated.[103] These inequalities are also reflected in death rates.

DEATH RATES

During the twentieth century there has been a sizeable decline in death rates in the UK.[104] However, inequalities remain:

- Life expectancy differences between social class I and V is 7 years in men and 5.5 years in women.
- Women in the lowest social class are 24 more times likely to die from complications in pregnancy than women in the top two classes.[105]
- Children in the bottom social class are 5 times more likely to die from an accident and 15 times more likely to die in a house fire than those at the top.[106]

DEATHS IN CHILDHOOD

Although overall death rates for babies and young children have declined over time, disparities remain. In 2001, infant mortality (ie, death within the first year) inside marriage was twice as high in unskilled manual social classes (7.2 per thousand) than in professional classes (3.6 per thousand).[107] Babies born into classes IV and V have a greater risk of low birthweight. Low birthweight is linked to death in infancy and associated with coronary heart disease and diabetes in later life.[108]

TABLE 4.1: **Perinatal* and infant mortality rates per 1,000 births (within marriage only) by social class 1978–79 and 2001**

Social class	Perinatal		Infant	
	1978–79	2001	1978–79	2001
I	11.9	5.6	9.8	3.6
II	12.3	5.7	10.1	3.6
III (non-manual)	13.9	8.1	11.1	4.5
III (manual)	15.1	8.1	12.4	5.0
IV	16.7	8.8	13.6	6.1
V	20.3	11.3	17.2	7.2
Other	20.4	10.1	23.3	7.1
Ratio Class V:I	1.71	2.0	1.8	2.0

* Perinatal deaths are stillbirths and deaths at ages up to six completed days of life

Source: *Mortality Statistics, Perinatal and Infant: social and biological factors 1978–79 and 1992*, HMSO, 1995; *Mortality Statistics, live births, stillbirths and infant deaths, 2001*, series DH3 no.34, Office for National Statistics, 2003 (Table 20 – all ages, within marriage)

ADULT DEATH RATES

As noted above for child deaths, there is a geographical pattern in premature adult death. In areas like Glasgow, Manchester and parts of London, death rates have risen rapidly, much of which could be accounted for by patterns of inequality, unemployment and poverty during the 1970s and 1980s.[109] Male residents in North Dorset or Christchurch can expect to live 10.6 years longer than those in Manchester, and female residents 7.2 years more.[110] Further statistics include:

- Unemployed men in England and Wales have a 20 per cent higher risk of death than average.[111]
- In Scotland, mortality rates in the 10 per cent most deprived areas are double those of the least deprived 50 per cent;[112] Glasgow City has the lowest life expectancy in the UK for men and women.[113]
- The death rate from coronary heart disease is three times higher in unskilled male workers than among professional men.[114]
- Suicide rates among young men in Manchester are twice the national average; 27 of its 33 wards are among the 10 per cent most deprived in the country.[115]

I used to belong to the Job Club and this chap was really looking for work hard, really really looking for work. And he thought he had a job and he came in to celebrate then they told him the job wasn't his and he tried to kill himself because he'd looked so long.

(Group of unemployed people, London)[116]

There are clear associations between housing conditions and death rates. In 2000–01 there were an estimated 25,000 'excess winter deaths' in England and Wales.[117] These death rates are higher than those in many European countries with much lower winter temperatures.[118]

POVERTY AND POOR HEALTH

Poverty is strongly associated with poor health. About two-thirds of the families interviewed in *Hardship Britain* reported sickness or disability, most commonly asthma, bronchitis and eczema. The prevalence of disability rises steeply with increasing levels of area deprivation, with residents in the most deprived areas more than twice as likely to have one or more disabilities as residents in the least deprived areas.[119] This association between area deprivation and disability persists after controlling for age, sex and social class characteristics of individuals. Ill-health was associated with the stress of poverty, inability to meet extra expenses caused by illness, and not being able to heat homes sufficiently.

I have asthma and when I get worried or I'm not warm, I get worse... we put on the heaters for the children because you have to, but for ourselves we say no.　　　　(R Cohen *et al, Hardship Britain*)[120]

Material disadvantage and subsequent poor health have an effect throughout the life cycle, from a higher risk of miscarriage and low birthweight to an increased risk of sickness and ill-health in childhood and a higher incidence of chronic diseases in adult life.

- People in the most deprived fifth of the population are more likely to suffer diabetes and are three and half times more likely to die of complications associated with the disease.[121]
- People on lower incomes are significantly more at risk from diet-related diseases such as heart attacks, cancers and strokes.[122]
- Thirty-five per cent of lone parents on income support suffer from a longstanding illness.[123]

- The 2001 *General Household Survey* revealed that the prevalence of longstanding illness was around 10 per cent higher for men and women from the routine and semi-routine groups than those from the managerial and professional group (see Table 4.2).[124]
- There are fewer GPs working in the most disadvantaged communities.[125]

Poverty also seems to be associated with poor mental health:

- A poor physical environment has a significant negative impact on physical and mental health.[126]
- A 2003 survey of 800 low-income households found a third of people reported suffering from stress, isolation and loneliness; 36 per cent of respondents said they were anxious or depressed.[127]
- One in four unemployed people have a neurotic disorder compared with only one in eight of those working full time, and for workless women the rate is twice as high as for workless men.[128]
- Higher reported stress also seems to be connected with isolation, and with economic inactivity for men and lone motherhood for women.[129]

As well as health, poverty can also affect relationships and participation in society.

TABLE 4.2: **Chronic sickness: percentage with reported limiting long-standing illness by socio-economic group (NS-SEC)[130], total of all ages, 2001**

Socio-economic group	Men	Women
Large employers and higher managerial	27	25
Higher professional	23	22
Lower managerial/professional	28	28
Intermediate	32	38
Small employer/own account	31	27
Lower supervisory/technical	35	32
Semi-routine	36	38
Routine	40	38
All	32	31

Source: Office for National Statistics, *Living in Britain 2001*, ONS, 2002

EXCLUSION

The *Poverty and Social Exclusion* surveys in Great Britain (1999) and in Northern Ireland (2002/03) also examined the links between poverty and other experiences, including being unable to afford to use services and exclusion from social relationships.

EXCLUSION FROM SERVICES

Lack of access to basic services can apply to services outside the home (such as transport) or inside it (such as power supplies). Outside the home, the *Poverty and Social Exclusion in Britain* (PSE) survey found that one in ten of the respondents found services unaffordable, mainly affecting evening classes and visits to the pub or cinema/theatre. Eleven per cent found train services unavailable or unaffordable.[131]

The *Poverty and Social Exclusion in Northern Ireland* (PSENI) survey in 2002/03 revealed similar exclusion from evening classes, visits to the pub or the cinema/theatre because such services were unaffordable. In addition, 1 per cent of respondents reported that they could not attend a place of worship because of lack of money.[132]

Within the home, 6 per cent of PSE survey respondents had experienced disconnection from a power supply, and 11 per cent had restricted their consumption.[133] In Northern Ireland, 5.4 per cent of PSENI respondents had been disconnected one or more times.[134] In Great Britain the number of gas disconnections for debt rose from 8,826 in 1996 to 21,780 in 2002 and from 477 to 995 for disconnections from electricity supply over the same period.[135] Although only 9 per cent of gas consumers and 15 per cent of electricity consumers use pre-payment, half of those in the lowest tenth of incomes do so for electricity and 58 per cent do so for gas, despite this being one of the most expensive and inconvenient forms of payment.[136] A recent Citizens Advice report found significant problems with pre-payment meters, which were often compulsory installed by suppliers because of customers missing payments.[137] The use of pre-payment meters gives rise to a significant incidence of self-disconnection; some people preferring this to being in debt. Nearly a quarter (24 per cent) of households with pre-payment meters reported self-disconnection from gas and 27 per cent self-disconnected from electricity in 2002.[138]

EXCLUSION FROM SOCIAL ACTIVITIES

Basic necessities included in the PSE survey were *social customs, obligations and activities.* Customs include celebrations on special occasions, such as Christmas, weddings and funerals, and presents for family and friends once a year. *Obligations and activities* include a hobby or leisure activity, as well as those involving reciprocation and care of others, such as visits to family or friends or having family/friends round for a meal.

The PSE survey found that:

- a fifth of the population were excluded from three or more social activities because they could not afford to participate;
- poor people were less likely to be active in their local community;
- 7 per cent could not afford a hobby or leisure activity;
- 18 per cent of adults could not afford a holiday away from home. [139]

The PSENI survey found that in 2002/03, 12 per cent of households could not participate in one social activity because of lack of money, 8 per cent were not able to participate in two, and 12 per cent were excluded from five or more activities because they could not afford to take part.

Other studies show the isolation, geographically, culturally and socially, experienced by people on low incomes. [140] Some lose contact with friends as their financial problems increase and they cannot afford to go out:

> We would like to visit relatives but we can't afford the bus fares.
> I get fed up with the four walls. It makes you feel down.
> (*Women and Men Talking about Poverty*) [141]

The *Expenditure and Food Survey for 2001–02* also showed that the poorest tenth of the income distribution spent £15.50 a week on 'recreation and culture' – over £38.50 a week less than the average (£54.00). [142]

PERCEPTIONS ABOUT BEING POOR

The PSE survey asked people whether they felt poor (leaving open how 'poor' was defined). Of those who said they felt poor all the time, 86 per cent were actually poor, though 11 per cent of those who were poor said they never felt poor. [143] The more often they believed they were poor in the past, the more likely they were to be poor at the time of the survey.

- Nearly three-quarters of people who felt isolated or depressed as a result of lack of money during the previous year were currently poor (at the time of the survey).
- Those who were dissatisfied with their area, or felt unsafe walking in the neighbourhood or being alone at home, were more likely to be poor.[144]

The PSENI also found that a subjective definition of poverty corresponded to an objective definition of poverty; of those people who claimed their income was a lot below that necessary to keep a household out of poverty, 82 per cent were poor, as were more than half (53 per cent) who said their income was a little below what was needed to prevent poverty.[145]

STIGMA AND MARGINALISATION

Many people on low incomes express feelings of marginalisation and exclusion. Although researchers organising group discussions in one study did not use the term 'stigma', it dominated the understanding of poor people about their poverty:

> Poor is stigma.
>
> (Group for low-income families)[146]

Many of those experiencing poverty view the words 'poor' and 'poverty' as demeaning descriptions. Being poor is a classification of difference which is experienced as stigmatising.[147] The public representations of poverty often reinforce the negative stereotyping of the poor and impact upon the self-identity of those in poverty.[148] In recent discussions with those experiencing poverty, many people articulated a sense of being made to feel different, and women reported feeling 'stigmatised and unwelcome' in 'better quality' shops:

> I never go into the big stores in town. [If you do] they're watching you. You feel right out of place – you feel like a tramp. You feel like they're following you in case you nick anything. You can feel eyes on you.
>
> (*Women and Men Talking about Poverty*)[149]

Many people also felt that where they lived could affect their chances of moving out of poverty, and perhaps of getting a job. They felt discriminated against, in terms of both employment and everyday services such as car insurance.[150] In a study of two poor estates in Sheffield and York, where only a third of residents were employed at the time of the survey, one resident said:

> As soon as you say you live on Bell Farm, you're some sort of deranged monster...a criminal, can't look after your children, you're in the pub all day.
>
> (P Lawless and Y Smith, 'Poverty, Inequality and Exclusion in the Contemporary City')[151]

PSYCHOLOGICAL EFFECTS OF POVERTY

Discussion groups of people living in poverty revealed some of its psychological effects, such as powerlessness, loss of self-esteem, stress, depression and anger.

> Constant worrying, 24 hours a day about money and having to manage for the rest of the week, month, year whatever.
>
> (Lone parents' group, Bristol)[152]

Another study found personal aspirations expressed by young people were low and very limited; younger people in poverty talked about their low self-esteem and the need to increase their confidence.[153]

Men and women can experience the effects of poverty differently; men may struggle to come to terms with failing to succeed as breadwinners, whilst women bear the brunt of having to manage inadequate resources and of trying to hide financial difficulties from other family members.[154]

TREATED AS POOR: DEALING WITH OFFICIALS

Being stigmatised – for example, by living in a disadvantaged area – may also lead to greater surveillance by state services. One mother with a new baby, whose father had just died, had her electricity cut off and was in debt. Asking social services for help, she found herself called to a case conference to assess her ability as a mother.[155]

Recent research found widespread criticism by those in poverty of Job Centres, the Benefits Agency, local authority housing departments, GPs, schools, and suppliers of gas and electricity.[156] Many people cited incidents where they felt they had been treated with a lack of respect by officials because of their financial circumstances:

> We feel like they think we are something to make fun of.
> (Father, referring to the 'dole office')[157]

Life on a low income entails form-filling, a great deal of contact with different offices, and queuing. Many people in poverty feel that officials have much power over their lives, and often believe they are treated disrespectfully by them.[158] Lack of choice is often a feature of poverty, one that may reinforce a sense of powerlessness. The compulsory introduction of electronic payment of most benefits and pensions from 2003, and the enforced instalment of many pre-payment meters, are examples of choices made by the state and the private sector on behalf of, rather than by, low-income consumers.[159]

Nevertheless, the diverse voices of people in poverty are being brought into the policy arena and the inclusion of people with experience of poverty and social exclusion is being called for at European level.[160] People in poverty are also active in fighting poverty in their own lives and in their communities.[161]

> ...despite structural and cultural constraints, people in poverty do exercise agency as actors in their own lives – from the everyday struggle of 'getting by', through instances of 'everyday resistance' and attempts to 'get out' of poverty, to more collective forms of 'getting organized' and demands for participation in decision-making that affects their lives.
> (P Beresford et al, *Poverty First Hand*)[162]

IMPACT ON FAMILY LIFE

Poverty has a negative impact on social relationships. In recent discussions involving groups of people in poverty all the respondents referred to the ways in which poverty created tensions at home and placed strains on family life.[163] People in poverty see their relationships with friends and family 'scarred' by financial circumstances. They also described frequent arguments between husbands and wives about money.[164]

Relationship breakdown can be another effect of poverty. Evidence from six years of the British Household Panel Survey (BHPS) revealed that people receiving income support were three times more likely to have a relationship breakdown than those not on income support.[165]

Research examining family change also found higher rates of splitting-up associated with levels of hardship, unemployment and social tenancy.[166]

One effect of family separation is that mothers with children are subject to the increased risk of poverty that lone parenthood brings. Divorce and separation mean the loss of any shared income and fewer than one in three lone parents receives any child maintenance from the child's father[167] despite attempts by recent governments to improve the calculation and collection of child support payments.

IMPACT ON CHILDREN

Many parents in poverty do not have sufficient income to provide the things identified by children themselves as essential for social interaction with their peers.[168] For instance, a child might miss out on school trips or going out with friends, simply because the parents cannot afford it:

> I don't usually go on school trips 'cos they are expensive and that… At our school they do loads of activities and they go to loads of different places… I don't bother asking.
>
> (Martin, 11)[169]

Faced with extensive advertising aimed at children, parents with a limited income try to reduce their children's expectations. Mothers in a recent study stated that they had worked hard to reduce children's aspirations; one mother said her children had learned to choose the cheapest items and 'not to ask for anything'.[170] Poverty can negatively impact upon child–parent relationships:

> For the respondents with young children, poverty was a significant element of their day-to-day relationships with their children. The difficulty of meeting the demands of children was a source of sadness, and generated a sense of failure and of guilt.
>
> (*Women and Men Talking about Poverty*)[171]

Poverty can also affect children by diminishing their parents' capacity and resources to bring them up.

> Good parenting requires certain permitting circumstances. There must be the necessary life opportunities and facilities. Where these are lacking even the best parents may find it difficult to exercise their skills.
>
> (Rutter, quoted in D Utting, *Family and Parenthood*)[172]

Chapter 5 considers the impact of poverty on children in more detail, including parental sacrifice to protect children from poverty and the longer-term impact of growing up in a low-income household.

CRIME AND FEAR OF CRIME

People on low incomes are often disproportionately affected by crime. First, while unemployed people have the same chance of experiencing crime as those in paid work, the former are more likely to be victims of different offences, such as car crime, burglary and household theft.[173] Second, being a victim of crime can have a more devastating effect on people on low incomes, for instance because they live in high-risk areas and are less likely to have home contents insurance.[174] Third, poor people are twice as likely to feel that their quality of life is significantly affected by fear of crime.[175]

Some poor people believed that the restricted choices faced by people on low incomes could push them into crime, though it was also recognised that this could simply result in a vicious circle of further financial limitations:

> You just can't get a car unless you just went illegal, then you get arrested and get into trouble, get fined and then it's taken out of your benefit so your benefit goes down.
>
> (Group of young people)[176]

CONCLUSION

Poverty casts a long shadow and can affect many aspects of life, from being unable to afford the basics to being excluded from social activities and services. Poverty can have many effects, and we have focused on just some of them, such as debt, a higher risk of ill-health and premature death, living in poor housing and sometimes homelessness. Whilst not all people who are poor experience these problems, and people who are not poor may also encounter them, people who live on low incomes, especially for a prolonged period, are more likely to be vulnerable to multiple deprivation.

NOTES

1 Department for Work and Pensions, *Opportunity for All: fourth annual report*, 2002, p83

2 R Lister, *Poverty*, Polity Press, 2004; P Beresford, D Green, R Lister and K Woodard, *Poverty First Hand: poor people speak for themselves*, CPAG, 1999

3 D Gordon, L Adelman, K Ashworth, J Bradshaw, R Levitas, S Middleton, C Pantazis, Demi Patsios, S Payne, P Townsend and J Williams, *Poverty and Social Exclusion in Britain*, Joseph Rowntree Foundation, 2000

4 E Kempson, *Life on a Low Income*, Joseph Rowntree Foundation, 1996

5 For example, J Mack and S Lansley, *Poor Britain*, Allen and Unwin, 1985

6 See note 3

7 P Hillyard, G Kelly, E McLaughlin, D Patsios and M Tomlinson, *Bare Necessities: poverty and social exclusion in Northern Ireland – key findings*, Democratic Dialogue No.16, 2003. Forty items and activities were considered 'necessities' by more than 50 per cent of the population surveyed. After various statistical tests for validity and reliability, 29 items were selected as 'deprivation items'. The consensual poverty threshold was established and defined a 'poor' household as one that lacked three or more deprivation items and have on average an equivalised income of £156.27 a week.

8 See note 3

9 H Burchett and A Seeley, *Good Enough to Eat?: The diet of pregnant teenagers*, Maternity Alliance/Food Commission, 2003

10 Quoted in S Leather, *The Making of Modern Malnutrition: an overview of food poverty in the UK*, The Caroline Walker Trust, 1996

11 See note 3 and note 7

12 S Middleton, K Ashworth and I Braithwaite, *Small Fortunes: spending on children, childhood poverty and parental sacrifice*, Joseph Rowntree Foundation, 1997

13 H Burchett and A Seeley, *Good Enough to Eat?: the diet of pregnant teenagers*, Maternity Alliance/Food Commission, April 2003

14 I Christie, M Harrison, C Hitchman and T Lang, *Inconvenience Food: the struggle to eat well on a low income*, Demos, 2002

15 E Holzhausen and V Pearlman, *Caring on the Breadline: the financial implications of caring*, Carers National Association, 2000

16 E Dowler and S Turner with B Dobson, *Poverty Bites: food health and poor families*, CPAG, 2001; *The Guardian*, 4 December 2002

17 J Pullinger and C Summerfield, *Social Focus on the Unemployed*, Office for National Statistics, 1999

18 See note 14

19 Lothian Anti Poverty Alliance, food poverty, www.lapa.org.uk.

20 C Farrell and W O'Connor, *Low-income families and Household Spending*, Research Report 192, Department for Work and Pensions, July 2003

21 See note 4

22 B Botting (ed), *Family Spending: a report on the Expenditure and Food Survey*, Office for National Statistics, 2003. The EFS report, published as *Family Spending*, replaced the *Family Expenditure Survey* (FES) and the *National Food Survey* (NFS) from April 2001

23 See, for example, the section on fuel poverty in Department of Trade and Industry, Energy Report, 1999

24 Department of Trade and Industry/Department for Environment, Food and Rural Affairs, *The UK Fuel Poverty Strategy: first annual progress report 2003*, 2003

25 A household is considered vulnerable if it meets one or more of the following criteria: one or more members of the household aged 60 or more, one or more children under 16, any member of the household being disabled or having a long-term illness – Department of Trade and Industry, *Fuel Poverty in England in 2001 Methodology: Update*, DTI, July 2003

26 See note 24

27 See note 3

28 E Kempson, A Bryson and K Rowlingson, *Hard Times? How poor families make ends meet*, Policy Studies Institute, 1994; S Yeandle, K Escott, L Grant and E Batty, *Women and Men Talking about Poverty*, working paper series No.7, Equal Opportunities Commission, 2003

29 T Ridge, *Childhood Poverty and Social Exclusion: from a child's perspective*, The Policy Press, 2002

30 S Yeandle, K Escott, L Grant and E Batty, *Women and Men Talking about Poverty*, Working Paper Series No.7, Equal Opportunities Commission, 2003

31 See note 30; see also J Goode, C Callender and R Lister, *Purse or Wallet?: gender inequalities and income distribution within families on benefit*, Policy Studies Institute, 1998

32 See note 4

33 See note 30, p5

34 P A Jones, 'Access to Credit on a Low Income', *How People on a Low Income Manage their Finances*, Economic and Social Research Council, 2002

35 Economic and Social Research Council, *How People on a Low Income Manage their Finances*, ESRC, 2002

36 See note 30, p7

37 S Edwards, *In Too Deep?: CAB clients' experience of debt*, Citizen's Advice/ Citizen's Advice Scotland, 2003

38 See note 37

39 E Kempson, *Over-indebtedness in Britain: a report to the Department of Trade and Industry*, September 2002

40 See note 37 and MORI, *Financial Over-Commitment Survey: research study conducted by MORI for Citizens Advice*, MORI, 2003

41 H Palmer with P Conaty, *Profiting from Poverty: why debt is big business in Britain*, New Economics Foundation, 2002

42 Citizens Advice press release on extortionate credit, March 2003; P Jones, *Access to Credit on a Low Income*, Co-operative Bank, 2001

43 CAP Summary – *Forgive Us Our Debts*, Church Action on Poverty, November 2002

44 Department for Work and Pensions, *Family Resources Survey Great Britain – 2001–2002*, 2003

45 Datamonitor, *UK Non-Standard and Sub-Prime Lending 2003*, 2003

46 E Kempson, 'Life on a Low Income: an overview of research on budgeting, credit and debt among the "financially excluded"', in *How people on Low Incomes Manage their Finances*, ESRC, 2002

47 Church Action on Poverty, *Forgive Us Our Debts*, CAP, December 2002

48 See note 47

49 See note 39

50 Department for Work and Pensions, *Opportunity For All: fifth annual report 2003*, The Stationery Office, 2003

51 National Consumer Council, *Everyday Essentials: meeting basic financial needs*, NCC, 2003

52 See note 51

53 See note 39

54 See note 39

55 'Profiting from Poverty' speech, Pat Conaty, 3rd Annual Community Finance Conference, January 2003

56 Shelter, *House Keeping: preventing homelessness through tackling rent arrears in social housing*, February 2003

57 National Association of Citizens Advice Bureaux, *Make or Break? CAB evidence on deductions from benefit*, NACAB, 1993

58 J Millar and T Ridge, *Families, Poverty, Work and Care: a review of literature on lone parents and low income couple families*, Research Report 153, Department for Work and Pensions, 2001

59 See note 39

60 See note 37

61 Leonard Cheshire, *Inclusive Citizenship, The Leonard Cheshire Social Exclusion Report 2002*, 2002

62 See note 39

63 See note 37

64 See note 30

65 D Kasparova, A Marsh, S Vegeris and J Perry, *Families and Children 2001: work and childcare*, Research Report 191, Department for Work and Pensions, 2003

66 See note 28

67 See note 28, *Hard Times? How poor families make ends meet*, p286

68 Office of the Deputy Prime Minister, *English House Condition Survey 2001*, 2003

69 Shelter, *Housing and Homelessness in England: the facts*, July 2002

70 See note 68

71 L Adelman, S Middleton and K Ashworth, *Britain's Poorest Children: severe and persistent poverty and social exclusion*, Save the Children/CRSP, 2003

72 Family Welfare Association/British Gas/Gingerbread, *House and Home Report*, Gingerbread and British Gas, April 2003

73 Shelter, *Home Sick: Shelter and Bradford & Bingley's campaign for healthy homes*, Shelter, 2002

74 See note 73

75 A Marsh, 'Housing and Health: the nature of the connection', *Radstats Journal*, No.76, Winter 2001

76 R Burrows, *Poverty and Home Ownership in Contemporary Britain*, The Policy Press, 2003

77 See note 4

78 *The Guardian*, Money section, 29 May 2003

79 S Wilcox, *Can Work – Can't Buy: local measures of the ability of working households to become home owners, Findings*, Joseph Rowntree Foundation, May 2003

80 Department for Transport, Local Government and the Regions, *More Than a Roof: a report into tackling homelessness*, 2002

81 Citizens Advice, *Possession Action – the last resort?*, Citizen's Advice Report, 2003

82 Additional applicants seen as in priority need: 18- to 20-year-olds who were previously in care, applicants vulnerable as a result of having to flee their home because of violence or the threat of violence

83 Office of the Deputy Prime Minister, *Statutory Homelessness: England fourth quarter*, Statistical Release, March 2003

84 J Newton, *All in One Place*, CHAS, 1994

85 C Summerfield and P Babb (eds), *Social Trends*, No. 33, Office for National Statistics, The Stationery Office, 2003

86 Department for the Environment, Transport and the Regions, *Housing in England: 1998/99 Housing Survey*, 2000

87 Own calculations from homelessness statistics, see note 68

88 Greater London Authority, *Homelessness in London*, GLA, 2001

89 Office of the Deputy Prime Minister, *Homeless Statistics June 2002*, September 2002

90 Crisis, *Statistics about Homelessness*, January 2003

91 Office of the Deputy Prime Minister, *Statutory Homelessness: England second quarter 2003*, Statistical Release, September 2003

92 Office of the Deputy Prime Minister, 'Local Housing Authority Homelessness Strategies', www.odpm.gov.uk, 2003

93 See note 4 and note 73

94 Office of the Deputy Prime Minister, *Statutory Homelessness: England fourth quarter 2002*, Statistical Release, March 2003

95 Crisis, *Out of Sight, Out of Mind? – the experiences of homeless women*, 1999

96 See note 47; see Citizens Advice, *Possession Action – the last resort?*, 2003

97 Shelter, *No Room to Play: children and homelessness*, Shelter, 2002

98 Crisis, *Health in Homelessness Strategies*, 2003

99 D Acheson, *Independent Inquiry into Inequalities in Health Report*, The Stationery Office, 1998

100 Crisis, *Still Dying for a Home*, 1996

101 Crisis, *Critical Condition: vulnerable single homeless people and access to GPs*, 2002

102 Neighbourhood Renewal Unit, Fact Sheet No.3, *Health and Neighbourhood Renewal*, April 2002

103 Department of Health, *Tackling Health Inequalities: summary of the cross-cutting review*, DoH, 2002

104 See for example, G Davey-Smith and D Gordon, 'Poverty Across the Life-Course and Health', in C Pantazis and D Gordon (eds), *Tackling Inequalities: where are we now and what can be done?*, The Policy Press, 2000

105 Department of Health, *Getting the Right Start: emerging findings*, April 2003

106 See note 103

107 See note 103

108 See note 103

109 R Mitchell, D Dorling and M Shaw, *Inequalities in Life and Death: what if Britain were more equal?*, The Policy Press, 2000

110 Office for National Statistics, *Life Expectancy at Birth: local health authorities in the UK, 1991–1993 to 1999–2001*, August 2003

111 See note 99

112 G Palmer, M Rahman and P Kenway, *Monitoring Poverty and Social Exclusion in Scotland*, Joseph Rowntree Foundation, 2003

113 See note 110

114 See note 103

115 *The Guardian*, 12 November 2002

116 See note 2, *Poverty First Hand: poor people speak for themselves*

117 Excess winter deaths are defined as the number of deaths in the four months from December to March, minus the average of the numbers in the preceding autumn (August–November) and the following summer (April–July); see note 101

118 Age Concern, *Hypothermia and Excess Winter Deaths*, Policy Unit, Age Concern England, January 2002

119 Department of Health, *Health Survey for England 2001*, 2001

120 R Cohen, J Coxall, G Craig and A Sadiq-Sangster, *Hardship Britain: being poor in the 1990s*, CPAG, 1992

121 See note 103

122 www.sustainweb.org

123 A Marsh, S McKay, Al Smith and A Stephenson, *Low-income families in Britain: work, welfare and social security in 1999*, Research Report 138, Department for Work and Pensions, 2001

124 General Household Survey, 'Self-reported sickness, socio-economic classification and economic activity status', Office for National Statistics, 2001

125 See note 103

126 See note 103

127 See note 72

128 See note 17

129 L Rainford and V Mason, *Health in England: investigating the links between social inequalities and health*, Office for National Statistics, 2000

130 From 2001 the National Statistics Socio-economic Classification (NS-SEC) replaced social class based on occupation and socio-economic groups (SEG). The information required to create NS-SEC is occupation coded to the unit groups (OUG) of the Standard Occupational Classification 2000 (SOC2000) and details of employment status (whether an employer, self-employed or employee; whether a supervisor; number of employees at the workplace).

131 See note 3

132 See note 7. The PSENI used the same set of questions relating to exclusion as used in the PSE survey.

133 See note 3

134 See note 7

135 Ofgem, *Social Action Plan Indicators*, http://www.ofgem.gov.uk, 2003. Disconnections for gas and electricity have not risen steadily, with fewer disconnections in 1999 (22,177 for gas and 373 for electricity) and 2000 (16,500 and 300)

136 National Energy Action, position paper, *Pre-Payment Meters*, July 2002

137 F Monroe and S Marks, *The Fuel Picture: CAB clients' experience of dealing with fuel suppliers*, CAB, 2002

138 See note 135

139 See note 3

140 See note 30

141 See note 30

142 B Botting (ed), *Family Spending: a report on the Expenditure and Food Survey*, Office for National Statistics, 2003

143 See note 3

144 See note 3; see also G Palmer, M Rahman and P Kenway, *Monitoring Poverty and Social Exclusion 2002*, New Policy Institute and Joseph Rowntree Foundation, 2002

145 See note 132, p53. Respondents were asked how much money was needed a week after tax to keep a household (such as theirs) out of poverty. A second question asked respondents how far above or below that level their household was.

146 See note 2, *Poverty First Hand: poor people speak for themselves*

147 See note 2, *Poverty*

148 See note 2, *Poverty*

149 See note 30

150 See note 30

151 P Lawless and Y Smith, 'Poverty, Inequality and Exclusion in the Contemporary City', in P Lawless, R Martin and S Hardy, *Unemployment and Social Exclusion: landscapes of labour inequality*, Regional Studies Association, 1998

152 See note 2, *Poverty First Hand*

153 See note 30

154 See note 30

155 ATD Fourth World, *Participation Works: involving people in poverty in policy-making*, 2000

156 See note 30

157 See note 30

158 UK Coalition Against Poverty, *Listen Hear – the right to be heard,* Report of the Commission on Poverty, Participation and Power, 2000

159 See note 137

160 See note 158 and Council of the European Union, *Fight against poverty and social exclusion: common objectives for the second round of National Action Plans*, REV 1 SOC 508, 14164/1/02, Brussels, 25 November 2002

161 Gellideg Foundation Group/Oxfam UK, *Fifty Voices are Better Than One: combating social exclusion and gender stereotyping in Gellideg, in the South Wales Valleys*, March 2003

162 See note 2, *Poverty First Hand*

163 See note 30

164 See note 30, p11

165 R Boheim and J Ermisch, *Breaking Up – financial surprises and partnership dissolution*, Institute for Social and Economic Research, University of Essex, 1999

166 A Marsh and J Perry, *Family Change 1999–2001*, Research Report 180, Department for Work and Pensions, 2003

167 See note 123

168 See note 29

169 See note 29

170 See note 29

171 See note 30

172 D Utting, *Family and Parenthood: supporting families, preventing breakdown*, Joseph Rowntree Foundation, 1995

173 See note 17

174 C Whyley, J McCormick and E Kempson, *Paying for Peace of Mind: access to home contents insurance for low-income households*, Policy Studies Institute, 1998

175 G Palmer, M Rahman and P Kenway, *Monitoring Poverty and Social Exclusion 2002*, New Policy Institute and Joseph Rowntree Foundation, 2002

176 See note 116

5 Children and poverty

Children growing up in low-income households are more likely than others to have poor health, to do badly at school, become teenage mothers or come into early contact with the police, to be unemployed as adults or to earn lower wages.

(HM Treasury, *Tackling Child Poverty: giving every child the best possible start in life*)[1]

The costs of a child, relative to income, can fall disproportionately on low-income households and the combination of higher costs and lower incomes can push some families into poverty. In Chapter 2 the higher risk of income poverty for children, as revealed by the *Households Below Average Income* statistics, was discussed, and in Chapter 3 the circumstances leading to poverty were examined. Here we consider the costs of children and the different measures which can be applied to child poverty, the persistence and severity of child poverty and the longer-term impact of a growing up in poverty (such as low educational achievement).

THE COSTS OF A CHILD

A child reaching her/his 17th birthday will have cost parents an estimated £50,000 (at 1997 prices).[2] These costs include one-off items like baby equipment and ongoing spending on essentials. One parent, usually the mother, may also have given up paid work, losing earnings.[3] Costs can be both direct (like food, clothing and toys) and indirect (such as earnings foregone).

DIRECT COSTS

The direct costs of a child have often been estimated through pricing a specific 'basket of goods and services' (the *budget standards* approach).[4] The *Small Fortunes* survey[5] used a different method – obtaining expenditure information from children and parents – and found that costs varied by age and income. More was spent on older children, but income constrained spending.

Using a similar approach, bringing up a disabled child has been costed as three times higher than the average for children as a whole.[6] Recent improvements to disability benefits still do not reflect fully the extra costs associated with disability, making little improvement to the incomes of many families with disabled children.[7]

TABLE 5.1: **Parent spending on children by age of child, 1997**

	Babies (under 2)		Pre-school (2–5)		Primary (full-time school, under 11)		Secondary (11–16)	
	Mean £	%	Mean £	%	Mean £	%	Mean £	%
Food	13.95	32	16.08	39	17.78	38	21.70	41
Clothes	7.45	17	5.26	13	4.12	9	3.51	7
Nappies	6.63	15	1.81	4	–	–	–	–
School	–	–	–	–	3.85	8	5.82	11
Babysitting	0.42	1	1.01	2	0.58	1	0.37	1
Phone	–	–	–	–	0.15	0	0.72	1
Other regular	5.91	13	5.97	14	3.32	7	3.72	7
Other	0.36	1	0.24	1	0.42	1	1.41	3
Christmas	2.38	5	2.59	6	3.06	7	4.03	8
Birthdays	1.36	3	1.62	4	1.49	3	1.85	4
Trips/holidays	3.77	9	4.30	10	5.78	12	4.28	8
Weekly average	44.21		41.28		46.30		52.38	
Childcare	7.64	17	10.52	25	3.16	7	0.86	2
Average including childcare	51.85		51.80		49.46		53.24	

Source: S Middleton, K Ashworth and I Braithwaite, *Small Fortunes: spending on children, childhood poverty and parental sacrifice*, Joseph Rowntree Foundation, 1997

For all parents, the costs of childcare can be high. In 2002 the estimated cost of a nursery place for one child under 2 was £6,650 a year.[8] The childcare element of working tax credit (and previously working families' tax credit) provides some payment towards childcare up to a maximum amount; but parents are still required to finance 30 per cent of costs and must use registered childcare to be eligible. Many parents do not have access to suitable or affordable childcare facilities, a problem partly being addressed by the National Childcare Strategy. In addition, many parents, especially lone parents, prefer to rely on family to meet their childcare needs.[9] As a result, many low-income working families are missing out on their tax credit entitlements; in February 2002, 668,000 lone parents were receiving working families' tax credit, of which only 140,000 received the childcare credit.[10]

INDIRECT OR OPPORTUNITY COSTS

The indirect cost of having a child (in giving up paid work) tends to be borne mainly by women. A report to the Cabinet Office Women's Unit showed that the gap in lifetime earnings between women with children and those without could be as great as half a million pounds, with those least skilled losing most.

- Earnings foregone by a low-skilled woman with two children were £269,000, and with four children £426,000.
- Earnings foregone by a high-skilled woman with two children were £19,000 and £90,000 with four children.[11]

CHILD POVERTY

The Labour Government has set ambitious targets to end child poverty within 20 years (2020), reducing it by a quarter by 2004/05 and halving it within 10 years. As part of this objective, measuring child poverty has been the recent focus of a consultation process between the Government and other interested parties (this is discussed in the Introduction).[12] Two approaches to measuring child poverty are considered in this chapter. The first uses the current Government 'poverty threshold' of below 60 per cent median income. The second is the consensual approach to establishing what are essential items and the numbers of families with children who lack these items because they cannot afford them.

TRENDS IN CHILD POVERTY

As noted in Chapter 2, child poverty rates have risen fast over the past 30 years, despite a fall in both average family size and numbers of families with children. The increase in child poverty since 1979 left the UK with one of the highest child income poverty rates relative to other countries by the mid-1990s[13] (discussed in Chapter 10).

- Child income poverty in 2001/02 was more than double that recorded in 1979; 30 per cent of all children were in income poverty in 2001/02 compared with 14 per cent of all children in 1979.[14]
- Child income poverty peaked in 1996/97, when 34 per cent of all children were income deprived.[15]
- Since 1997 child income poverty in Great Britain has fallen by around 500,000 to 3.8 million children, the lowest figure since 1991. Despite the reduction this still means that almost one in three children remain in income poverty.

CHILDREN AT RISK OF POVERTY

Families with children make up 53 per cent of those in income poverty. Children are more likely than other groups to be poor, one-third more likely than the population as a whole in the UK. Some children, such as those in lone-parent households, from workless families and many from ethnic minority families, are more at risk of income poverty than others.[16] The 2001/02 *Households Below Average Income* (HBAI) revealed that:

- 54 per cent of children in lone-parent households and 22 per cent of children in couple families lived in households with an income below 60 per cent of the median (after housing costs – AHC);
- 75 per cent of children in lone-parent families and 81 per cent of children in couple families where no one was in paid work lived in income poverty;
- children from ethnic minority households were more at risk of falling into a low-income group: while 27 per cent of children in white households lived in households with an income below 60 per cent of the median (AHC), 36 per cent of Indian, 41 per cent of Black Caribbean, 47 per cent of Black non-Caribbean, and 69 per cent of Pakistani and Bangladeshi children lived in households with incomes below this level;[17]

- disabled children, or those children with a disabled parent, were much more likely to experience poverty, live in unsuitable housing and suffer exclusion from public and community services.[18]

Children are more likely to live in households in receipt of means-tested benefits, such as income support; 17 per cent of households with children receive half or more of their income from means-tested benefits, compared with 6 per cent of households without children. In lone-parent households, 49 per cent received more than half their income from means-tested benefits, increasing to 68 per cent in house-holds with three or more children.[19] Of those children in income poverty, 38 per cent lived in a household in receipt of income support.[20]

PERSISTENT AND SEVERE CHILD POVERTY

Children, particularly those under five, have a greater risk of staying in poverty for extended periods than adults.[21] The latest data shows that 16 per cent of children lived in persistent income poverty for at least three out of four years between 1998 and 2001, a figure relatively unchanged for the past decade.[22] A recent analysis used data from the *British Household Panel Survey* (BHPS) (1991–99) and the *Poverty and Social Exclusion in Britain* (PSE) survey to examine the incidence of severe and persistent child poverty in Great Britain. Children were defined as experiencing severe poverty if poor on all three of the following measures:

- the child's own deprivation (if lacking one or more necessities because her/his parents could not afford them);
- the deprivation of their parents (if the parent went without two or more items seen as necessary because they could not afford them);
- the income poverty of their household (households with an income of below 40 per cent of median).[23]

Children were defined as experiencing *non-severe* poverty if poor on at least one of the above measures. The analysis found that 29 per cent of children were persistently poor, 13 per cent were severely poor for at least one year and 9 per cent of children experienced both severe *and* persistent poverty. Of those children who moved out of severe poverty the majority, 72 per cent, moved into non-severe poverty. Persistent and severe childhood poverty appeared more likely to occur around times of change in children's households, especially movements between paid work and benefits.[24] This may have been due to the inflexibility of the

TABLE 5.2: **Proportions at risk of persistent income poverty by family type, 1991–2000**

	% in bottom 30% in all years		
	1991–94	1995–98	1997–2000
Couples with children	23	23	21
Lone parents	62	55	56
Couple no children	7	8	8
Single no children	13	14	13

Source: Department for Work and Pensions, *Households Below Average Income 1994/5–2001/02*, 2003, p 129

benefit system, leaving families on a very low income during these transitional periods.

According to HBAI, lone parents are more likely to remain poor relative to couples with children and childless working-age adults (see Table 5.2).

DEPRIVATION

The PSE survey in 1999 defined a child as 'deprived' if lacking one or more necessities because her/his parents could not afford them.[25] On this measure 34 per cent of children lacked one or more items; 18 per cent lacked two or more. The *Poverty and Social Exclusion in Northern Ireland* (PSENI) survey (2002/03) used a similar list to determine which necessities children were lacking because their parents could not afford them.[26]

Children who were deprived of essentials in the PSE survey did not necessarily equate to those who were poor by income measures; 45 per cent of children who lived in 'income-poor' households (defined as below 60 per cent of median household income) were not 'necessity deprived' (according to the 'one item' threshold). For those deprived of two or more essentials, 65 per cent were income poor but not necessities-deprived.[27]

TABLE 5.3: **Percentage of children lacking certain basic necessities, PSE (1999) and PSENI (2002/03) surveys**

	PSE		PSENI
	% lacking one	% lacking two	% who cannot afford item/activity
Food			
Fresh fruit and vegetables daily	5	9	(4)
Three meals a day	(3)	(5)	(1)
Meat/fish/vegetarian twice daily	11	21	5
Clothing			
New fitted shoes	7	12	(2)
Warm waterproof coat	6	11	(3)
School uniform	6	18	(1)
Participation/activities			
Celebrations	10	20	(1)
Hobby/leisure	5	(10)	4
Swimming once a month	21	34	–
Holiday away from home	64	68	28
Leisure equipment	9	17	8
Friends round for tea/snack	11	21	–
Developmental			
Books of own	0	(1)	(1)
Play group	(4)	(7)	(3)
Educational games	12	21	5
Toys	(1)	(3)	(0.4)
Construction toys	10	19	(4)
Bike: new/secondhand	10	18	7
Environmental			
Bed and bedding for self	(2)	(3)	(1)
Bedrooms for each child of different sex over age 10	10	10	7
Bedroom carpet	(4)	(9)	–
Garden for play	10	8	5

Note: Figures in brackets indicate less than 20 weighted cases; – indicates that these items were not on, or were different from, the list of necessities in the PSE survey

Source: D Gordon et al, *Poverty and Social Exclusion in Britain*, Joseph Rowntree Foundation, 2000; P Hillyard et al, *Bare Necessities: poverty and social exclusion in Northern Ireland – key findings*, Democratic Dialogue No.16, 2003

THE IMPACT OF GROWING UP IN POVERTY

Despite the best efforts of parents to protect their children, it is simply not possible for children to avoid the realisation that they are poor, particularly if poverty persists for a significant length of time.

(S Middleton, 'Coping for the Children: low income families and financial management')[28]

PARENTAL SACRIFICE

The *Britain's Poorest Children* study showed that many parents were deprived of necessities when their children were not, suggesting a significant degree of parental sacrifice.[29] This finding parallels other research, which has found that parents are often more likely to go without basic items than their children.[30] Figure 5.1 shows that the parents of children who were poor on all three measures in *Britain's Poorest Children* were the most likely to lack necessities. However, while these parents often lacked personal necessities (41 per cent of these parents had no warm waterproof coat and 34 per cent lacked fresh fruit or vegetables daily) they were no more likely to lack household

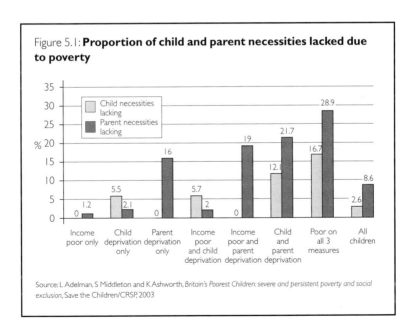

Figure 5.1: **Proportion of child and parent necessities lacked due to poverty**

Source: L Adelman, S Middleton and K Ashworth, *Britain's Poorest Children: severe and persistent poverty and social exclusion*, Save the Children/CRSP, 2003

necessities. The authors suggest that parents are sacrificing their own health and well-being by cutting back on personal necessities, rather than on household items that would affect their children.[31]

In another recent study of low-income families, parents, especially mothers, viewed the children as the household's main priority and any extra income was spent on them, often to the detriment of parental needs.[32] Two-parent families seem more able to protect their children from poverty than lone-parent families.[33] This may be due to the longer periods that lone parents spend out of paid work and on income support or the necessary reliance on just one wage for lone-parent families when in paid work.

STIGMA AND SCHOOL MEALS

Parents may also be wary of poverty 'stigmatising' their children; one example is free school meal entitlement.[34] Twenty per cent of those children entitled to free school meals in 2001 did not take up their entitlement. Poor quality of school meals and an unawareness of entitlement partially explained non-take-up but a further reason given by parents and children was embarrassment or fear of stigma.[35] In many schools children can be identified as having free school meals (such as by separate queues or tokens) which, in some cases, can result in bullying from other pupils.[36]

> I realised when I was in year 7 that the people who got free school meals were teased...I couldn't handle that as I was already getting teased enough so I don't get free school meals.[37]

Although the risk of stigma is apparent, many children and parents view free school meal provision as a valuable resource. It enables children to have an adequate main meal when there may be cut-backs on food at home. It also acts as a 'budgeting mechanism' for parents and as such its absence, for example in the school holidays, may cause an extra financial strain on a limited family budget.[38]

POOR CHILD HEALTH

> Babies born to poorer families are more likely to be born prematurely,
> are at greater risk of infant mortality and have a greater likelihood of
> poverty, impaired development and chronic disease in later life.
>> (Department of Health, *Tackling Health Inequalities*)[39]

Inability to afford essentials like food means a poor diet, which can lead
to poor health. CPAG research has shown that people on low incomes
know how to eat healthily but high food prices make it hard to do so.[40]
Children in households receiving income support are at risk from a
nutritionally poor diet and hunger.[41] Children in poverty are also at
increased risk of suffering Illness.

- The Food Commission calculated the average cost of a healthier
  'basket of food' to be 51 per cent more expensive than 'standard'
  alternatives.[42]
- A study of pregnant teenagers found that most had nutritionally
  inadequate diets, largely because they could not afford to eat
  properly; this posed a health risk for themselves and their children's
  future health.[43]

Children's and young people's mental well-being is affected by poverty
and social hardship.[44] Poverty and family discord seem to be the most
important factors in increasing the risk of childhood mental health
problems; both are more likely to occur when the parents are unemployed, divorced or heading lone-parent families.[45] The prevalence of
self-harm and attempted suicide by children was more than twice as
high for those in class V than in class I.[46]

Furthermore, *some* poor children may be at risk of abuse or neglect.
Although the association is complex, there is a link between poverty
and the physical abuse and neglect of children.[47] It may, though, simply
be that poor families are more easily detected by social welfare
agencies.

The poor physical environment also affects children's well-being.
Children in deprived areas are five times more likely to be killed in road
accidents. This is because they are more likely to be pedestrians than
their more affluent peers, and less likely to have access to a safe play area
or garden.[48]

CHILD DEVELOPMENT

Poverty can also affect child development; low birthweight and shorter height are both more pronounced in deprived areas.[49]

- Birthweight on average is 130 grams lower in children from social classes IV/V (the two lowest socio-economic classes) than I/II (the two top socio-economic classes). Low birthweight is closely associated with infant death and chronic diseases in later life.[50]
- Between 15 and 20 per cent of children attending one Glasgow children's hospital showed signs of malnutrition, being either under-height and/or under-weight for their age – 60 per cent of Glasgow's population live in areas of multiple deprivation.[51]
- Involvement with many services considered universal, such as ante-natal classes and health visiting, are not well known about or are unavailable in poor areas.[52]

Poverty can also have effects on a child's intellectual development, as the following research shows.

- An analysis of children aged 6 to 17 in the National Child Development Study found those in the top fifth of incomes scored on average 3.7 per cent higher on a test of cognitive functioning, the Peabody Picture Vocabulary Test, than children on the lowest incomes.[53]
- From as early as 22 months, children of parents in social classes I/II with higher educational levels are already 14 percentage points higher up the scale of educational development than children of class IV/V parents with low educational attainment.[54]

Recent strategies such as Early Excellence centres, Sure Start projects and Children's Centres aim to promote the development of young children and equalise opportunities. Although funding has significantly increased in deprived areas, availability remains problematic.

- There are 600,000 children under three living in income poverty and only 42,740 free or subsidised places for disadvantaged families. That is one place for every 14 children living in poverty.[55]
- It has been estimated that Sure Start, an initiative targeting children living in deprived areas, will only reach a third of all children in poverty by 2004.[56]

EDUCATIONAL DISADVANTAGE

The links between poverty, social class and poor educational attainment are strong. They are evident before primary school, increase throughout a child's school career and are reflected in differential qualifications and rates of access to further education. Although there has been some improvement in the attainment levels of pupils at 'disadvantaged' schools, there is still considerable underachievement.

- In 2002, 59 per cent of children receiving free school meals (FSM) reached expected attainment levels in Key Stage 2 for English, compared to 70 per cent of those not receiving free school meals (non-FSM). The gap in attainment levels between FSM and non-FSM children was even wider by Key Stage 3 in all subjects and regardless of prior achievement.[57]
- Schools in the poorest areas have 10 to 25 per cent of pupils achieving five GCSE passes at grades A*–C against a national average of just under 50 per cent.[58]
- Nearly 90 per cent of 'failing schools'[59] are located in deprived areas and have a large proportion of children eligible for free school meals.[60]
- Research has found a close link between truanting and child poverty. Money problems in the family were a significant factor in younger children's non-attendance at school.[61]
- Suspension, exclusion and, in particular, truancy from school are more likely for children whose families are in receipt of working-age means-tested benefits.[62] Children excluded from school are unlikely to return to mainstream education.[63]
- Children growing up in poverty are more likely to expect to leave school at 16 – a factor that decreases the chance of receiving high-grade GCSEs.[64]
- Lack of material resources such as space to work, books and computers at home and money for equipment and trips were identified by professionals in education as key factors in children's low performance.[65]

Children in poverty offer an account of school life in which they are not only educationally disadvantaged, by missing out on school activities, but also socially disadvantaged. They are excluded from participating in the everyday opportunities and experiences shared by their peer group because of their poverty.[66] Tess Ridge concludes from her recent research examining poverty from a child's perspective that 'children living in households receiving low-income means-tested benefits are having qualitatively different experiences at school to their non-benefit peers'.[67]

In 2002, 13 per cent of 18-year-olds and 7 per cent of 16-year-olds in England and Wales were not in any education, training or employment; 30 per cent of these 16-year-olds had no reported GCSEs. One-third of children who were persistent truants in the last year of secondary school were not in paid work, training or education at 18. About two-fifths of those out of work at 16 were not in education, training or employment by 18.[68] These young people were more likely to have parents who were poor or unemployed.[69]

'POOR' CHILDREN AND FAMILY FINANCES

> …if you're poor when you're a child, you don't expect to be rich when you grow up.
>
> (C Willow, 'Bread is free')[70]

Interviews with children aged between 5 and 16 revealed that children living in poverty had learned to moderate their demands on parents.[71] Children of lone parents were more likely than those in two-parent families to restrict their requests for items, believing their parent could not afford them (57 per cent and 47 per cent respectively). The same behaviour was found for children in income support families (54 per cent) compared with those not on income support (48 per cent).

Other discussions with children in poverty have shown children's considerable awareness of their parent's financial circumstances and has revealed that for some children, the moderation of their demands and a denial of their own needs was a means of trying to protect their parents from the impact of poverty.[72] Children's self-sacrificing behaviour was one way many children managed their poverty, but the discussions also revealed the children's resourcefulness in obtaining money and material goods. For example, many children did household chores for a small sum (when a parent was able to pay) or undertook paid work outside the home, such as babysitting, cleaning and paper-rounds, benefiting themselves and their family. 'Income from work both sustains children and contributes to family budgets directly and in kind'.[73] For some children, however, having a job had a negative impact on their schoolwork and on their social life.[74]

Possibly because of the financial exclusion experienced by many people in poverty, children in low-income families often see their parents operate a cash-based lifestyle, with little use of mainstream financial institutions (see Chapter 4). Poorer children consequently have little knowledge of the role of banks and building societies and may be disadvantaged in terms of financial skills as they become adults.[75]

LONGER-TERM OUTCOMES OF CHILDHOOD POVERTY

> In general, children of poverty are more likely to form lower expectations about their success at school or work, and they in fact turn out to be less successful in achieving higher levels of education or getting jobs or avoiding getting pregnant.
>
> (J Ermisch, M Francesconi and D J Pevalin, *Outcomes for Children of Poverty*)[76]

Children growing up in poorer families are more likely as adults to have a low income and other disadvantages.

- Living in poverty as a child was likely to lead to lower wages and more unemployment in men at age 33.[77]
- Children who grew up in a low-income family are more likely to be economically inactive, have lower self-esteem and have a fatalistic attitude to health.
- The experience of childhood poverty for females is also associated with a significantly higher risk of early childbearing.[78]
- Ambitions for the future among disadvantaged teenagers were found to be largely unrealistic, for example being a famous pop star or footballer, or limited; girls in particular displayed very limited work ambitions.[79]

The Social Exclusion Unit notes that teenage pregnancy is often both a cause and a consequence of social exclusion.[80] The UK still has the highest rate of teenage pregnancies in Western Europe – 42.5 conceptions per 1,000 women aged 15 to 17 in 2001 – despite seeing a 10 per cent reduction in teenage conceptions (and therefore the prevention of 8,000 pregnancies) since 1998.[81] The rate of teenage conception and pregnancy is higher in some of the poorest areas; between 1992 and 1997, 48 per cent of teenage conceptions occurred in the 20 per cent most deprived wards.[82] Teenage conception and pregnancy rates are also very high for those who have been in care or excluded from school. Many teenagers face very restricted access to social security benefits and are therefore especially vulnerable to income poverty. Just over one-third (35.5 per cent) of teenage mothers aged 16–19 participated in education, training or employment in 2002; although low, this is double the comparable figure for 1997 (16 per cent).[83] Sure Start Plus, which aims to reduce the risk of long-term social exclusion resulting from teenage pregnancy, has offered one-to one advice and group activities for an estimated 4,000 pregnant teenagers or teenage parents since April 2001.[84]

GOVERNMENT POLICIES AND CHILD POVERTY

The eradication of child poverty is a much-stated ambition of the present Government. In addition to tax and benefit changes designed to raise the income of poorer families (see Chapter 2), more innovative policies have also been introduced to tackle current and future child poverty.

The Child Trust Fund will provide (in April 2005) an initial 'endowment' voucher of £250 for every child born in the UK since September 2002 (£500 for low-income families), which is used to open a savings account, or alternative, in the child's name.[85] A further Government payment will be made into the account when children are 7 years old. The 'endowment' can be boosted by contributions, of up to £1,200 a year, from relatives and the child-recipient her/himself. The initiative is designed to encourage saving among low-income families and provide available capital for the child on reaching adulthood. However, although proposed as a measure to help low-income families, it is unlikely that many poor families will have the resources to contribute.

'Early years' schemes such as Sure Start, providing free part-time early education for 3- and 4-year-olds in deprived areas, and the creation of Children's Centres, are also central to the Government's anti-poverty agenda. The long-term aim is for all young children living in the 20 per cent most disadvantaged wards in England to have access to Children's Centre services, providing early education, in addition to child and family health services.[86] While welcomed, the scheme has been criticised for failing to reach the two-thirds of children in poverty who live outside the 20 per cent targeted area.[87] The extension of Children's Centres to cover the 30 per cent most disadvantaged wards, and therefore reaching a further 340,000 children in poverty, was recommended by a recent Commons Committee, along with a call for extra childcare funding in order to meet the child poverty and lone parent employment targets by 2010.[88] The Government rejected these recommendations in October 2003.[89]

Another initiative aimed at secondary-school-age children, education maintenance allowances (EMAs), have already been piloted and will be introduced nationally in England from September 2004. EMAs will provide weekly financial support of up to £30 a week, depending on parental income, to 16–19 year olds who enter further education, with additional bonuses of £100 for attendance and achievement.[90] This may have the effect of encouraging young people from poorer backgrounds to continue with post-compulsory studies.

In June 2003, Margaret Hodge was appointed Minister for Children and Young People. Responsibility for social care policy for children and for the teenage pregnancy programme transferred from the Department of Health to the Department for Education and Skills. In July 2003, the House of Commons Work and Pensions Committee announced an inquiry 'to examine the extent of child poverty in the UK and the effectiveness of the Government's strategy to eradicate it'.[91]

CONCLUSION

The birth of a child may be enough to push many low-income families into poverty. Families with children tend to spend more on the basics than households without children. Whether measured by incomes, spending or deprivation of basic necessities, families with children tend to be 'poor', with lone-parent families the poorest of all.

Although parents may sacrifice their own needs to protect their children from having to go without or face the stigma of being poor, for many this is a losing battle, with poor children facing greater risks of ill-health, poor development and low educational attainment. Poverty can follow a child into adulthood, inhibiting aspirations and leading to under-achievement and educational and employment disadvantage. As a result, plans to reduce child poverty need to tackle both the immediate and longer-term effects of childhood deprivation.

NOTES

1 HM Treasury, *Tackling Child Poverty: giving every child the best possible start in life*, a Pre-budget Report Document, December 2001

2 S Middleton, K Ashworth and I Braithwaite, *Small Fortunes: spending on children, childhood poverty and parental sacrifice*, Joseph Rowntree Foundation, 1997

3 K Rake K (ed), *Women's Incomes Over the Lifetime*, Women's Unit/Cabinet Office, The Stationery Office, 2000

4 N Oldfield and A C S Yu, *The Cost of a Child: living standards for the 1990s*, CPAG, 1993

5 See note 2

6 B Dobson and S Middleton, *Paying to Care: the cost of childhood disability*, Joseph Rowntree Foundation, 1998

7 N Sharma, *Still Missing Out? Ending Poverty and Social Exclusion: messages to government from families with disabled children*, Barnardo's, 2002

8 DayCare Trust, *Childcare Facts – about childcare costs*, www.daycaretrust.org.uk, January 2003

9 W O'Connor and R Boreham, *Investigating Low Labour Market Participation Among Lone Parents in London: a review of the methods*, Department for Work and Pensions In-house Report 104, November 2002

10 Inland Revenue, *Working Families' Tax Credit Statistics*, Quarterly Enquiry, February 2002, www.inlandrevenue.gov.uk/wftctables/wftc_feb_02.pdf

11 See note 3

12 Department for Work and Pensions, *Measuring Child Poverty*, December 2003

13 M Brewer, T Clark and A Goodman, *The Government's Child Poverty Target: how much progress has been made?*, Institute for Fiscal Studies, April 2002

14 Department for Work and Pensions, *Households Below Average Income 1994/5–2001/02*, The Stationery Office, March 2003; Department of Social Security, *Households Below Average Income 1979–1996/97*, Corporate Document Services, 1998

15 See note 14, *Households Below Average Income 1994/5–2001/02*

16 See note 1

17 See note 14, *Households Below Average Income 1994/5–2001/02*

18 See note 7

19 Office for National Statistics, *Family Resources Survey 2001–2002*, Department for Work and Pensions, 2003, Table 3.9

20 See note 14, *Households Below Average Income 1994/5–2001/02*

21 M S Hill and S P Jenkins, 'Poverty Among British Children: chronic or transitory', in B Bradbury, S P Jenkins, J Micklewright (eds), *The Dynamics of Child Poverty in Industrial Countries*, Cambridge University Press, 2001

22 See note 14, *Households Below Average Income 1994/5–2001/02*; Department for Work and Pensions, *Opportunity for All: fifth annual report 2003*, The Stationery Office, 2003

23 L Adelman, S Middleton and K Ashworth, *Britain's Poorest Children: severe and persistent poverty and social exclusion*, Save the Children/Centre for Research in Social Policy, 2003. The report used two thresholds for severe and non-severe persistent income poverty. These thresholds were 27 per cent and 59 per cent of weekly median household income respectively.

24 See note 23, p136

25 D Gordon, L Adelman, K Ashworth, J Bradshaw, R Levitas, S Middleton, C Pantazis, D Patsios, S Payne, P Townsend and J Williams, *Poverty and Social Exclusion in Britain*, Joseph Rowntree Foundation, 2000

26 P Hillyard, G Kelly, E McLaughlin, D Patsios and M Tomlinson, *Bare Necessities: poverty and social exclusion in Northern Ireland – key findings*, Democratic Dialogue No.16, 2003. Although a list of child necessities was established and respondents were asked from this what necessities their children were lacking, a child poverty threshold based on children's items and activities together with low income was not formulated for the report.

27 See note 25

28 S Middleton, 'Coping for the Children: low income families and financial management', in *How People on Low Incomes Manage their Finances*, Economic and Social Research Council, 2002

29 See note 23

30 See note 2

31 See note 23, p 22

32 C Farrell and W O'Connor, *Low-income Families and Household Spending*, Research Report 192, Department for Work and Pensions, July 2003

33 See note 2

34 Children entitled to free school meals include: those with parents in receipt of income support or means-tested jobseeker's allowance or support provided under Part VI of the Immigration and Asylum Act 1999, or families who are in receipt of child tax credit but who are not entitled to working tax credit, and whose annual income (as assessed by the Inland Revenue) does not exceed £13,230. Parents in receipt of working tax credit are excluded.

35 P Storey and R Chamberlain, *Improving the take-up of free school meals*, Department of Education and Employment, 2001

36 W McMahon and T Marsh, *Filling the Gap: free school meals, nutrition and poverty*, CPAG, 1999

37 T Ridge, Childhood *Poverty and Social Exclusion: from a child's perspective*, The Policy Press, 2002

38 See note 37

39 Department of Health, *Tackling Health Inequalities: summary of the cross-cutting review*, Department of Health, 2002

40 E Dowler, S Turner with B Dobson, *Poverty Bites: food health and poor families*, CPAG, 2001; H Burchett and A Seeley, *Good Enough to Eat?: The diet of pregnant teenagers*, Maternity Alliance/Food Commission, April 2003

41 See note 40

42 Food Commission, 'Healthier diets cost more than ever', *Food Magazine*, issue 55, 2001. 'Standard' alternatives were processed foods such as white bread and white pasta instead of wholemeal.

43 See note 40, *Good Enough to Eat?: The diet of pregnant teenagers*

44 Wired for Health, 'What stresses kids out', www.wiredforhealth.gov.uk/doc.php?docid=7242

45 K Darton and G Stewart, Mind Factsheet, 'Children and young people and mental health', *Mind*, 2001; Department of Health, *Getting the Right Start: emerging findings*, 2003

46 Department of Health, *Children and Adolescents Who Try to Harm, Hurt or Kill Themselves*, 2001

47 P Cawson, C Wattam, S Brooker and G Kelly, *Child Maltreatment in the UK: a study of the prevalence of child abuse and neglect*, NSPCC, 2000; D Quilgars, 'Child Abuse', in J Bradshaw (ed), *Poverty: the outcomes for children*, Family Policy Studies Centre, 2001

48 T Grayling, K Hallam, D Graham, R Anderson and S Glaister, *Streets Ahead: safe and liveable streets for children*, IPPR, 2002; Department of Health, *Getting the Right Start: emerging findings*, 2003

49 S Holtermann, *All our Futures: the impact of public expenditure and fiscal policies on Britain's children and young people*, Barnardo's, 1995

50 Department of Health, *Tackling Health Inequalities: summary of the cross-cutting review on health inequalities*, November 2002

51 NCH Scotland/Scottish Executive, *Factfile 2002*, 2002

52 End Child Poverty, *Supporting Poor Families*, Briefing Paper, December 2002

53 A McCulloch and H Joshi, *Child Development and Resources: an exploration of evidence from the second generation of the 1958 British birth cohort*, Institute for Social and Economic Research Paper 99-15, 1999

54 HM Treasury, *Tackling Poverty and Extending Opportunity: the modernisation of Britain's tax and benefits system*, March 1999

55 See note 8

56 T Marsh, *End Child Poverty Newsletter*, Issue 3, Winter 2002, p3

57 Department for Education and Skills, *Statistics of Education: pupil progress by pupil characteristics: 2002*, June 2003, p20

58 R Lupton, *Places Apart? The initial report of CASE's areas study*, CASE Report 14, CASE, 2001

59 Failing schools refers to those schools on 'special measures' – those which have been found 'likely to fail to give its pupils an acceptable standard of education' as decided by an Ofsted Registered Inspector and agreed to by Her Majesty's Chief Inspector of Schools (HMCI), www.standards.dfes.gov.uk/schoolimprovement/siweak/siguidance/sispecial/

60 R Lupton, 'School Quality, Free School Meals and Area Deprivation: reading between the lines', paper presented at the LSE Research Laboratory All-Centre Event, 3 July 2002

61 M Zhang, 'Links Between School Absenteeism and Child Poverty', *Pastoral Care in Education*, March 2003

62 See note 37, pp115–116. Benefits: Income support, jobseeker's allowance and a small number of those in receipt of family credit. Ridge's analysis of the *British Household Panel Survey* (1997, Wave 7) showed that children living in a family in receipt of benefit were twice as likely to truant as those children in a family not in receipt of benefits.

63 G Palmer, M Rahman and P Kenway, *Monitoring Poverty and Social exclusion 2002*, Joseph Rowntree Foundation, 2002

64 J Ermisch, M Francesconi and D J Pevalin, *Outcomes for Children of Poverty*, Research Report 158, Department for Work and Pensions, 2001

65 See note 60

66 See note 37

67 See note 37, p129

68 Department for Education and Skills, *Youth Cohort Study: The activities and experiences of 16 year olds: England and Wales 2002*, February 2003; DfES, *Youth Cohort Study: The activities and experiences of 18 year olds: England and Wales 2002*, February 2003

69 Strategy Unit, *Ethnic Minorities and the Labour Market: interim analytical report*, 2002

70 C Willow, *'Bread is free': children and young people talk about poverty*, Children's Rights Alliance for England/Save the Children, 2001, cited in Euronet, *Including Children? Developing a coherent approach to child poverty and social exclusion across Europe*, 2001

71 J Shropshire and S Middleton, *Small Expectations: Learning to be poor?*, Joseph Rowntree Foundation, 1999

72 See note 37, p109

73 See note 37, p57

74 See note 37

75 J Loumidis and S Middleton, *A Cycle of Disadvantage?: Financial exclusion in childhood*, Financial Services Authority, 2000; S Middleton, 'Coping for the Children: Low income families and financial management', in *How People on Low Incomes Manage their Finances*, Economic and Social Research Council, 2002

76 See note 64

77 P Gregg, S Harkness and S Machin, 'Poor Kids: trends in child poverty in Britain, 1968–96', *Fiscal Studies*, Vol. 20, No. 2, June 1999

78 See note 64

79 Teenage Pregnancy Unit, *Lifestyles and Media Consumption of Disadvantaged Teenagers*, www.teenagepregnancyunit.gov.uk, March 2001

80 Teenage Pregnancy Unit, *National Evaluation of Sure Start Plus – summary* January 2002, August 2002

81 Office for National Statistics, 'Conceptions: Numbers, rates and percentages leading to legal abortion: by age of woman at conception', *Health Statistics Quarterly*, No 17, February 2003

82 Neighbourhood Renewal Unit, *National Deprivation – related targets 2000 – teenage pregnancy*, www.neighbourhood.gov.uk

83 Department of Health, *Tackling Health Inequalities: a programme for action*, July 2003

84 M Wiggins, H Austerberry, M Rosato, M Sawtell and S Oliver, *Service Delivery Study: interim findings*, Social Science Research Unit, Institute of Education, May 2003

85 Unit trusts and life products can also be used as well as standard savings accounts

86 The Government's National Childcare Strategy only covers England. Scotland and Wales have their own childcare strategies, which are the responsibility of the devolved administrations.

87 House of Commons Work and Pensions Select Committee, *Childcare for Working Parents: fifth report of session 2002–03*, Volume 1, 2003

88 See note 87

89 House of Commons Work and Pensions Committee, *Government Response to the Committee's Fifth Report into Childcare for Working Parents*, First Special Report of Session, 2002–03 HC 1184, The Stationery Office, October 2003

90 Department for Education and Skills, *Education Maintenance Allowance – an introduction*, DfES, 2003. Any young person who lives in a household with an annual income of £30,000 or less is entitled to an EMA. Weekly allowances of £10 will be given to young people living in households nearer the EMA threshold and £20 EMA a week provided for mid-income threshold households. Young people in families with household income levels below £19,000 will receive the full £30 a week rate.

91 House of Commons Work and Pensions Committee homepage, www.parliament.uk, 'Child Poverty in the UK', Session 2002/03

6 Women and poverty

People's sex is a key determinant of who is poor. Women and men have different experiences of poverty, different livelihood options and different potential routes out of poverty.
(J Rowlands, *Alive and Kicking: women and men's responses to poverty and globalisation in the UK*)[1]

The incidence and experience of poverty are deeply gendered. In much of the world women are more likely than men to experience poverty.[2] Within the UK the gendered nature of poverty is clear. The *Poverty and Social Exclusion in Northern Ireland* (PSENI) survey found that 29 per cent of women lived in poor households, compared with 25 per cent of men, and 57 per cent of adults in poor households were women.[3] In Great Britain 21 per cent of women, compared to 18 per cent of men, had incomes below 60 per cent of the median in 2001/02.[4] Some women are at even greater risk of income poverty; unemployed women, women from particular ethnic minorities, female tenants and female single-pensioners are more likely to experience poverty than are men with the same characteristics.[5] A recent analysis of the *Poverty and Social Exclusion in Britain* (PSE) survey data found that the chances of a woman being in poverty were 14 per cent higher than for a man.[6] Furthermore:

> In some dimensions women are also more likely be socially excluded – labour market excluded, excluded from services, from social activities and restricted in going out.[7]

Focusing on women's poverty raises crucial issues for the examination of poverty as a whole.[8] Caroline Glendinning and Jane Millar's *Women and Poverty in Britain* brought together many of the central aspects of women's poverty.[9] The authors argue that looking at women's risk of poverty is not simply a question of illuminating the disparate levels of income that exist between men and women. It is also about:

- women's *access* to incomes and other resources;
- the *time* spent in generating income and resources; and
- the *transfer* of these resources from some members of a household to others.

This approach facilitates a much more complete understanding of the gendered nature of poverty which is not captured by straightforward statistics on family or household incomes. The structural disadvantages women face in the labour market, the gap between women and men's average pay, women's high rates of part-time and low-paid work and time out of the labour market to care for relatives or bring up children, and the unequal sharing of household resources all contribute to women's poverty.

INDICATORS OF WOMEN'S POVERTY

LOW INCOME

Looking at the individual incomes of men and women reveals major gender inequalities. Women are over-represented at the lower end of the income distribution and under-represented in the top income brackets; for men, the situation is reversed (see Table 6.1).[10] Women in general are more vulnerable to having a lower income than men are and receive a higher proportion of their income from benefits than from employment. In 2001/02, around 40 per cent of all women had total and net individual incomes of less than £100 a week, compared to less than one in five of all men; women in pensioner couples and in couple families with children had the lowest total weekly individual income of all women.[11] The weekly median total individual income for all men was twice that for all women (see Figure 6.1).

In addition to the disparity in the *amount* of income for men and women the *sources* of income are also markedly different. Although the major source of income for both sexes is earnings, a lower proportion of women – 42 per cent –received most (at least three-quarters) of their

TABLE 6.1: **Percentage distribution of all women and all men within the all adult total individual income quintiles, 2001/02, Great Britain**

	Percentage					
	Bottom quintile	Second quintile	Third quintile	Fourth quintile	Top quintile	Population size (millions)
All women	28	26	21	15	11	22.4
All men	12	14	19	25	30	21.8
All adults	20	20	20	20	20	44.2

Source: Women and Equality Unit/Department of Trade and Industry, *Individual Income 1996 to 2001/02*, June 2003

FIGURE 6.1: **Median total individual income by gender and family type, 2001/02, Great Britain**

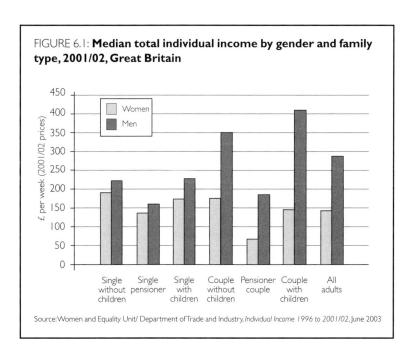

Source: Women and Equality Unit/ Department of Trade and Industry, *Individual Income 1996 to 2001/02*, June 2003

income from employment, compared with 60 per cent of all men in Great Britain.[12] Earnings also made up 42 per cent of the total individual income of female lone parents, with a further 37 per cent coming from benefits. However, over half of all female lone parents received 75 per cent or more of their income from benefits or tax credits.[13] Women are also more likely to be recipients of means-tested benefits, rather than contributory benefits. In 2003, almost two-thirds of claimants reliant on income support were women.[14]

EMPLOYMENT AND UNEMPLOYMENT

Women's participation in the labour market has increased from 38 per cent of the workforce in 1971 to around 45 per cent of the total workforce today.[15] While entry to the labour market allows women access to independent income, women continue to be paid less than men doing similar work. Women also remain concentrated in particular areas of low-pay (and low-status) employment – 85 per cent of workers in personal services, 79 per cent of workers in administrative and secretarial jobs and 69 per cent of those in sales and customer services are women, reflecting the continuation of a gendered labour market.[16] Around 80 per cent of part-time workers are women; such employment is often low-paid and insecure[17] and may be 'chosen' by women to fit in with caring responsibilities in the face of limited access to, or availability of, full-time employment.[18] As well as affecting women's choice of employment, childbirth and unpaid caring responsibilities may also interrupt time in the labour market, impacting upon women's immediate earnings and possible contributions to state and occupational pension schemes for support in later life.

The International Labour Organization (ILO) unemployment measure records 582,000 women as currently unemployed – the lowest number in the UK since records of this kind began in 1984.[19] According to the claimant count, far fewer – 236,600 women – were unemployed in May 2003. The lower claimant count statistics are based on the numbers claiming benefit or national insurance credits and may hide the full extent of women's unemployment. For example, many unemployed women do not qualify for income-based jobseeker's allowance because their partner is in paid work. One recent study of 'hidden' unemployment in the East Midlands estimated that four out of five women suffering 'real unemployment' are actually 'hidden' statistically, compared to only about one in two men.[20] In addition, some of the 4.7 million women described as 'economically inactive' in 2003 labour market analyses may not define themselves as unemployed when undertaking unpaid caring work or looking after the home and as a consequence are statistically absent from the unemployment figures.

LOW PAY

Women are nearly three times more likely to be in low paid employment than men are.[21] Part-time jobs, largely undertaken by women, are about five times more likely to be low paid than full-time jobs; but a full-time job held by a woman is still about twice as likely to be low paid as one held by a man.[22] 'Low pay is an issue not only for those women on low wages, but also for those who depend on them – such as their children.'[23]

The national minimum wage, introduced in 1999 and uprated each year, has benefited low-paid workers, especially women; 70 per cent of beneficiaries from the main 2001 uprating were women, and around two-thirds of jobs that gained were part time.[24] However, of the 330,000 people estimated to be in jobs paying below the national minimum wage in 2002, 230,000 were in jobs occupied by women.[25]

The National Group on Homeworking (NGH) reported that many homeworkers, mainly women, and especially women from Pakistani and Bangladeshi communities, are particularly likely to be very low paid and are less aware than other employees of their right to a minimum wage.[26]

LONE MOTHERS

In 2002, one in five children lived in a lone-parent family. Over 90 per cent of the 1.5 million lone-parent households in the UK are headed by women; such households are much more likely to be in poverty than other family groups.[27] While caring for dependent children affects all mothers' ability to undertake paid work, the impact on lone parents appears greater – 53 per cent of lone mothers were in paid work in 2003, compared with over 70 per cent of mothers in couples.[28] As well as missing out on the possibility of a partner's support with childcare, which may affect mothers' ability or desire to enter paid work,[29] lone parents may also lose out on the prospect of sharing a partner's income and thus reliance on a single wage if employed, or benefits if not, leads to a low household income and a greater vulnerability to poverty and deprivation (see Chapter 3). One feature of lone-parenthood and poverty is that, 'Poorer fathers are more likely to be non-resident and in less contact with their children',[30] which may create further financial and emotional strain on lone mothers and undermine their ability to get out of poverty.

In recent years government policies have promoted paid work as a route out of poverty for lone parents with a specific target to get 70 per cent of lone parents into paid work by 2010. One scheme designed to achieve this goal, the New Deal for Lone Parents (NDLP), provides help, through a lone-parent adviser, with looking for and applying for jobs or training and offers advice about childcare and in-work benefits. The NDLP appears to have been successful in moving lone parents into paid work – 53 per cent of programme leavers entered employment of 16 hours a week or more.[31] However, most of the jobs lone parents moved into after the NDLP were low-skilled or elementary occupations.[32] Consequently the earnings from such work alone may not be enough to escape poverty. In addition, 7 per cent of lone parents on the scheme were participating for the third time or more and 29 per cent of all NDLP leavers returned to income support within a year.[33]

The combination of coping with bringing up children on their own and the difficulties of managing on a single wage, very often at low levels, with little access to affordable childcare, means that many lone mothers find themselves forced to rely on means-tested benefits for long periods.

BENEFITS

> The economic disadvantages experienced earlier in the life course, mainly as a result of caring activities, extend into later life. As a result, a much greater proportion of women's resources derive from means-tested cash transfers.[34]

One of the main features of the current social security system in the UK is the division between national insurance, non-contributory and means-tested benefits and tax credits. As long as sufficient contributions have been made, national insurance benefits are paid on an individual basis regardless of income. Non-contributory benefits are not means-tested, but they are usually at lower rates than national insurance benefits. Means-tested benefits are assessed on the basis of income and capital and are based on the 'benefit unit' of a household (with joint assessment for heterosexual couples living together). Because women are more likely to have breaks in employment and to work part time and earn low wages, many fall below the threshold for making national insurance contributions. Women are therefore less likely than men to have national insurance benefits in their own right, and as a result are more dependent on means-tested benefits (see Table 6.2). For 30 per

TABLE 6.2: **Percentage of benefit claimants by sex, February 2003***

Great Britain	per cent	
Benefit	Men	Women
Income support	35	65
Jobseeker's allowance	76	24
Incapacity benefit	65	35
Minimum income guarantee	38	62
Attendance allowance	30	70
Disability living allowance	51	49
Carer's allowance	25	75
Industrial injury disablement benefit*	87	13
State pension	37	63
Widow's benefit	0	100
Bereavement benefits	36	64
Child benefit	5	95

*Industrial injuries disablement benefit – figures for December 2002

Source: Department for Work and Pensions, *Statistical Summary – First Release,* June 2003

cent of all women, benefits and tax credits made up at least 75 per cent of their overall income; this compares with only 16 per cent of all men.[35]

Of people below pension age, more men are claiming contributory benefits and more women are claiming means-tested and non-contributory benefits.[36] Retirement pension (a contributory benefit) is an exception to this pattern because of the high proportion of women pensioners.[37] However, the average amount of entitlement to state pension in 2002 was substantially lower for women – £67 a week, compared to men's £92 a week. In addition, men in pensioner couples received more of their income from occupational pensions (41 per cent), compared with less than a fifth (18 per cent) of the income of women in such couples[38] – leaving women pensioners more reliant on state benefits. A much higher proportion of women than men over pension age have been dependent on minimum income guarantee (MIG – income support for those over 60); 920,000 single women received MIG in 2000/01 and a further estimated 230,000 to 380,000 single women were entitled but did not claim.[39]

The pension credit replaced the MIG in October 2003 (see Chapter 3). While the pension credit continues to offer a minimum income for pensioners, the 'savings' part of the pension credit is only available to those over 65, which excludes women from qualifying until five years after state pension age.[40] Furthermore, in order to receive the savings element of the pension credit, pensioners must be receiving income above the level of the full basic state pension; 51 per cent of women do not qualify for a full state pension, thus excluding half of all female pensioners. After the pension credit reforms, it is estimated that three-quarters of single women over 60 will be entitled to one of the principal means-tested benefits,[41] indicative of their greater longevity and lower income than men.

EXCLUSION

The indicators of poverty used so far look at hard facts, like income; but there are less quantifiable aspects to poverty, such as not being able to go out for a drink or a meal, or missing out on seeing friends. The PSE survey revealed that women were more likely than men to be excluded from social activities because they could not afford them. Women are also more likely than men to be excluded from services and to face substantial labour market exclusion.[42] Pakistani and Bangladeshi women are particularly likely to suffer exclusion from higher education and from the labour market.[43]

One study found that poorer young women in rural areas faced particularly high levels of social exclusion. Young women had limited access to employment opportunities, and were denied access to decision-making and the shared cultural life of the community. Such social exclusion was compounded by poverty and unchallenged gender stereotyping, which further restricted their job opportunities and aspirations.[44]

THE CAUSES OF WOMEN'S POVERTY

Underpinning the ... causes of poverty is the assumption that women are, or should be, financially dependent upon men and that their role within the family is as carer, rather than earner. Ending women's poverty and deprivation will, to some extent, rely on reducing their economic dependence on men.

(Bradshaw *et al*, *Gender and Poverty in Britain*)[45]

Many women's lives are still shaped by the family responsibilities they have traditionally been expected to take on: the tasks of childcare, caring for the elderly and maintaining the home. These tasks shape women's paid work patterns, the type of occupations they work in, their earnings and their social security benefits. They push women into financial dependence upon men or upon state benefits. Although women, and even lone mothers, increasingly are being seen as 'workers' in social and economic policy, it is still often assumed that women's income is less important than men's and that money, food and other resources are shared evenly within the family. For many women, neither employment nor social security can keep them out of poverty.

WOMEN'S UNPAID WORK

DOMESTIC LABOUR

The UK *Time Use* survey reveals that a traditional, gendered, division of household tasks remains very much the norm, both in terms of the types of chores carried out and what women and men say they 'like' doing. Within couple households in 2000/01:

- 42 per cent of men did no ironing and 39 per cent of men did no laundry;
- 46 per cent of women did not do DIY repair work compared to 16 per cent of men;
- over half of women said they 'liked' food shopping, 69 per cent 'liked' cooking, 49 per cent 'liked' tidying the house and 44 per cent 'liked' washing clothes;
- women spend an average of 3 hours and 40 minutes on housework and family care a day; men spend an average of 2 hours a day on the same tasks.[46]

Despite their increased participation in the labour market, women continue to be responsible for the bulk of domestic work. British women do four times the amount of housework as their male partners, with married women in part-time paid work having a total weekly workload 13 hours greater than that of married men, time mostly spent on housework.[47] Although there have been some changes in the amount of time spent on housework and paid work between men and women over the past decade, narrowing the differentials, this has been due to the reduction in women's time spent on domestic chores rather than an increase of men's work within the household.[48]

The continuation of a gender ideology that places the burden of housework and childcare on women has consequences for women's ambitions and ability to work outside the home. Part-time or casual work is 'chosen' to fit around expected domestic responsibilities or as a way back into the labour market for women with young children. As discussed, such work is often low-paid with little training opportunities and therefore has implications for women's immediate economic position as well as future employment opportunities and pension provision.[49]

CARING FOR CHILDREN

With changing attitudes towards parenting and the increasing participation of mothers in the labour market, caring for children is starting to be seen as an issue for fathers as well as mothers.[50] However, the persistence of a pay gap – women earned 18.9 per cent less than men in 2002 – means that it often makes financial sense for mothers, rather than fathers, to give up paid work or reduce their hours to care for dependent children.[51] The cultural expectation that mothers will be the primary carer and fathers the 'breadwinner' is also an enduring one that results in women usually undertaking the role of looking after children. Caring for children has a knock-on effect on women's employment and earning capacity: years out of paid employment, working part time and having lower earnings, loss of pension rights and skills which become outdated are consequences for many women who withdraw from the labour market in order to care. Women may also experience downward mobility on their return to paid work; one recent study found that 48 per cent of women who had been managers before having children suffered downward mobility.[52]

Fathers on low incomes may be under pressure to work longer hours to compensate for the loss of the mother's earnings after childbirth, causing a further obstacle to sharing childcare.[53] To some extent this problem is being recognised and was partially addressed by the Employment Act 2002 and the introduction of 'family-friendly' policies in April 2003. The recent legislation extends parents' rights in work and may enable fathers to become more involved in child-rearing; paternity leave became a statutory requirement and new fathers receive two weeks' paid leave, although the payment of £100 a week may not be enough to encourage fathers to take time out of paid work.

Possibly the most significant change was the introduction of flexible working rights. This allows parents and guardians with a child under 6 or a disabled child under 18 to request changes in working hours, working times and the place of work. However, an employer is not legally obliged to meet employee requests. Although designed to allow flexible working arrangements for fathers and mothers, a survey of human resource professionals found that 60 per cent said the flexible work regulations would adversely affect their decision to employ women.[54] The legislation may therefore have unintended detrimental consequences on women's employability. In addition, men are reluctant to work flexibly; 46 per cent of men say that working non-standard working hours can adversely affect their career.[55]

Recent research has also found that while flexible working practices may allow women to balance domestic and paid work, structural inequalities limited mothers' access to flexible working arrangements; many women in low-paid, low-status jobs are not eligible to use them.[56] In addition, 'family-friendly' policies did not change the gendered division of labour in the mothers' homes.[57]

CARING WORK

> With the exception of spouse care, women predominate among those providing care in the home for adults and, in particular, among those providing the most intensive care.
> (R Lister, *Citizenship: Feminist Perspectives*)[58]

It is not only caring for children that has a knock-on effect on women's lost earnings, but also caring for adult relatives who are elderly or sick or have a disability:

- 6.8 million adults provided informal care either inside or outside their home in 2002;[59]
- 58 per cent of informal carers are women; of those caring for at least 20 hours a week, 61 per cent were women and 39 per cent men;
- almost a third of married or cohabiting women aged 45–64 were carers in 2000;
- 18 per cent of all women and 14 per cent of all men over 16 are informal carers; 11 per cent of women are the main carers, compared with 7 per cent of men;
- caring had a marked impact on employment, especially for women: 23 per cent of female carers were economically inactive compared with 17 per cent of male carers;[60]

- 21 per cent of women carers spent over 35 hours a week on caring work.[61]

Among carers of working age who spent 20 or more hours a week on caring, 54 per cent of men were working compared with 42 per cent of women; male carers were almost three times as likely to be working full time as female carers.[62]

The inability to take up paid work because of caring responsibilities and the low payment of carers' benefits means that the financial cost of caring is substantial. One study found that many carers were unable to afford basic household bills; one in three were in debt and one in five cut back on food to save money.[63]

When women do return to the labour market after an 'interruption', such as care work, especially that of children, they face a greater 'wage penalty' than do men; women's jobs after re-entry will pay an average of 16.1 per cent less than their former jobs, whereas men will suffer a 6.5 per cent drop in wages.[64] The more time spent out of the labour market, the greater the loss.[65]

WOMEN'S PAID WORK

Women's growing participation in the labour market, from 38 per cent of the total labour force in 1971 to around 45 per cent in 2003,[66] is in part triggered by the growth of the service sector, increasing flexibility in work patterns and part-time employment and the continuing decline of manual jobs. But despite women's increasing presence, occupational segregation between 'men's jobs' and 'women's jobs' remains entrenched. The division between women and men in the world of paid work reflects and reinforces the division of labour in the home, and in paid work women are concentrated in particular occupations and industries. The latest *Labour Force Survey* shows that in 2002/03:

- around 40 per cent of employed women were working in public administration, education and health;
- almost a quarter of employed women were working in administrative and secretarial posts compared with just 5 per cent of men;
- 14 per cent of women were working in personal service occupations (healthcare, childcare and related personal services) compared with around 2 per cent of men.[67]

Average gross earnings of full-time male employees were £514 per week in April 2002 compared to women's average gross full-time weekly earnings of £383.[68] Part of the disparity in pay is accounted for by the occupations in which women predominate – ones that have high proportions of low-paid workers. According to the *New Earnings Survey 2002*, more than twice the proportion of women (27 per cent) than men (12 per cent) among full-time employees earned under £250 a week, with much higher proportions of women than men earning below this level in particular occupations. Sixty-four per cent of full-time childcare workers were paid under £250 a week (gross), as were:

- 59.1 per cent of full-time workers in catering;
- 49.4 per cent of full-time workers in health and related occupations;
- 31.3 per cent of full-time workers in clerical and secretarial occupations, with 40.2 per cent of 'other secretarial', personal assistants and typists and 58.9 per cent of receptionists earning below this level.

One of the five most common jobs for women, retail cash desk and check-out operator, was also the lowest paid occupation in 2002: 89 per cent of full-time workers earned under £250 a week.[69]

The gender pay gap in hourly earnings for full-time employees narrowed from 28 per cent in 1982 to 20 per cent in the mid-1990s but has barely changed since this time.[70] Women working full time currently earn 81 per cent of a full-time male worker's hourly earnings; this 19 per cent difference represents a slight widening of the gender pay gap in 2002 and a return to levels recorded in 2000.[71] There was an especially large pay gap – 41 per cent – between women who worked part time and men in full-time employment. This differential in hourly earnings between women who work part time and men who work full time is as wide now as it was in the late 1970s.[72] Table 6.3 shows the differences between men and women's earnings and the gender pay gap.

Although women are increasingly entering managerial and professional occupations, they tend to be located at the lower levels of the profession.[73]

Elsewhere, occupational segregation seems firmly in place and seems likely to remain so for the near future; the gender breakdown of Foundation Level Modern Apprenticeships in 2001–02 illustrates the very gendered nature of particular industries (see Table 6.4).

TABLE 6.3: **Earnings differentials between men and women, 2002 – average earnings (£) of employees, Great Britain, 2002**

	Hourly*	Weekly	Annual
Average earnings (£ per hour):			
Women			
Full-time	10.22	383.4	19,811
Part-time	7.42	143.8	7,593
All	**9.48**	**283.5**	**14,619**
Men			
Full-time	12.59	513.8	27,437
Part-time	8.82	165.3	9,485
All	**12.46**	**484.1**	**26,020**
Gender pay gaps (%):			
Women F/T and men F/T	18.8	25.4	27.8
Women P/T and men P/T	15.9	13.0	19.9
Women P/T and men F/T	41.1	72.0	72.3
All women and all men	**23.9**	**41.4**	**43.8**

*Hourly earnings exclude overtime hours and pay, whilst weekly earnings include overtime and other additional payments

Source: Equal Opportunities Commission, *Women and Men in Britain: pay and income, March 2003*, p4. All data are from the *New Earnings Survey 2002*.

TABLE 6.4: **Women and men in Foundation Level Modern Apprenticeships, 2001–02**

Industry	Women (%)	Men (%)
Construction	1	99
Engineering manufacturing	4	96
Childcare	97	3
Information and communication technology	33	67

Source: Equal Opportunities Committee, 'Jobs for the boys and jobs for the girls' press release, June 2003

Such gender segregation in the labour market has consequences for women's income. Female-dominated occupations, such as childcare, are associated with lower earnings. If segregation were reduced to equal numbers of men and women in each industry, women's wages would rise by 33 pence an hour.

PATTERNS OF WOMEN'S PAID WORK

Patterns of women's work are directly linked to responsibilities for caring for children or others. Within families with dependent children, as the youngest child gets older the mother is more likely to be in paid work. A large proportion of women with children in the youngest age groups are not 'economically active' (this category includes those who are not seeking paid work, or are not available to work, such as the long-term sick, disabled people and those looking after children or the home) (see Table 6.5).

When women are in paid work they are far more likely to be working part time than men — 42.4 per cent of women worked part time in 2002, with 65.5 per cent doing so when their children were under 4, in contrast to just 9 per cent of men working part time.[75]

TABLE 6.5: **Employment rates for women of working age with children in 2002/03**

	All women	Women with dependent children					All men
		(By age of youngest dependent child)					
	16–59	All (0–18)	0–4	5–10	11–15	16–18	16–64
In employment	69.5	65.0	52.0	69.2	77.4	78.2	79.1
Full-time	57.6	40.9	34.5	37.2	49.3	53.7	91.0
Part-time	42.4	59.1	65.5	62.8	50.7	46.3	9.0
Unemployed (as % of the population)	3.1	3.0	3.0	3.5	2.3	2.4	4.8
Economically inactive	27.3	32.1	45.0	27.3	20.3	19.4	16.1

Source:, Office for National Statistics, *Labour Market Trends*, Vol. 111, No. 5, May 2003

Because of the structure of the labour market, women's choices of part-time work are limited; jobs within the professional and managerial sectors are much less likely to have part-time work available.[76] Typically, part-time work is concentrated in low-skilled, low-pay occupations, often with few opportunities for training or economic advancement. The low pay associated with part-time work is a large factor in women's poverty.

> Women's earnings, particularly where they are part time, are frequently insufficient to provide genuine economic independence...or the ability to maintain an independent poverty-free household.[77]

Part-time work also has financial implications for women in later life; only 37 per cent of women working part time have access to any kind of pension scheme.[78]

Much of women's dependence on part-time work can be seen as a 'solution' to balancing childcare and paid work in the absence of a comprehensive system of childcare. In the *Labour Force Survey 2002*, 54 per cent of female part-time employees said they worked part time because they wanted to spend time with their family, had domestic commitments or they felt insufficient childcare facilities were available.[79] The provision of affordable childcare is central to mothers' decision to undertake paid work and their ability to do so. According to one study:

> 63% of non-working mothers and 78% of non-working lone mothers said they would prefer to go out to work or study if they had access to good quality, convenient, reliable and affordable childcare.[80]

However, the cost of childcare in the UK remains expensive and therefore inaccessible to many low-income parents; nursery provision for one child under two was estimated to cost £6,650 a year in 2002.[81] Even with a proportion of costs paid by the childcare element of working tax credit up to a ceiling, parents must still pay 30 per cent, a sizeable amount for low-earning parents and possibly enough to make paid work an economically unfeasible option.[82]

The National Childcare Strategy (NCS), launched in 1998, aimed to increase the quantity, quality and affordability of childcare, primarily to enable more women to enter paid employment. Since its introduction childcare provision has grown substantially.[83] A recent Work and Pensions Committee report noted that if the NCS meets its target of providing 1.6 million childcare places by 2004, and a further 250,000 by 2006, it may facilitate mothers, especially low-income mothers, to take up paid work.[84] Nevertheless, at present there are too few child-care places; even with the Government's investment there are doubts that current measures will create the childcare places needed to meet the Government target for increasing lone-parent employment.[85] There is also concern that many women and children living in poverty will miss out, since most low-income families live outside of the 20 per cent most deprived wards targeted by the scheme.[86] An additional concern with the Government's promotion of childcare facilities is the unambiguous connection made by them between paid childcare and paid work. As Peter Moss points out, 'childcare should not just be about freeing parents so that they are able to work'.[87] A labour-market driven strategy underlying current childcare policies could pressurise women into paid employment, which may not be in their own, or their children's, best interests in the long term.

'Making work pay' has been fundamental to the Government's anti-poverty strategy. The introduction of working families' tax credit, replaced by working tax credit (combined with child tax credit for those with children) in April 2003, has been particularly beneficial to women, largely because they are among the lowest-paid workers.[88] Child tax credits payments are designed to go directly to the main carer, usually the mother in couple families, and therefore raise the income and living standards of all family members.[89] One possible shortcoming of the tax credit scheme is that many parents are not claiming the childcare element. In 2002, just 22 per cent of lone parents and 3 per cent of couple families who received working families' tax credit also claimed the childcare element.[90] Such a low rate of claimants may partly be because parents are only eligible if registered childcare is used and therefore cannot claim if childcare is unavailable in their area or if informal childcare is used.

Despite the evidence that women are disadvantaged in the world of paid work in comparison with men, women's earnings are increasingly important to family income; 17 per cent of households with one partner in paid work were in poverty in 2001/02 compared with 3 per cent of households in which both partners were in paid employment.[91]

WOMEN'S HIDDEN POVERTY

The distribution of money, food and other goods inside the home is an area that is seen as private and is therefore very difficult to research. A number of studies of low-income households have shown that women often put the needs of their families above their own.[92] In this way women help to prevent or reduce poverty for other members of their family but at the cost of impoverishing themselves:

> 'Hidden poverty' among women manifests itself through the unequal distribution of both income and consumption within families. It can mean either that women are poor when their male partners are not or that women experience poverty more intensely than their partners.[93]

Studies have shown that income is not shared equally within families, with men having greater 'personal spending money' than women[94] and more control over financial decisions.[95] Bringing money into the household seems to bring a sense of entitlement as to how it is spent, with men generally as the higher earner being the one with greater control over family expenditure.[96] Overall, women bring in less than a third of the total family income of couples (31 per cent), with 69 per cent coming from the individual income of men.[97] Even women working full time contribute an average of 46 per cent to family resources, with the majority coming from the male partner. Low-earning women are likely to have less control in household financial decisions than women earning more, and they are the least likely to be the main user of a joint account between couples.[98] Many women, therefore, still live in households where there are considerable financial imbalances and a large proportion of women continue to be economically dependent on their partner's income and on his decision as to how it should be shared and spent.

However, within many low-income families women are more likely to be in charge of the 'family budget', which often entails attempting to stretch a limited income and manage debt[99] and therefore is potentially burdensome rather than empowering. Managing on a low family income may also involve the concealment of bills and money owing[100] and so brings particular stresses and anxieties for women. For some women in poverty, though, managing on a small budget is seen as a source of pride.[101]

It is not only the sharing of money and resources that can be unequal within a home, but also the impact of things that a family does not have. For example, living in an overcrowded flat with damp and heating problems has a greater effect on a mother at home with a child than on her husband who is out at work, simply because of the amount of time the woman spends at home.

CONCLUSION

Many of the numerous measures introduced by the Government to tackle poverty will be of considerable benefit to women, but tackling gender inequality in poverty is not an explicit outcome or objective in current Government policy.

(J Bradshaw, N Finch, P Kemp, E Mayhew and J Williams, *Gender and Poverty in Britain*)[102]

Despite a government commitment in 1998 to focus on gender, this has not fully materialised within the subsequent 'welfare reform' agenda.[103] Women continue to be seen as a member of a 'couple' or a 'family',[104] papering over inequalities between women and men and the differential opportunities and limitations facing them within the home and in the world of paid work.

Women's poverty is compounded over a lifetime. Their lower rates of pay, work patterns interrupted because of caring for others, the trap of part-time work, and the diminished social security, occupational and private benefits received as a result of their work patterns, combine to impoverish women throughout their lives. Women's longer life expectancy and their reduced access to pensions means that a high proportion of women are also disproportionately susceptible to poverty in their old age.

NOTES

1 J Rowlands, *Alive and Kicking: women and men's responses to poverty and globalisation in the UK*, Oxfam GB, November 2002

2 UNIFEM, *Progress of the World's Women 2002: gender equality and the millennium development goals*, Volume 2, 2002; K Christopher, P England, S McLanahan, K Ross Phillips, Timothy M Smeeding, 'Gender Inequality and Poverty in Affluent Nations: the role of single motherhood and the state', *JCPR Working Paper* 108, August 2000 – Sweden was the only affluent European country of those examined where men's poverty was higher than women's

3 P Hillyard, G Kelly, E McLaughlin, D Patsios and M Tomlinson, *Bare Necessities: Poverty and Social Exclusion in Northern Ireland – key findings*, Democratic Dialogue Report No.16, 2003

4 Department for Work and Pensions, *Households Below Average Income 1994/5–2001/02* Corporate Document Services, 2003

5 J Bradshaw, N Finch, P Kemp, E Mayhew and J Williams, *Gender and Poverty in Britain*, Working paper Series No.6, Equal Opportunities Commission, Spring 2003

6 Equal Opportunities Commission, *Gender and Poverty in Britain*, Research Findings, 2003

7 See note 5

8 J Millar and C Glendinning, 'Gender and poverty: a survey article', *Journal of Social Policy*, Vol 18, Part 3, July 1989.

9 C Glendinning and J Millar (eds), *Women and Poverty in Britain*, Wheatsheaf, 1987

10 Department of Trade and Industry/Women and Equality Unit, *Individual Income 1996 to 2001/02*, 2003

11 See note 10 – 'Total income is gross income plus tax credits. Net income deducts National Insurance contributions and income tax from gross income', pv

12 See note 10

13 This same analysis is not possible for men given the small number of male lone parents

14 Department for Work and Pensions, *First Release*, Statistical Summary, June 2003

15 Women and Equality Unit, *Changing World, Changing Lives: women in the UK since 1999*, 2003

16 Equal Opportunities Commission, *Facts about Women and Men in Great Britain 2003*, 2003

17 See note 15; Low Pay Commission, *The National Minimum Wage: fourth report of the low pay commission, building on success*, The Stationery Office, 2003

18 See note 5

19 Office for National Statistics, *Labour Market Statistics Headlines – July 2003*, July 2003

20 C Beatty, S Fothergill, T Gore and A Green, *Hidden Unemployment in the East Midlands*, commissioned by the East Midlands Observatory, 2002

21 Office for National Statistics, 'Patterns of Low Pay', *Labour Market Trends*, Vol. 111, No. 4, April 2003, p175

22 See note 21

23 Fawcett Society, *Fawcett Briefing on Women and Low Pay*, 2002, p1

24 See note 17, *The National Minimum Wage: fourth report of the low pay commission, building on success*, p13

25 Office for National Statistics, *Jobs Paid Below Minimum Wage Rates*, 2002, www.statistics.gov.uk

26 See note 17, *The National Minimum Wage: fourth report of the low pay commission, building on success*

27 C Summerfield and P Babb (eds), *Social Trends*, No. 33, Office for National Statistics, The Stationery Office, 2003; see note 4

28 Department for Work and Pensions, *Opportunity for All: fifth annual report 2003*, The Stationery Office, 2003

29 W O'Connor and R Boreham, *Investigating Low Labour Market Participation Among Lone Parents in London: a review of the methods*, In-house Report 104, Department for Work and Pensions, November 2002

30 Fawcett Society/Equal Opportunities Commission/Fathers Direct, *Men and Women: who looks after the children? Report on three joint seminars*, November 2002

31 M Evans, J Millar and S Sarre, *New Deal for Lone Parents: second synthesis report of the national evaluation*, Research Report 163, Department for Work and Pensions, June 2003

32 See note 31

33 See note 31

34 K Rake and M Daly, 'Gender, household and individual income in France, Germany, Italy, the Netherlands, Sweden, the USA and the UK', *Luxembourg Income Study working paper no.332*, November 2002, p12

35 See note 10

36 R Lister, *Women's Economic Dependency and Social Security*, Equal Opportunities Commission, 1992

37 This is because of women's greater longevity (almost two-thirds of pensioners are women). Less than 12 per cent of women receive the full basic state pension in their own right, through their own contributions record. This is compared to 91 per cent of men who receive the full basic state pension; 51 per cent of women do currently receive the full basic state pension but, for the majority, based on their late husband's contribution record (Equal Opportunities Commission, Press Release, *Government must act for future female pensioners*, October 2003).

38 See note 10

39 Office for National Statistics, *Income Related Benefits Estimates of Take-Up in 2000/2001*, Department for Work and Pensions, 2003

40 Age Concern, State Pension Credit Bill, House of Lords, 2nd Reading, 18 December 2001

41 J Banks, R Blundell, R Disney and C Emmerson, *Retirement, Pensions and the Adequacy of Saving: a guide to the debate*, Institute for Fiscal Studies, Briefing Note 29, October 2002

42 See note 5

43 A Dale, 'Social Exclusion of Pakistani and Bangladeshi Women', Sociological Research Online, vol.7, no.3, 2002, www.socresonline.org.uk/7/3/dale.html

44 R Alsop, S Clisby, G Craig, R Evans and J Hockey, *Beyond the Bus Shelter: young women's choices and challenges in rural areas*, YWCA, 2002

45 See note 5, piv

46 C Aliaga and K Winqvist, 'How Women and Men Spend their Time: results from 13 European countries', *Population and Social Conditions*, Theme 3, Eurostat, 2003

47 X Ramos, *Domestic Work Time and Gender Differentials in Great Britain 1992–1998: facts, value judgements and subjective fairness perceptions*, presented at the British Household Panel Survey 2003 conference, 4 July 2003

48 See note 47

49 M Grace, 'The Work of Caring for Young Children: priceless or worthless?', *Women's Studies International Forum*, Volume 21 (4), 1998, pp401–413

50 See note 30

51 See note 30

52 S Walby and W Olsen, *The Impact of Women's Position in the Labour Market on Pay and Implications for UK Productivity*, Report to Women and Equality Unit, November 2002

53 See note 30

54 Survey conducted by Croner, cited in *The Guardian*, 5 April 2003

55 Women and Equality Unit, *Work–Life Balance Survey*, 2000

56 T Reynolds, C Callender and R Edwards, 'Caring and Counting: the impact of mothers' employment on family relationships', *Findings*, Joseph Rowntree Foundation, July 2003, p4

57 See note 56

58 R Lister, *Citizenship: Feminist Perspectives* (second edition), Palgrave, 2003, p132

59 Carers UK – www.carersonline.co.uk

60 J Mayer and H Green, *Carers 2000*, Office for National Statistics, The Stationery Office, 2002

61 Department for Work and Pensions, *Family Resources Survey 2001–2002*, 2003

62 See note 60

63 M Howard, *Paying the Price: carers, poverty and social exclusion*, CPAG, 2001

64 P Gregg, 'The Impact of Unemployment and Job Loss on Future Earnings', HM Treasury, *Persistent Poverty and Lifetime Inequality: the evidence*, Occasional Paper No.10, 1998

65 See note 64

66 See note 15

67 Office for National Statistics, *Labour Market Trends*, Vol. 111, No. 5, May 2003

68 Office for National Statistics, *Labour Market: New Earnings Survey 2002*, 2002

69 See note 68

70 J Bulman, 'Results of the 2002 New Earnings Survey', Office for National Statistics, *Labour Market Trends*, Vol. 110, No. 10, October 2002

71 See note 70

72 Equal Opportunities Commission, *Men and Women in Britain*, March 2003

73 S Walby and W Olsen, *The Impact of Women's Position in the Labour Market on Pay and Implications for UK Productivity*, Report to Women and Equality Unit, 2002

74 See note 73

75 See note 67

76 See note 73

77 R Lister, *Poverty*, Polity Press, 2004

78 Trades Union Congress, Report to TUC Women's Conference 2003, *Beating the Gender Poverty Trap*, March 2003

79 K Hurrell, *Statistics on Reasons for Working Part-time*, Equal Opportunities Commission, 2003

80 S Woodland, M Miller and S Tipping, *Repeat Study of Parents' Demand for Childcare*, Research Report 348, Department for Education and Skills, 2002, cited in House of Commons Work and Pensions Select Committee, *Childcare for Working Parents: fifth report of session 2002–03*, Volume 1, 2003, p6

81 DayCare Trust, *Childcare Facts – about childcare costs*, www.daycaretrust.org.uk, January 2003

82 House of Commons Work and Pensions Select Committee, *Childcare for Working Parents: fifth report of session 2002–03*, Volume 1, 2003, p25

83 See note 82

84 See note 82

85 See note 82, p14

86 See note 82

87 See note 82, p12

88 See note 5

89 Several studies have shown that men's management of the family budget in low-income families is often associated with female disadvantage. When women are responsible for the family budget they prioritise other family members' needs, especially children's, above their own. J Goode, C Callender and R Lister, *Purse or Wallet?: gender inequalities and income distribution within families on benefit*, Policy Studies Institute, 1998

90 Inland Revenue, *Working Families' Tax Credit Quarterly Enquiry*, November 2002, 2003

91 Department for Work and Pensions, *Households Below Average Income 2001/02*, March 2003, Table 3.5 (AHC)

92 S Middleton, K Ashworth and I Braithwaite, *Small Fortunes: spending on children, childhood poverty and parental sacrifice*, Joseph Rowntree Foundation, 1997; C Farrell and W O'Connor, *Low-income Families and Household Spending*, Research Report 192, Department for Work and Pensions, July 2003

93 See note 77

94 J Pahl, *Money and Marriage*, Macmillan, 1989

95 S Payne, *Women, Health and Poverty: an introduction*, Harvester Wheatsheaf, 1991; see also K Rake and G Jayatilaka, *Home Truths: an analysis of decision making within the home*, Fawcett Society, April 2002

96 See note 95, *Home Truths: an analysis of decision making within the home*; see note 89

97 See note 10

98 See note 95

99 See note 94; L Adelman, K Ashworth and S Middleton, *Intra-household Distribution of Poverty and Social Exclusion: evidence from the 1999 PSE survey of Britain*. Working Paper no.23, Centre for Research in Social Policy, 2000

100 S Yeandle, K Escott, L Grant and E Batty, *Women and Men Talking about Poverty*, Working Paper Series No. 7, Equal Opportunities Commission, 2003

101 P Beresford, D Green, R Lister and K Woodard, *Poverty First Hand: poor people speak for themselves*, CPAG, 1999; see note 89, *Purse or Wallet?: gender inequalities and income distribution within families on benefit*

102 See note 5, p38

103 F Bennett, 'Gender Implications of Current Social Security Reforms, *Fiscal Studies*, Vol.23, No.4, 2002, p562. The 1998 document referred to is: Department of Social Security, *Women and Social Security: a policy appraisal by the Department of Social Security*, DSS, 1998.

104 See note 103

7
Ethnicity and poverty

In comparison to their representation in the population, people from ethnic minority communities are more likely than others to live in deprived areas; be poor; be unemployed, compared with white people with similar qualifications; suffer ill-health and live in overcrowded and unpopular housing. They also experience widespread racial harassment and racial crime and are over-represented in the criminal justice system, from stop and search to prison. But there is much variation within and between ethnic groups in all of these areas.

(Social Exclusion Unit, *Ethnic Minority Issues in Social Exclusion and Neighbourhood Renewal*)[1]

In the latest (2001) census, 4.6 million people in the United Kingdom (UK) described themselves as belonging to an ethnic minority group – 7.9 per cent of the population – many of whom are living in poverty.[2] Until relatively recently, few studies explored the nature and extent of poverty faced by people from ethnic minority communities in Great Britain.[3] Information has not always been available by ethnic group, or the numbers involved have been too small for the analysis to be robust.[4] However, *Households Below Average Income* (HBAI)[5] now contains information about ethnicity, and 'race' is increasingly recognised as a policy concern. Many people from an ethnic minority share a disadvantaged economic and social position in comparison to the white majority, but more research is revealing the varying experiences *between* different ethnic minority groups.[6]

CPAG's latest publication examining ethnicity and poverty reveals that many people from ethnic minorities are leading *Parallel Lives* to those of the population as a whole.[7] This chapter considers some of the indicators of poverty, notably low incomes and unemployment, followed by other associated aspects of poverty, such as educational disadvantage, poor housing and poor health. Finally we consider ethnicity and the benefits system.

Throughout this chapter we use the term 'ethnic minority', though in tables and figures the terminology follows the classification used in the original source.

INDICATORS OF POVERTY

INCOMES

Poverty, the lack of an adequate income, does not automatically flow from ethnic minority status, but it can be a common experience, such as for Pakistani and Bangladeshi individuals.[8] People from ethnic minority groups are over-represented in the bottom fifth of the income distribution; in 2001/2002, 61 per cent of Pakistani and Bangladeshi individuals were in the bottom fifth – three times more than White, and almost twice as many as Black Caribbean, individuals.

TABLE 7.1: **Percentage of individuals in income fifths, after housing costs (AHC), by ethnic group, including the self-employed, Great Britain, 2001/02**

	Percentage					
	5 (bottom)	4	3	2	1 (top)	'000s
White	18	20	20	21	21	52.1
Black Caribbean	34	21	17	13	16	0.8
Black Non-Caribbean	43	22	14	12	9	0.6
Indian	26	15	26	16	17	1.0
Pakistani/Bangladeshi	61	20	11	6	3	1.0
Other	37	18	15	12	18	1.5
All individuals	20	20	20	20	20	57.0

Source: Department for Work and Pensions, *Households Below Average Income 1994/5–2001/02*, 2003, Table 3.1, p25

The composition of families varies by ethnic group. Pakistani and Bangladeshi households tend to be larger than those of other ethnic groups, partly due to the younger demographic of such households. The average size of Bangladeshi households in 2002 was 4.7 people per household and for Pakistani households the average was 4.2 people. In comparison, the average sizes of Black Caribbean, Mixed origin and White households were each around 2.3 people.[9] More than half of Caribbean (54 per cent) and Mixed origin (61 per cent) households with children were lone-parent families, compared to 23 per cent of White households and 9 per cent of Asian families.[10]

Ethnic minority households overall were more likely to be receiving means-tested benefits than White households,[11] Pakistani/Bangladeshi households in particular because they were at a higher risk of unemployment, Caribbean households because more were lone-parent families.[12]

Table 7.2 illustrates a greater reliance on means-tested benefits and tax credits by ethnic minorities. Unfortunately, the most recently published data from the survey has been re-classified in line with the 2001 Census and no longer disaggregates figures for the Asian category – ie,

TABLE 7.2: **Percentage of benefit units* receiving means-tested benefit by ethnic origin, 2001/02**

State support received	White	Mixed	Asian or Asian British	Black or British Black	Chinese/ other ethnic group	All groups
Working families' tax credit	3	4	6	6	1	**3**
Income support/ Minimum income guarantee	10	18	16	20	14	**11**
Housing benefit	12	20	13	24	16	**12**
Council tax benefit	15	22	18	26	19	**16**
Income-based jobseeker's allowance	2	5	3	6	3	**2**
On any income-related benefit	18	30	26	34	24	**19**

* 'Benefit unit' is a standard DWP term, which relates to the tighter family definition of 'a single adult or couple living as married and any dependent children'

Source: Adapted from Department for Work and Pensions, *Family Resources Survey Great Britain, 2001/02*, 2003, Table 3.17

no longer distinguishes between Indian and Pakistani and Bangladeshi groups. Previous data shows that these groups have very different patterns in terms of employment, family structure, income and resources. Indian groups are much less likely to be in poverty than other ethnic minorities, whereas Pakistani and Bangladeshi groups, especially Bangladeshi, are at the bottom end of the income distribution, with a high reliance on means-tested benefits.[13]

Older ethnic minority people also tend to be over-represented in the bottom of the income distribution. Many arrived in the UK in the middle of their working lives, leaving less time to build up pension entitlements, and they spend longer periods being unemployed or low paid, so have limited national insurance or occupational provision.[14]

UNEMPLOYMENT

In 2002, unemployment among men and women from all ethnic minorities was substantially higher than for Whites and was three times higher for African and Pakistani/Bangladeshi people.[15]

Research at the end of the 1990s showed that ethnic minority jobseekers completed more job applications than White jobseekers, but did not achieve any more interviews. Over two years, fewer people from ethnic minorities (66 per cent) left benefit for paid jobs than other claimants (76 per cent), and even when finding paid work, spells of employment were shorter.[16]

Despite a fall in unemployment levels in the late 1990s, the overall employment position of ethnic minorities by 2001 generally remained considerably worse than that of the White population.[17] Black workers were hit harder by the last recession than white workers and they did not benefit as much as White workers in the subsequent economic upturn.[18] For people of Pakistani and Bangladeshi origin, unemployment has remained consistently high compared to white workers.

- In 1992, the unemployment rate of Bangladeshi, Pakistani and Black Caribbean men was 15 to 20 percentage points higher than that of their White counterparts; by 2000, although reduced, the difference was still approximately 10 to 15 percentage points.[19]
- Pakistani/Bangladeshi households were the least likely to be 'work-rich' households in 2002, with only 10 per cent of households with all working-age adults in employment in autumn 2002, compared with 57 per cent of White, 46 per cent of Black Caribbean and 35 per cent of Indian households.[20]

- The rate of unemployment among Black African male graduates is currently seven times that of White graduates.[21]

Young ethnic minority people also tend to be disadvantaged in work schemes, consequently jeopardising their chances in the labour market. For example, in 2002/03, while 40.3 per cent of White people left the New Deal to enter sustained employment only 31 per cent of young people from ethnic minority groups did so.[22] Young people from ethnic minority groups were also much less likely to be put on the subsidised employment option; 14 per cent of White young people were on this option but for young people from a minority ethnic group this figure falls to just 5.6 per cent.[23]

EMPLOYMENT RATES

The gap in the employment rate between White and ethnic minority workers has increased between 1997 and 2001.[24] In winter 2002/03, 58 per cent of people from an ethnic minority group were in employment compared to 76 per cent of the White population.[25] Pakistani and Bangladeshi men had the lowest employment rate and Pakistani and Bangladeshi women were less than half as likely to be in paid work as all

TABLE 7.3: **Proportion in employment by ethnic origin (by thousands and per cent of population), 2002, Great Britain**

Ethnic groups	Women in employment		Men in employment	
	'000s	%	'000s	%
All in employment	12, 306	67	14,925	79
Black/Black British	221	56	237	65
– Caribbean	121	62	128	66
– African	81	49	96	62
Asian/Asian British	324	44	525	68
– Indian	195	58	259	73
– Pakistani and Bangladeshi	70	25	178	61
Chinese	39	53	47	68
Non-White/Mixed	736	49	991	66
White	11,570	68	13,929	80

Source: Equal Opportunities Commission, *Facts about Women and Men in Great Britain 2003*, January 2003

other minority women and three times less likely to be economically active than their Black Caribbean counterparts – perhaps due to religious or cultural factors,[26] the structure of the labour market and an increased disadvantage due to a combination of ethnicity and gender.

LABOUR MARKET SEGREGATION

> Ethnic minorities are disadvantaged in the labour market, in ways and to degrees that go beyond the experiences of whites.
> (Strategy Unit, *Ethnic Minorities and the Labour Market: Final Report*)[27]

Different immigration histories, the time frames of these and the geographical area and industry in which ethnic minority groups become established have contributed to differential labour market experiences *between* and *within* minority groups.[28] Segregation into particular industries and being concentrated in former industrial, often deprived, areas, made many ethnic minority workers especially vulnerable to the decline in manufacturing and the rise in unemployment during the 1980s and 1990s. Pakistani groups, who were heavily concentrated in heavy manufacturing and textile industries of Birmingham and Yorkshire in the 1970s, were hit particularly hard by the recession of the late 1970s and early 1980s.[29] Black Caribbean men have been, and remain, overly concentrated in manual work whereas Chinese and Bangladeshis are particularly concentrated in the catering industries.[30]

There is evidence that some segregation may occur because ethnic minorities perceive certain industries or employers as 'White'. In addition, employers may see ethnic minorities as 'outside their recruitment pool'.[31] This has led to concentrations of ethnic minorities in certain areas of employment and their absence in others.[32]

- Pakistanis are nearly twice as likely as Whites to fall under the socio-economic classification of semi-skilled or unskilled.
- With the exception of Indian and Chinese male workers, people from ethnic minorities are less likely to be in the top occupational category and fewer are in supervisory or managerial positions compared with White employees.
- Of male Bangladeshi workers in Great Britain 52 per cent are in the restaurant industry, an especially low-paid sector, compared with only 1 per cent of White male workers.
- Indian men are ten times more likely to be medical practitioners than are the general population.[33]

- Black African and Black Caribbean men are over-represented in manual occupations within transport and communication industries.[34]

Indian and Pakistani women are more likely than other women to work in manufacturing, particularly textiles, and one-third of Black women work in health or social work compared to one-fifth of all women. With the exception of Indian women, ethnic minority women are less likely to be in a professional position; this is especially so for Black women, who are half as likely to be in a professional status occupation than White women.[35]

While labour market changes have had an impact on these patterns, racial or cultural discrimination also appears to have been a factor. Although overt discrimination has been combated by legislation, *indirect discrimination*, through policies and practices that systematically disadvantage ethnic minorities, continues.

- A survey, conducted in 2003, found that workers from ethnic minorities experience 'hidden' discrimination. They reported being overlooked for promotion and having to put up with racist language, and said that only lip service was paid to equal opportunities policies in their workplaces.[36]
- Cultural or religious factors may also influence the labour market position of ethnic minorities. Sikhs and Indian Muslims are almost twice as likely to be unemployed as Hindus.[37]

LOW PAY

Some ethnic minority employees are also more likely to be low paid, especially Bangladeshi and Pakistani workers.[38] In 2002, Pakistani and Bangladeshi full-time workers had the lowest average gross hourly rates of pay in Great Britain (£5.90 for women and £7.61 for men) and were the most disadvantaged group, with average weekly net earnings being between 45 per cent and 52 per cent below those of their White counterparts.[39] Black African women's average pay was also low, at £7.42 per hour. However, White, Black and Indian men were paid at over £9 per hour, with Indian men's earnings the highest, at £11.16.[40] The position of Indian men's earnings levels has improved over the past decade and is now around 3 per cent higher than that of White workers.[41]

Homeworkers, many of whom are women from Pakistani and Bangladeshi communities, are vulnerable to extremely low pay, often working by piece rate work amounting to as little as £1.50 per hour. Low pay may go unreported by homeworkers because of fear of losing work and being seen as betraying their community.[42] Recent plans by the Government propose an amendment to the minimum wage legislation requiring employers to pay all homeworkers the minimum wage for all hours worked or a 'fair piece rate', in effect abolishing previous loopholes in the legislation which allowed employers to legally pay homeworkers only four-fifths of the minimum wage or pay less because of employers estimates of the hours needed to complete the task.[43]

OTHER ASPECTS OF POVERTY

EDUCATIONAL DISADVANTAGE

Educational progress varies by ethnic origin; the gap between ethnic minority and White children widens during primary school but at secondary school the trend reverses for Indian and Chinese pupils, who tend to do better in GCSE final examinations than their White counterparts.[44]

Office for Standards in Education (OFSTED) research, published in 2000, found that Black pupils' position relative to their White peers *worsened* between the start and end of compulsory schooling; in one large urban authority, African-Caribbean children entered school as the highest-achieving group but left as the group least likely to attain five high-grade GCSEs.[45]

In 2001, Black children were three times more likely to be excluded from school than white pupils,[46] but no more likely to be persistent truants.[47] The exclusion rate for other minority groups (Chinese, Indian, Bangladeshi, Pakistani) is below average.[48]

While increasing numbers of ethnic minority pupils have gained five or more GCSEs at grades A–C since the late 1990s, disparities in achievement between pupils from different ethnic groups remains. In 2002, only 36 per cent of Black pupils, 40 per cent of Pakistani and 41 per cent of Bangladeshi pupils had reached that level, compared with 52 per cent of White and 60 per cent of Indian pupils.[49] Attainment of GCSEs for Black children, especially Black boys, has fallen in recent years and the gap between White and Black boys has increased by four percentage points in the past decade.[50] Within each ethnic group, girls had higher average attainment than boys; but ethnic inequalities remained, even when controlling for gender and class.[51]

- Over 30 per cent of Pakistani and Black pupils and over 50 per cent of Bangladeshi pupils are eligible for free school meals. Within each gender and ethnic group, those entitled to free school meals were least likely to obtain five or more GCSE grades; boys tended to do less well than girls.[52]
- Proportionately more Black, Pakistani and Bangladeshi pupils are recorded as having special educational needs compared to White, Chinese and Indian pupils.
- Pakistanis and Bangladeshis were most likely to have no qualifications. Nearly half (48 per cent) of Bangladeshi women and 40 per cent of Bangladeshi men and Pakistani women had no qualifications in 2002.[53]

However, young people from ethnic minority groups are more likely to be in post-16-year-old, full-time education than White young people.[54] Three-quarters of Indian young people were in full-time education at 18, twice the proportion for Whites; 51 per cent of Indian 18-year-olds were in full-time higher education compared with just over a fifth of Pakistanis/Bangladeshis and a quarter of Whites.[55] However, although people from ethnic minority groups are more likely to hold degree-level qualifications compared to white people, they are less

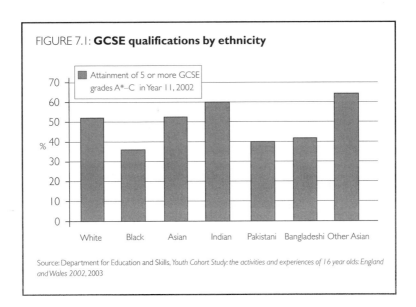

FIGURE 7.1: **GCSE qualifications by ethnicity**

Attainment of 5 or more GCSE grades A*–C in Year 11, 2002

Source: Department for Education and Skills, *Youth Cohort Study: the activities and experiences of 16 year olds: England and Wales 2002*, 2003

likely to obtain a first or upper second class degree[56] and are largely concentrated in the modern (post-1992) universities.[57]

LIVING IN DEPRIVED AREAS

Ethnic minority households are not evenly spread across Great Britain; instead, many are substantially over-represented in deprived areas. In 2002, 78 per cent of Black Africans and 56 per cent of Bangladeshis lived in London, many in the most deprived boroughs.[58]

- Nearly half (48 per cent) of all ethnic minorities lived in Greater London, compared to 10 per cent of the white population.[59]
- 70 per cent of all people from ethnic minorities lived in the 88 most deprived local authority districts in 2000, often in inadequate housing.[60]
- Only 1 in 20 Black and Asian people lived in an area of low unemployment in 1998, compared with one in five Whites.[61]

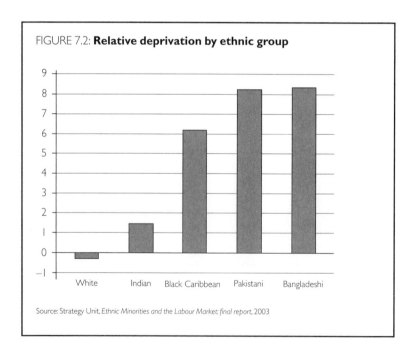

FIGURE 7.2: **Relative deprivation by ethnic group**

Source: Strategy Unit, *Ethnic Minorities and the Labour Market: final report*, 2003

Living in a deprived area can damage people's employment prospects, limit their access to good quality public services and contribute to poor physical and mental health.[62] Figure 7.2 illustrates the deprivation experienced by certain ethnic groups relative to other ethnic groups. The deprivation index combines several indicators including: 'unemployment rate, children in low-income households, lacking amenities (bath/shower/toilet), lacking a car, children in unsuitable accommodation, and educational participation'.[63]

POOR QUALITY HOUSING

There are significant ethnic differences in housing tenure patterns, affected by migration patterns and discrimination in the housing market as well as income.[64] A high proportion of Bangladeshi and Black African households live in the social rented sector (57 per cent and 50 per cent respectively in 2002). In contrast, 55 per cent of Indian and 47 per cent of Pakistani heads of household were owner-occupiers with a mortgage.[65] Home ownership for Pakistani families has often been the result of restricted options, rather than a positive choice.[66] Often such housing is low quality, in undesirable inner-city areas, and owned by families without the resources to improve or maintain their home.[67] Recent research has found that many such homeowners are living in poverty.[68] The proportion of people in Great Britain living in unfit dwellings is higher for ethnic minority groups overall than for Whites; in 2000, over three times more people of Bangladeshi and Pakistani origin lived in unfit housing than White and Indian people.[69]

People from ethnic minority communities are also more likely than Whites to live in overcrowded accommodation – 15 per cent of ethnic minority households live in overcrowded conditions compared to 2 per cent of White households; this figure rises to 30 per cent for Bangladeshi households.[70] Overcrowding may be a factor in the disproportionate rates of homelessness experienced by ethnic minorities. A quarter of those accepted as homeless in London in 2001 were from African and Caribbean households although they make up only 11 per cent of London households.[71]

POOR HEALTH AND PREMATURE DEATH

Ethnic minority groups can be more at risk of poor health. Pakistani and Bangladeshi people are three to four times more likely than the general population to report bad health; Indian men and women and Black-Caribbean women were also more likely to describe their health as bad or very bad.[72] Some conditions, such as diabetes, are more common in certain ethnic minority groups; compared with Whites, Pakistani/Bangladeshi people are over five times, and Indian/South Asian people three times, more likely to have diabetes.[73] Furthermore, health service providers' insensitivity to cultural, religious and language issues can have a negative impact on the use of health services by ethnic minority groups.[74] Families living in poverty make less use of health services relative to need, especially preventive health services, and demonstrate poorer health and social outcomes.[75] For example:

- women of Bangladeshi origin are half as likely as the average to attend cervical cancer screening;
- babies of mothers born in Pakistan are twice as likely to die in infancy as the general population;[76]
- African Caribbean women have 80 per cent higher rates for diagnosed high blood pressure than Whites;[77]
- the higher prevalence of learning difficulties in South Asian communities has been linked to high levels of material and social deprivation.[78]

Health variations may be explained in part by the socio-economic status of ethnic minority groups as well as being associated with the process and consequences of migration and discrimination.[79]

The diagnosis of mental health problems also varies across ethnic groups. People from ethnic minorities are more likely to be diagnosed, admitted to hospital and have a poorer outcome from treatment than Whites. Such differences may be explained by a number of factors, including poverty and racism.[80] They may also be due to mainstream mental health services failure to understand or meet the needs of ethnic minority communities.[81] Although the link between mental ill-health and ethnicity is complicated, recent in-depth research examining mental illness and ethnicity found:

- a twofold higher prevalence rate of psychotic illness for Black Caribbean people compared with the White population – those who were in poorer economic positions appeared to have a higher risk;
- Irish men and Pakistani women had significantly higher, and Bangladeshi women lower, rates of common mental disorders;
- depressive episodes and anxiety disorders were most common among Indian and Pakistani women.[82]

Experiencing racism, unemployment, benefit-level incomes and over-crowding were identified as impacting upon the physical and mental health of many people from ethnic minority groups.[83]

ETHNICITY AND THE BENEFITS SYSTEM

Ethnic minority communities can face particular problems within the benefits system:[84]

- The emphasis on non-interruption of contributions for some benefits, such as pensions, militates against those who have irregular earnings, absences abroad or short working lives in the UK from qualifying for them.
- The consequent over-reliance on means-tested benefits can result in an increased likelihood of ethnic minority families suffering from the associated problems, such as low take-up, administrative complexity and the poverty trap.
- Direct and indirect discrimination can occur through conditions placed on 'people from abroad' such as sponsorship and tests of residence.
- Direct and indirect discrimination can occur in the administration of social security, including the failure to provide interpretation and translation facilities.

IMMIGRATION STATUS AND SOCIAL SECURITY

Most social security benefits now have immigration conditions attached to them; immigration status[85] can affect benefit entitlement, and vice versa. Although immigration status is not the same as ethnicity, these issues may have a greater impact on ethnic minority claimants.[86] Some people may also be deterred from claiming benefits, fearing that their immigration status would be questioned.[87]

The 'habitual residence test' was introduced to determine entitlement to the main means-tested benefits but there is evidence that it has been administered inappropriately and that Black and Asian people have been disproportionately affected.[88] Awareness of differential treatment based on racist assumptions may lead to the non take-up of benefit entitlements, already a problem with means-tested benefits for older people from ethnic minority groups.[89]

Underclaiming by certain ethnic groups may also be influenced by culture and religion; with negative perceptions of benefit claiming found amongst Chinese and Bangladeshi households.[90] Shame and stigma were most strongly felt amongst Bangladeshi, Pakistani and Chinese households and least strongly by African-Caribbeans.

ASYLUM SEEKERS AND REFUGEES

Asylum seekers are prohibited from working until a decision has been made about their asylum claim and are barred from claiming social security benefits. Restricted financial provision is given by the National Asylum Support Service (NASS), but at subsistence levels – ie, £37.77 a week for a single asylum seeker in 2003[91], which is £20.88 less than a basic income support payment. An asylum-seeker family with two children would receive 24 per cent less than an equivalent family on income support. There are also restrictions on access to the maternity grant for asylum seekers and no entitlement to child benefit, further lowering the income of such families with children. In January 2003, the Government further restricted access to financial help by withdrawing eligibility to NASS provision (for those with no dependent children) unless an asylum claim was made 'as soon as reasonably practicable' after arrival in the UK and destitution could be proved. Although a legal challenge resulted in a ruling that asylum-seekers were suffering 'inhuman and degrading treatment' by being forced to sleep rough and beg for food or money with which to buy it, the Home Office won its appeal in the case of one asylum-seeker in September 2003 and the legislation currently stands.[92]

The restrictive measures placed on asylum-seekers result in very low incomes, leaving even those with provision from the NASS extremely vulnerable to poverty. A recent report collected evidence from 40 organisations working with asylum-seekers and found extreme levels of hardship and exclusion:

- 85 per cent of organisations reported that their clients experience hunger;
- 95 per cent reported that their clients cannot afford to buy clothes or shoes;
- 80 per cent said their clients are not able to maintain good health.[93]

Even if refugee status is granted, refugees often face additional problems because of language difficulties, lack of awareness of their rights or unfamiliarity with the process. People who were previously supported by the NASS often experience bureaucratic difficulties in obtaining housing and child benefit, such as long delays in receiving a national insurance number and documentation establishing entitlement to benefits.[94] Refugees face the worst employment prospects, markedly worse than people from ethnic minorities generally; refugees in 2001 were more likely to be in temporary work and be low paid, were less likely to be offered training, received little holiday entitlement and were more frequently working beneath their skills and qualification level.[95]

BENEFITS ADMINISTRATION

People whose residency status is not in doubt may still encounter problems. Several reports have documented excessive delays in processing claims, with some files lost due to incorrect use of some Black claimants' names.[96] Some evidence may not be easy to produce, such as a marriage licence; the increasing emphasis on national insurance numbers for benefit claims may also have led to delays.[97] A Commission for Racial Equality report on claims by Asian people in Manchester showed that supporting evidence was more often required, and fraud officers drawn in more frequently, for Asian than for other claims.[98] Lone Asian women, particularly orthodox Muslim women who had a dependent economic role prior to the death of, or separation from, a spouse, have also encountered difficulties as a result of their social role not normally involving them in dealing with outside authorities.[99]

CONCLUSION

The ethnic minority population has been at greater risk of being excluded from many aspects of society as a result of discrimination in employment and in the wider society. People from most ethnic minority groups are more at risk of unemployment and worklessness, low pay and poor working conditions, poor health, housing and low incomes, with some ethnic groups suffering extreme poverty.

NOTES

1 Social Exclusion Unit, *Ethnic Minority Issues in Social Exclusion and Neighbourhood Renewal*, Cabinet Office, 2000

2 Office for National Statistics, *Minority Ethnic Population*, February 2003; Department for Work and Pensions, *Households Below Average Income 1994/5–2001/02*, Corporate Document Services, 2003

3 See L Platt, *Parallel Lives?: Poverty among ethnic minority groups in Britain*, CPAG, 2002

4 See for example, Social Exclusion Unit, *Ethnic Minority Issues in Social Exclusion and Neighbourhood Renewal*, Cabinet Office, 2000

5 See note 2, *Households Below Average Income 1994/5–2001/02*

6 See for example T Modood and R Berthoud, *Ethnic Minorities in Britain: diversity and disadvantage*, Policy Studies Institute, 1997; see note 3

7 See note 3

8 R Berthoud, *The Incomes of Ethnic Minorities*, Essex University, 1998

9 A White (ed), *Social Focus in Brief: ethnicity 2002*, Office for National Statistics, December 2002

10 See note 9

11 Department for Work and Pensions, *Family Resources Survey Great Britain 2001–2002*, DWP, 2003

12 Office for National Statistics, 'Work and Worklessness among Households by Ethnic Origin', *Labour Market Trends*, Vol. 111, No. 4, April 2003

13 See for example Department for Work and Pensions, *Family Resources Survey Great Britain, 2000/01*, 2002

14 Department of Social Security, *The Changing Welfare State: pensioner incomes*, Department of Social Services Paper No 2, March 2000

15 Women and Equality Unit, *Ethnic Minority Women in the UK*, Department of Trade and Industry, October 2002

16 J Shropshire, R Warton and R Walker, *Unemployment and Jobseeking: the experience of ethnic minorities*, Research Report RR106, Department for Education and Employment, 1999

17 Strategy Unit, *Ethnic Minorities and the Labour Market: final report*, 2003

18 Performance and Innovation Unit, *Ethnic Minorities and the Labour Market: interim analytical report*, 2002

19 See note 18

20 See note 12

21 See note 17

22 Trades Union Congress, *Ethnicity and Poverty*, www.tuc.org.uk/welfare, September 2003

23 See note 22. Overall, 12.3 per cent of New Deal for Young People participants were on the subsidised employment option, generally seen as the best option. The original planning assumption was that 40 per cent of those on an option would be in subsidised employment.

24 See note 18

25 Office for National Statistics, *Labour Market Trends*, Vol. 111, No. 6, June 2003

26 See note 18

27 See note 17

28 See note 3

29 See note 3, p101

30 See note 3

31 See note 18

32 See note 17

33 See note 17

34 See note 18

35 See note 18

36 Trades Union Congress, *Black Voices at Work*, April 2003

37 M Brown, 'Religion and Economic Activity in the South Asian Population', *Ethnic and Racial Studies*, Vol 23, No 6, 2000

38 Low Pay Commission, *The National Minimum Wage, Fourth Report of the Low Pay Commission: building on success*, 2003

39 See note 17

40 Women and Equality Unit, *Ethnic Minority Women in the UK*, Department of Trade and Industry, October 2002

41 See note 17

42 See note 38, p161

43 Department of Trade and Industry, *National Minimum Wage Regulations – consultation on draft regulations to introduce fair piece rates for output workers*, November 2003

44 J Sparkes, *Schools, Education and Social Exclusion*, CASE paper 29, STICERD, LSE, November 1999; see also Department for Education and Skills, *Youth Cohort Study: the activities and experiences of 16 year olds: England and Wales 2002*, First Statistical Release, February 2003

45 D Gillborn and H Mirza, *Educational Inequality: mapping race, class and gender: a synthesis of research evidence*, Office for Standards in Education, 2000

46 See note 9

47 Social Exclusion Unit, *Truancy and School Exclusion*, Cm 3957, 1998

48 Home Office, *Race Equality in Public Services: driving up standards and accounting for progress*, 2000

49 See note 44, *Youth Cohort Study: the activities and experiences of 16 year olds: England and Wales 2002*

50 See note 17

51 See note 44, *Schools, Education and Social Exclusion*

52 G Bhattacharyya, L Ison, M Blair, *Minority Ethnic Attainment and Participation in Education and Training: the Evidence*, Department for Education and Skills, 2003

53 See note 9

54 See note 44, *Youth Cohort Study: the activities and experiences of 16 year olds: England and Wales 2002*

55 See note 44, *Youth Cohort Study: the activities and experiences of 16 year olds: England and Wales 2002*

56 See note 52

57 M Shiner and T Modood, 'Help or Hindrance? Higher Education and the Route to Ethnic Equality', *British Journal of Sociology of Education*, Vol 23, No 2, 2002, pp209–232

58 See note 9

59 See note 17

60 Office of the Deputy Prime Minister, Factsheet 14, *Housing and Neighbourhood Renewal*, 2002

61 B Parekh, *The Future of Multi-Ethnic Britain*, The Runnymede Trust, 2000

62 See note 18

63 See note 17, p30

64 See note 3

65 C Summerfield and P Babb (eds), *Social Trends*, No. 33, Office for National Statistics, The Stationery Office, 2003

66 See note 3

67 R Dorsett, 'Ethnic Minorities in the Inner City', Policy Studies Institute/Joseph Rowntree Foundation, 1998

68 R Burrows, Poverty and Home Ownership in Contemporary Britain, The Policy Press, 2003. Homeowners are not entitled to housing benefit and cannot get state financial support for mortgage payments or repairs.

69 See note 17

70 Tony McNulty MP, House of Commons, *Hansard*, 19 December 2002, Column 956W, from Shelter Press Release, 2002

71 Shelter, *Housing and Homelessness: the facts*, July 2002

72 See note 9

73 Department of Health, *The Health of Britain's Ethnic Minority Groups: health survey for England*, 1999

74 Department of Health, *Tackling Health Inequalities: summary of the 2002 cross-cutting review*, November 2002

75 Department of Health, *Getting the Right Start: national service framework for children: emerging findings*, April 2003

76 See note 74

77 Commission for Racial Equality, Factsheet, www.cre.gov.uk

78 M Ghazala, A Nocon and W Ahmad, with L Jones, *Learning Difficulties and Ethnicity*, Department of Health, March 2001

79 Social Exclusion Unit, *Ethnic Minority Issues in Social Exclusion and Neighbourhood Renewal*, Cabinet Office, June 2000

80 The Mental Health Foundation, *Minority Ethnic Groups and Mental Health*, www.mentalhealth.org.uk, updated August 2003

81 See note 80

82 J Nazroo and M King, 'Psychotic Symptoms and Estimated Rates', and S Weich and S McManus, 'Common Mental Disorders', *Ethnic Minority Psychiatric Illness Rates in the Community* (EMPIRIC Report), Department of Health, April 2002

83 National Centre for Social Research, *Ethnic Differences in the Context and Experience of Psychiatric illness, A Qualitative Study*, Department of Health, May 2002

84 G Craig, 'Race, Social Security and Poverty' in J Ditch (ed), *Introduction to Social Security*, Routledge, 1999

85 For a more detailed discussion of immigration policy see note 61; for its interaction with benefit rules, see CPAG's *Migration and Social Security Handbook* and note 3

86 S McKay and K Rowlingson, *Social Security in Britain*, Macmillan, 1999

87 A Bloch, 'Ethnic inequality and social security policy', in Walker and Walker (eds), *Britain Divided: the growth of social exclusion in the 1980s and 1990s*, CPAG, 1997

88 National Association of Citizens Advice Bureaux, *Failing the Test: CAB clients' experience of the habitual residence test in social security*, February 1996; see note 3, p134

89 National Audit Office, *Tackling Pensioner Poverty: Encouraging take-up of entitlements*, Report by the Comptroller and Auditor General, HC 37 Session 2002–2003, 2002

90 I Law, C Hylton, A Karmani and A Deacon, *Racial Equality and Social Security Service Delivery: a study of perceptions and experience of black ethnic minority people eligible for benefit in Leeds*, Leeds University, 1994

91 Commission For Racial Equality, *Refugees and Asylum Seekers – the facts*, www.cre.gov.uk, 2003. The 'poverty line' here is below 60 per cent of median income.

92 Refugee Council, 'Update: withdrawal of in-country asylum support', *Refugee Council Briefing*, www.refugeecouncil.org.uk, October 2003. The legal challenges to the Government's withdrawal of in-country asylum support under section 55 of the Nationality, Immigration and Asylum Act 2002 (NIA Act) were undertaken by the Refugee Council, in conjunction with other concerned agencies.

93 J Penrose, *Poverty and Asylum in the UK*, Oxfam/Refugee Council, July 2002

94 J Neuburger, *House Keeping: preventing homelessness through tackling rent arrears in social housing*, Shelter, 2003

95 A Bloch, *Refugees' Opportunities and Barriers to Employment and Training*, Research Report Summary 179, Department for Work and Pensions, 2002

96 National Association of Citizens Advice Bureaux, *Barriers to Benefit: Black claimants and social security*, CAB evidence E/1/91, 1991

97 National Association of Citizens Advice Bureaux, *A Person Before the Law: the case for a statement of rights for people with limited leave to remain in the UK*, February 2000

98 Commission for Racial Equality, *The Provision of Income Support to Asian and Non-Asian Claimants*, Manchester CRE, 1995

99 R Cohen, J Coxall, G Craig and A Sadiq-Sangster, *Hardship Britain: being poor in the 1990s*, CPAG, 1992

8 Unequal shares

*Given the definition of poverty as low income relative to the national
average, both child and overall poverty rates are highly correlated with the
degree of income inequality.*
(J Micklewright, *Child poverty in English-speaking countries*)[1]

The UK has one of the most unequal distribution of incomes in the
industrialised countries of the world (international comparisons are
further discussed in Chapter 10). While income inequality declined
during the 1960s, it began to rise at the end of the 1970s and continued
to do so dramatically throughout the 1980s; incomes in the top income
bracket (decile) grew by around 60 per cent during the 1980s
compared with almost zero growth at the bottom.[2] From the mid-
1990s income inequality again increased, and was higher in 2000/01
than at any point in recent decades.[3]

Wealth is even more unevenly distributed than incomes. Currently
wealth inequality is increasing and the numbers of people with no
wealth at all has not altered since 1997.[4] Inequalities in income and
wealth have significant consequences for individuals' health,
opportunities and quality of life.

This chapter examines the unequal shares in income, expenditure,
earnings and wealth, and the impact of government policy (tax and
social security) on these trends.

UNEQUAL INCOMES

There are a number of ways of measuring income inequality, sometimes giving rise to a degree of difference in results. One widely used measure is the Gini coefficient, which 'collapses the entire income distribution into a single number between zero and one' (or 100 per cent); the higher the number, the greater the degree of income inequality.[5] Complete equality results in a Gini coefficient of zero; complete inequality, where only one person has all the income and the rest have none, is given by a Gini coefficient of 1 (or 100 per cent).[6]

Another measure is to look at the share of total income for each group (decile or quintile) in the income distribution. The gap between income groups can also be examined by looking at the ratio of the top tenth (decile) or top fifth (richest quintile) of the income distribution to that of the bottom tenth (poorest decile) or bottom fifth (poorest quintile) of the population. A comparison with those in the middle of the income distribution can also be explored, showing how the poorest groups are faring in relation to both the middle and richest income groups in the population.

Each measure indicates a significant increase in income inequality during the 1980s.

- In 1979 the Gini coefficient (for disposable income) was 27 per cent, rising to 36 per cent by 1990.[7]
- In 1979 the richest group (top quintile) had a 36 per cent share of disposable income compared to a 9 per cent share held by the bottom quintile; by 1990 the income share for the richest group had risen to 43 per cent while the poorest quintile's share fell to 7 per cent.[8]
- Between 1979 and 1990 the income growth of the richest group (top decile) was more than eight times greater than that of the poorest group (bottom decile).[9]

Income inequality, as measured by the Gini coefficient, remained fairly stable over the 1990s but began to rise by the middle of the decade; by 2000/01 income inequality was greater than at any other period in recent history.[10] Figure 8.1 illustrates the changes in inequality from 1979 to 2002, as measured by the Gini coefficient. The share of total income received by those in the top and bottom deciles also reflects a pattern of rising inequality between 1994/95 and 2001/02, with the richest group (top decile) gaining 2 per cent more of total income (29 per cent) over this period while the poorest group's share (bottom decile) remains unaltered at 2 per cent.[11]

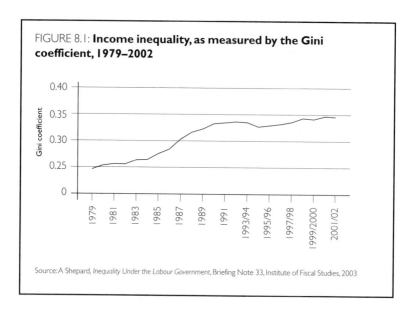

FIGURE 8.1: **Income inequality, as measured by the Gini coefficient, 1979–2002**

Source: A Shepard, *Inequality Under the Labour Government*, Briefing Note 33, Institute of Fiscal Studies, 2003

Despite some indication of increasing income inequality in recent years, the latest figures for household incomes (1996/97 to 2001/02) reveal a more equal growth across the income distribution, with the real-term incomes of those in the lower deciles (deciles 2, 3 and 4) rising fastest; however, the percentage change for the very poorest group remains lower than for the other deciles (see Table 8.1).[12] Additionally, if examined by family group rather than income bracket, some groups fared less well; the bottom quintile median income for unemployed families saw a fall in income in real terms over the period 1994/5 to 2001/02.[13] In addition, income growth has also occurred in the richest group and accordingly vast income inequality remains. Although the recent income growth among poorer income groups is to be welcomed, the real income levels of the poorest tenth have scarcely improved compared with 25 years ago.[14]

Income can be analysed at different 'stages':

- 'original income' is income from sources such as earnings, occupational pensions and investments before taxes or benefits;
- 'disposable income' is income from employment and benefits, after direct taxes (including employee's national insurance, council tax, etc);
- 'post-tax income' is income after direct and indirect taxes are taken and benefits have been paid;

TABLE: 8.1: **Percentage changes in real incomes for decile medians**

Between 1979 and 1996/97, including self-employed

Decile group	Income BHC	Income AHC
1 (bottom 10%)	12	–9
2 (10%–20%)	18	5
3 (20%–30%)	21	12
4 (30%–40%)	24	23
5 (40%–50%)	30	31
6 (50%–60%)	34	36
7 (60%–70%)	38	41
8 (70%–80%)	41	46
9 (80%–90%)	49	54
10 (top 10%)	62	70
Total population (mean)	**42**	**44**

Between 1996/97 and 2001/02, including self-employed

Decile group	Income BHC	Income AHC
1 (bottom 10%)	10	(+9 to+21)
2 (10%–20%)	17	24
3 (20%–30%)	17	25
4 (30%–40%)	17	24
5 (40%–50%)	16	20
6 (50%–60%)	14	17
7 (60%–70%)	14	17
8 (70%–80%)	14	16
9 (80%–90%)	15	18
10 (top 10%)	17	21
Total population (mean)	**17**	**21**

BCH = before housing costs, ACH = after housing costs
Figures in brackets denote uncertainty due to sampling variation; more than one figure in brackets indicates the range of possible percentage change

Source: Department of Social Services, *Households Below Average Income 1979–1996/7*; Department for Work and Pensions, *Households Below Average Income 1996/7–2001/02*, 2003, Table A1 [15]

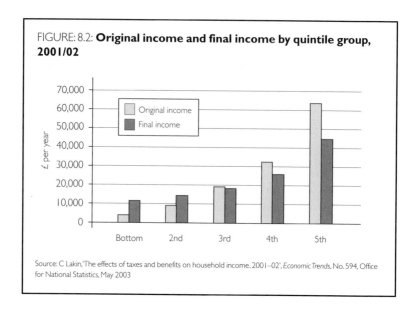

FIGURE: 8.2: **Original income and final income by quintile group, 2001/02**

Source: C Lakin, 'The effects of taxes and benefits on household income, 2001–02', *Economic Trends*, No. 594, Office for National Statistics, May 2003

- 'final income' takes 'in kind' benefits into account, such as education and health services.[16]

At each income stage the top fifth have gained an increased share of income; between 1979 and 2001/02 the richest fifth's share of original income grew from 43 per cent to 52 per cent and their share of post-tax income rose from 37 per cent to 45 per cent.[17]

In 2001/02 the original income of the top fifth of households was 18 times more than that of the bottom fifth's (£62,900 a year compared with £3,500). Taxes and social security benefits reduce income inequalities between households but the income of the wealthiest fifth of households remains four times greater than that of the lowest-income households, even after the redistributive effect of tax and benefits is taken into account (see Figure 8.2).[18] From 1996/97 to 2001/02, the post-tax income of the bottom fifth of households fell by 1 per cent; for the top tenth, it rose by 2 per cent.[19]

Assessing income inequality by considering the income of the richest relative to the poorest can be undertaken by calculating the ratio between income groups. This can be done by taking the ratio of the income at the 90th percentile to that at the 10th percentile (these percentiles are the income values which divide the population, when ranked by income, into 100 equal-sized groups – ie, 10 per cent of the population have incomes below the 10th percentile)[20] or the income at the 75th percentile to that at the 25th. The ratios for disposable income (which excludes VAT, etc) on both measures are shown in Table 8.2.[21]

These ratio measures show a growth in income inequality in the 1980s, with a steadier, but fluctuating, distribution in the 1990s. During 1999/2000, however, the figures show a worrying drop in the share of the poorest fifth of original incomes as well as an increase in inequality as measured by disposable income. While this pattern has not continued there has been relatively little change in income inequality in recent years on these measures.

Each of the measures shows a rise, by different degrees, in income inequality from the mid-1990s. One explanation could be the significant rise in pay of top earners, causing a considerable differential between the average-paid worker and the highest-paid, so much so that now more employees earn below the weekly average than above it.[22]

TABLE: 8.2: **Ratios for disposable income, 1978–2001/02**

	P90/P10	P75/P25
1978	3.2	1.9
1980	3.5	2.0
1982	3.3	2.0
1984	3.3	2.0
1986	3.7	2.1
1988	4.4	2.4
1990	4.9	2.5
1992	4.6	2.4
1993/94	4.5	2.3
1995/96	4.2	2.2
1996/97	4.4	2.3
1997/98	4.5	2.3
1998/99	4.5	2.3
1999/2000	4.6	2.4
2000/01	4.5	2.3
2001/02	4.5	2.3

Source: C Lakin, 'The effects of taxes and benefits on household income, 2001–02', *Economic Trends*, No 594, Office for National Statistics, May 2003

UNEQUAL EXPENDITURE

Household spending (expenditure) can be another important indicator of inequality, though it may not reflect income trends (for example, people may choose to spend beyond their means by using savings or borrowing or falling into debt; alternatively some income may be diverted into savings). In reflecting expectations of future income, expenditure may be more stable than measures of current income. A poverty line defined by income concerns the right to a minimum level of resources, while one defined by expenditure is about a standard of living.[23]

Hence, spending and income trends may be different. For example, the Institute for Fiscal Studies (IFS) analysed changes in expenditure between 1979 and 1992, showing that the rise in spending inequality was not as large as the growth in income inequality (which could be evidence of more permanent inequality and more short-term uncertainty and risk in incomes).

Spending by the bottom fifth of spenders rose by 14 per cent, whereas the income of the bottom tenth of the income distribution fell by 18 per cent.[24] Over the early 1990s income inequality stabilised and expenditure inequality fell, but from the mid-1990s income inequality has risen faster than spending inequality.[25]

The *Expenditure and Food Survey* (formerly the *Family Expenditure Survey*) examines spending differences among households. The most recent analysis revealed that families in the top income bracket (wealthiest 10 per cent) spent an average of £885 per week in 2001/02, £36 more than the year before, while families in the lowest income group spent £127, a figure unchanged from the previous year.[26]

In addition to differential expenditure between households, significant inequalities exist in areas of spending. Households in the three lowest income groups spend the largest proportion on 'basics' – food, followed by housing. By contrast, two of the three highest income groups spent a greater proportion of their income on restaurants and hotels than on food or housing.[27]

Low-income households have spending priorities which have been found to be more complex than those of better-off households.[28] For example, debt repayments may be paid before rent or council tax because of the lower penalties of non-payment for these outgoings. An increase in income in these lower-income households saw an increase in expenditure on improvements in food quality, housing and clothing, with children benefiting most.[29]

UNEQUAL EARNINGS

Earnings can generate inequality as those without paid work lag further behind earnings growth and those in paid work but who are low paid may find it hard to increase their earnings. The gap between the highest-paid and lowest-paid workers has escalated since the 1980s.

- Earnings for men in the richest tenth of the income distribution rose at double the rate of the poorest tenth over 20 years; for women, earnings at the top grew by five times as much as at the bottom.[30]
- In 2002 the lowest-paid workers received a tenth of the earnings of the highest-paid group.
- For full-time working adults the richest tenth of weekly earnings was 196 per cent of the median, while the poorest tenth was 56 per cent.
- Hourly earnings of the richest 10 ten per cent were more than three and a half times those of the bottom 10 per cent for full-timers and three times those of the bottom 10 per cent for part-timers.[31]
- In the last 10 years the earnings of the wealthiest 10 per cent has risen by 53.7 per cent while that of the lowest has grown by 45.6 per cent.[32]

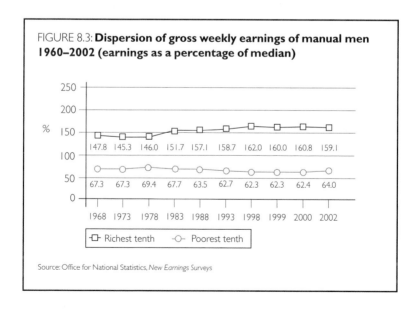

FIGURE 8.3: **Dispersion of gross weekly earnings of manual men 1960–2002 (earnings as a percentage of median)**

Source: Office for National Statistics, *New Earnings Surveys*

- In 1978 the poorest tenth of men in full-time manual work earned 69 per cent of the average and the richest tenth earned 146 per cent of the average; by 2002, the poorest tenth earned 64 per cent and the richest 159 per cent (see Figure 8.3) of the average.[33]

The earnings dispersion in the 1980s could be explained in part by:

- higher wages for more experience or qualifications, especially for young people;
- the declining importance of trade unions and wages councils;
- a growing polarisation between 'work-rich' and 'work-poor' households;
- a rise in self-employment.[34]

Significant earnings inequality remains between male and female employees. In 2002, women's hourly full-time earnings were 81.1 per cent of men's full-time earnings, indicating a slight widening of the gender pay gap since 2001 and a return to April 2000 levels.[35] Women are also more likely than men to work part time and in low-paid occupations, such as shelf-filling, cleaning, care and catering work. Table 8.3 illustrates the differential earnings between the lowest-paid and the highest-paid workers and the disparity in pay between men and women.

Research shows that wage mobility is limited and the individuals who do increase their earnings tend not to move very far.

- Only 30 per cent of employed men in the bottom decile in 1989 had moved up the wage distribution by 1994 (mainly to the next two deciles), whereas almost half (48 per cent) in the top decile were still there five years later.[36]

TABLE 8.3: **Distribution of pay in Great Britain, 2002**

Gross weekly earnings (£) including overtime pay and overtime hours

	Men	Women	All
10 per cent earned less than:	196.2	74.2	102.5
50 per cent earned less than:	399.7	239.8	320.3
10 per cent earned more than:	812.7	536.6	683.3

Source: J Bulman, 'Results of the 2002 Earnings Survey', *Labour Market Trends*, Office for National Statistics, 2002

- During a three-year period to 1994, 28 per cent of men saw their wages rise by a fifth, but 12 per cent experienced a fall of a fifth or more.[37]
- Those in the lower deciles of the wage distribution are much more likely to exit into unemployment or worklessness.[38]

CONTEMPORARY LOW PAY

The Labour Government introduced a national minimum wage in April 1999, initially set at an hourly rate of £3.60 for workers over 22, and £3 for workers aged 18–21. This has been uprated several times and in October 2003 stood at £3.80 for 18–21-year-olds and £4.50 for workers over 22. This amount, however, still represents relatively low pay in the UK and younger workers (those under 18) remain excluded from the right to a minimum wage, although the Department of Trade and Industry has recently indicated that a minimum wage for 16- and 17-year-olds will be introduced, but at a lower rate than that for other workers.[39]

- In 2002, 11 per cent of part-time workers were paid at less than 10p above the national minimum wage; 34 per cent were paid less than £5 per hour.[40]
- Women are far more likely to be earning low pay. In 2002 men's annual earnings total was 38 per cent greater than the annual total for women.[41]

Fewer people than expected have gained from the introduction of the minimum wage – just 1.2 million initially and an estimated 1 to 1.5 million from the main 2001 uprating, approximately 6 to 7 per cent of all workers.[42] The smaller October 2002 uprating benefited fewer workers as the increase had fallen behind a rise in average earnings and prices over the period. However, the minimum wage has been particularly beneficial for women, those in part-time jobs and some ethnic minority workers.[43] Nevertheless, in 2002 an estimated 330,000 people were still being paid below the minimum wage.[44]

The continuance of low-paid jobs is in marked contrast to the escalation of the salaries and bonuses of high earners. While average-paid workers have seen increases of 3 to 4 per cent in recent years, the highest-paid executives had salary increases of 21 per cent in 2000, 19 per cent in 2001 and 16 per cent in 2002[45], widening an already existing gap in income inequality. At least 123 directors are now paid more than £1m a year, with a further 364 paid between £500,000 and £1m.[46]

UNEQUAL WEALTH

Wealth is far more unequally distributed than incomes. Assets included in 'marketable wealth' are houses, stocks and shares, and other saleable resources. Marketable wealth therefore comprises assets that can be sold, and their value realised, and excludes things such as an individual's stake in an occupational pension scheme.[47] The top 2.4 million households own assets worth around £1,300 billion, while the bottom 12 million own assets of around £150 million.[48] By 2001 the wealthiest 1 per cent of the UK population owned almost a quarter – 23 per cent – of the UK's marketable wealth (see Table 8.4) and the wealthiest half owned almost all the wealth – 95 per cent.[49] If housing is excluded from the amount of estimated wealth then the results become even more skewed, with 33 per cent of marketable wealth in the UK concentrated in the hands of the wealthiest 1 per cent of the population.[50] Having financial resources has substantial effects on people's life chances; wealth not only helps people to cope with unexpected life events but also allows individuals to 'take opportunities that might otherwise be closed to them'.[51]

During the 1980s and 1990s the wealth gap widened dramatically. Ownership of assets like housing and pensions grew, while simultaneously the number of those without assets doubled – from 5 per cent in 1979 to 10 per cent by 1999.[52] Comparing the identifiable wealth of the richest thousand people and families in the UK and

---

TABLE 8.4: **Marketable wealth, 1979–2001**

	1979	1983	1987	1992	1996	1997	2000	2001
Percentage of marketable wealth owned by:								
Most wealthy 1%	20	20	18	18	20	22	22	23
Most wealthy 10%	50	50	51	50	52	55	55	56
Least wealthy 50%	8	9	9	7	7	7	6	5

Source: Inland Revenue statistics, *Personal Wealth*, 2003, Table 13.5

the least wealthy half of the population (some 28 million people), the former had, on average, *15,000 times more* wealth than the least wealthy at the turn of the millennium.[53] While virtually all those in the top half of the income distribution have at least one asset, 31 per cent of those in the lowest decile have none.[54]

Analysis of the *British Household Panel Survey* (BHPS) data by the Institute for Fiscal Studies reveals huge inequalities in the amount of financial wealth in the population (financial wealth is defined as savings plus investments minus debts and does not include housing wealth); one quarter of the population are £200 or more in debt while a further quarter have £9,050 or more of assets.[55]

50 per cent of the population has:

- net financial wealth of £600 or less;
- savings of £1,000 or less;
- no investments.

On the other hand, 10 per cent hold:

- net wealth of £35,000 or more;
- savings of £18,000 or more;
- investments of £15,000 or over.[56]

Many households have no assets but this can be a dynamic process; some people currently without assets having had them in the past, and perhaps are likely to have them in the future.[57] Some disparity in the

---

TABLE 8.5: **The distribution of financial wealth in the UK, 2000**

Wealth distribution (percentiles)	Savings (£)	Investments (£)	Debt (£)	Net financial wealth (£)
10th	0	0	0	−4,248
25th	1	0	0	−200
50th	1,000	0	0	600
75th	6,000	2,000	2,000	9,050
90th	18,000	15,000	6,500	35,000
Average (mean)	7,005	7,445	2,087	12,363

Source: J Banks, Z Smith, M Wakefield, *The Distribution of Financial Wealth in the UK: evidence from 2000 BHPS data*, Institute for Fiscal Studies, November 2002

ownership of wealth partly concerns age and stage of the life cycle – for instance, new households having less time to accumulate wealth than older ones. However, nearly half (47.3 per cent) of all 'benefit units' (a family group) who had no wealth in 1995 also had no wealth by 2000.[58] A quarter of those in the bottom 10 per cent of the income distribution have no financial assets.[59] In addition, 70 per cent of lone parents have no financial assets and three-quarters of low income 16–24-year-olds have no savings,[60] indicating that some groups are much more likely to have no wealth or access to the means of accumulating wealth. Nearly half (47 per cent) of households with an income under £200 per week had no savings compared to 19 per cent of those with an income of £500–£600 per week.[61]

According to the 2001/02 *Family Resources Survey*, the following had no current or savings account of any kind:

- 24 per cent of lone-parent households;
- 36 per cent of households with a member who is sick or disabled;
- 27 per cent of households where the head or spouse is unemployed;
- 10 per cent of pensioner households.[62]

HOUSING AS A SOURCE OF WEALTH

In Chapter 4 some of the effects of poverty on housing, including homelessness, were documented. Here, housing is examined as an increasingly important source of *wealth*. A recent Institute for Public Policy Research (IPPR) report argues that 'Housing poverty is now the most extreme form of social inequality in Britain'.[63] The research shows that over the past 50 years there has been a growing wealth divide between home-owners and people who rent; the value of the net equity (the total value of a property minus the owner's outstanding mortgage balance repayments) of personally-owned housing in Great Britain increased from £36 billion in 1970 to £1,525 billion in 2001.[64] The housing market has seen burgeoning house prices in recent years and consequent increases in wealth for homeowners. By the end of 2003, those with a typical house worth £120,000 will have seen their wealth increase by £12,000 tax free in one year.[65] A recent analysis of the BHPS data also suggests a significant widening of the wealth-gap between homeowners and tenants over the period 1995–2000.[66] Table 8.6 shows the association between wealth-holding and tenure status.

TABLE 8.6: **Financial and total net wealth by household type – BHPS 2000/01**

	Number of households	Mean net financial wealth	Median net financial wealth	Mean net wealth (incl housing)	Median net wealth (incl housing)
Owners	2,863	14,335	1,882	103,632	69,186
All tenants	1,366	2,695	0	5,233	0
Social tenants	1,022	2,509	0	3,711	0
All households	4,229	10,575	250	71,848	37,500

Source: Adapted from W Peterson, *Housing and the Dynamics of Wealth-Holding in the UK*, preliminary report for BHPS User Group, July 2003

The Policy Studies Institute examined housing wealth across 'life cycle' groups, finding that lone parents and single people were least likely to have housing wealth at the end of the 1990s, as Table 8.7 shows. Such groups will have been unable to share in the increasing wealth gained during the recent housing boom, further widening the gap between the haves and the have-nots.

TABLE 8.7: **Median housing wealth by life cycle groups**

Life cycle group	£
Young singles	0
Older singles	0
Young childless couples	8,900
Lone parents	0
Young couples, young children	14,000
Older couples, young children	37,000
Couples, school-age children	43,800
Older childless couples	48,500
Pensioner couples	59,400
Single pensioners	0

Source: K Rowlingson, C Whyley and T Warren, *Wealth in Britain: a lifecycle perspective*, Policy Studies Institute, 1999

THE IMPACT OF SOCIAL SECURITY AND TAX POLICY

While income and wealth are clearly extremely unequally shared among the population, redistribution can occur through tax and benefits. Social security benefits and taxation systems can be tools to either reduce (or increase) inequality. Overall, households in the top half of the income distribution pay more in taxes than they receive in benefits while those in the lower half pay less in direct tax (except local taxes) and receive more in cash and in-kind benefits.

Direct taxes (with the exception of local taxes, such as council tax) tend to be progressive, taking a larger proportion of income from the richest, thus contributing towards reducing inequality, though not by |as much as cash benefits. While the higher-income groups also pay more in *local taxes* in absolute terms, if viewed as a proportion of gross income the impact of local taxes is actually higher on the lower half of the income distribution.[67]

Indirect taxes, such as VAT, take relatively more from people on low incomes, partly due to the proportionately higher spending of some low-income households on items which attract indirect tax. In addition, some higher-income households channel their income into savings and mortgages, which do not attract indirect taxation.[68]

Cash benefits are higher for households lower down the income distribution than at the top, so have a more equalising effect on the distribution of income. Households in the bottom two quintile groups together receive about 60 per cent of total cash benefits.[69]

Benefits in kind, such as education and health services, mainly benefit those on lower incomes; households in the bottom quintile group receive the equivalent of around £5,200 from all benefits in kind, twice the amount received by the top fifth.[70]

Figure 8.4 shows the effect of direct and indirect taxes on each quintile group

It is clear that tax and benefit policies are important drivers for changing the distribution of income and wealth; during the 1980s when income inequality grew, the top rate of income tax dropped from 83 per cent to 40 per cent.[71] Changes to the tax system between 1985 and 1995 entailed a reduction in the tax rates (income tax) and also in national insurance rates and a shift towards indirect taxation. As a result, the poorest tenth lost on average £3 a week (2.9 per cent of their net

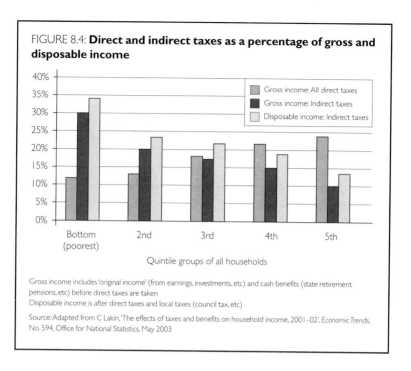

FIGURE 8.4: **Direct and indirect taxes as a percentage of gross and disposable income**

Legend:
- Gross income: All direct taxes
- Gross income: Indirect taxes
- Disposable income: Indirect taxes

Quintile groups of all households

Gross income includes 'original income' (from earnings, investments, etc) and cash benefits (state retirement pensions, etc) before direct taxes are taken
Disposable income is after direct taxes and local taxes (council tax, etc)

Source: Adapted from C Lakin, 'The effects of taxes and benefits on household income, 2001–02', *Economic Trends*, No. 594, Office for National Statistics, May 2003

income), whilst the top tenth gained £31 (5.8 per cent of their net income).[72] The Joseph Rowntree Foundation's inquiry into income and wealth also concluded that the tax system had little impact, as the shift in the tax burden from higher-income to lower- and middle-income groups cancelled out the progressivity of income tax.[73]

An analysis of tax and benefit changes since 1997 suggests some turnaround. It has been estimated that the bottom three deciles of the income distribution have experienced average gains of £20 or more a week, with losses in the richer tenth of the population. Pensioners and low-income families with children were found to benefit most from the reforms.[74] An estimated 4.1 million families with children are predicted to gain, and 300,000 lose, from the new tax credits introduced in 2003, with average gains being made in the lower-income groups and losses among those with higher incomes.[75] However, apart from the extension of tax credits to some workers without children or a disability, the new tax credits can be seen largely as a restructuring of current benefits and tax credits rather than as a system of innovative payments.[76]

Examining just 'benefits in kind' or the 'social wage' also shows a significant change, with a 50 per cent increase in real terms across the population since 1979.[77] Between 1996/97 and 2000/01, the value of the social wage increased by £260 per person for those in the poorest fifth, and by £50 for those in the richest fifth and is therefore an important, if not necessarily deliberate, means of redistribution.[78] However, although the social wage favours those with lower incomes, because cash incomes have grown at a faster rate than the social wage between 1996/97 and 2000/01 increases in the social wage have not prevented inequality in final incomes.[79]

The accumulation of wealth or assets, such as savings and investments, is no longer seen as the privilege of the rich; instead the idea of wealth-holding is being incorporated into the Government's anti-poverty strategies. Such 'asset-based welfare' is a new approach to social security reform that has been claimed to directly challenge aspects of wealth distribution.[80] The savings gateway (see Chapter 4) and the Child Trust Fund (see Chapter 5) are two of the Government's asset-based policies which seek to encourage saving among those with low incomes by providing an account-based financial incentive. It is hoped by the Government that an initial financial incentive will encourage the accumulation of capital and, as such, provide a financial safeguard or 'buffer' that would help avert poverty for low-income families.[81] The problem with such asset-based policies is that those who are being encouraged to save are the least likely to be able to do so and those with higher incomes and greater financial know-how may be the real beneficiaries of the policy. There is also a danger that 'asset-based policies could fill the space needed for more radical solutions'.[82]

CONCLUSION

There is no doubt that the gap between rich and poor, however measured, remains vast. Income and wealth inequality are greater now than at any time in recent decades. Nonetheless, changes in taxation and social security policies, which have played a part in maintaining these divisions over the previous two decades, have recently given way to more progressive changes which may, in time, reduce the inequalities between rich and poor. However, the Prime Minister has made it clear that while tackling poverty is a priority, reducing inequality is not.[83]

NOTES

1 J Micklewright, *Child poverty in English-speaking countries*, Innocenti Working Papers, No 94, UNICEF, 2003

2 P Johnson and S Tanner, *Ownership and the Distribution of Wealth*, Institute for Fiscal Studies, 1998

3 A Shephard, *Inequality Under the Labour Government*, Briefing Note 33, Institute for Fiscal Studies, 2003

4 W Paxton, *Wealth Distribution – the evidence*, Institute for Public Policy Research, Centre for Asset-based Welfare – evidence report, September 2002

5 See note 3, p4

6 Office for National Statistics, *Measuring inequality in household income: the Gini coefficient*, www.statistics.gov.uk/about/methodology_by_theme/gini/default.asp

7 C Lakin, *The Effects of Taxes and Benefits on Household Income, 2001–02*, Office for National Statistics, 2003, Table 27 (Appendix 1)

8 C Lakin, *The Effects of Taxes and Benefits on Household Income, 2001–02*, Office for National Statistics, 2003

9 A Goodman and A Shephard, *Inequality and Living Standards in Great Britain: some facts*, Briefing Note 19, 2002

10 See note 3, p4. The reference period used is from 1979 to 2001/02. Figures for 2001/02 show a slight fall in income inequality (from 0.348 in 2000/01 to 0.346 in 2001/02) but this fall is statistically insignificant; see also Department for Work and Pensions, *Households Below Average Income 1994/5–2001/02*, Corporate Document Services, March 2003, Table A3, p135

11 See note 11, *Households Below Average Income 1994/5–2001/02*

12 Department for Work and Pensions, *Households Below Average Income 1996/7–2001/02*, 2003

13 See note 11, p13

14 See note 9, p16

15 Comparisons for the period to 1998/99 can only be made from 1994/95 when the larger *Family Resources Survey* was used in the HBAI series, replacing the earlier *Family Expenditure Survey*; the two series are not directly comparable

16 See note 8

17 C Lakin, 'The effects of taxes and benefits on household income, 2001–02', *Economic Trends*, No. 594, Office for National Statistics, May 2003

18 See note 17

19 See note 8

20 See note 11, Appendix 1, p224

21 The figures are for disposable income and therefore no account is taken for indirect taxes (VAT, duties, etc)

22 Editorial from *IDS Report 874*, February 2003. Pay rises for top earners have outstripped the rest of the workforce, resulting in two-thirds of full-time employees in 2002 receiving less than average gross weekly earnings.

23 A Atkinson, *Poverty and Social Security*, Harvester Wheatsheaf, 1989

24 A Goodman and S Webb, 'The Distribution of UK Household Expenditure, 1979–1992', *Fiscal Studies*, Vol. 16 No. 3, pp55–60, 1996. Spending change is measured on an after housing costs (AHC) income measure.

25 See note 9

26 Office for National Statistics, *Family Spending: a report on the 2001–2002 Expenditure and Food Survey, 2003*

27 See note 26

28 C Farrell and W O'Connor, *Low-income Families and Household Spending*, Research Summary, Department for Work and Pensions, 2003

29 See note 28

30 HM Treasury, 'Tackling Poverty and Extending Opportunity', *The Modernisation of Britain's Tax and Benefit System*, Number 4, March 1999

31 Office for National Statistics, *New Earnings Survey*, 2002

32 See note 22

33 Office for National Statistics, *New Earnings Survey 2002: streamlined and summary analyses*, 2003

34 J Hills, *The Joseph Rowntree Foundation Inquiry into Income and Wealth, Volume 2: a summary of the evidence*, Joseph Rowntree Foundation, 1995

35 J Bulman, 'Results of the 2002 Earnings Survey', *Labour Market Trends*, Office for National Statistics, October 2002

36 R Dickens, 'Wage Mobility in Great Britain', in CASE, *Persistent Poverty and Lifetime Inequality: the evidence*, proceedings from a workshop held at HM Treasury 17 and 18 November 1998, CASE report 5, March 1999

37 A Gosling, P Johnson, J McCrae and G Paull, *The Dynamics of Low Pay and Unemployment in Early 1990s Britain*, Joseph Rowntree Foundation, 1997

38 R Dickens, 'Caught in a Trap: Wage Mobility in Great Britain 1975–94', *Economica*, Vol. 67 Issue 268, p477, November 2000

39 *The Guardian*, 'Minimum wage likely for 16 year olds', 3 January 2004. The findings of the Low Pay Commission were to be published around the time of going to press in February 2004.

40 D Heasman, 'Patterns of low pay', *Labour Market Trends*, Office for National Statistics, April 2003

41 Office for National Statistics, *New Earnings Survey 2002*, October 2002

42 See note 39. A lack of good statistics on low-paid workers makes an analysis of their situation difficult.

43 Low Pay Commission, *The National Minimum Wage: fourth report of the Low Pay Commission: building on success*, The Stationery Office, March 2003

44 Office for National Statistics, *Jobs Paid Below Minimum Wage Rates*, 2002, www.statistics.gov.uk/downloads/theme_labour/jobs_paid_below_minimum_wage_rates.xls

45 M Meacher, 'Worse than under Thatcher', *The Guardian*, 15 July 2003

46 See note 45

47 Office for National Statistics, *Composition of the net wealth of the household sector, 1987 to 1998*, Social trends dataset 30, 2002

48 See note 4

49 Inland Revenue, *Personal Wealth, Distribution among the adult population of marketable wealth* (Series C), 2003

50 See note 49

51 W Paxton, 'Asset-based welfare – a solution to child poverty?', *End Child Poverty Newsletter*, Winter 2002, Issue 3, p6; W Paxton and M Taylor, 'Bridging The Wealth Gap', *New Statesman*, July 2002

52 See note 51, 'Bridging The Wealth Gap'

53 D Gordon, 'Inequalities in Income, Wealth and Standard of Living in Britain', in C Pantazis and D Gordon (eds), *Tackling Inequalities: where are we now and what can be done?*, The Policy Press, 2000

54 See note 4

55 J Banks, Z Smith, M Wakefield, *The Distribution of Financial Wealth in the UK: evidence from 2000 BHPS data*, IFS, 2002, p2

56 J Banks, Z Smith, M Wakefield, *The Distribution of Financial Wealth in the UK: evidence from 2000 BHPS data*, Institute for Fiscal Studies, 2002

57 K Rowlingson, C Whyley and T Warren, *Wealth in Britain: a lifecycle perspective*, Policy Studies Institute, 1999

58 Benefit unit relates to 'a single adult or couple living as married and any dependent children' – Department for Work and Pensions, *Family Resources Survey 2001/02*, 2003, p15

59 C Emmerson and M Wakefield, 'Should we encourage saving among those with low(er) incomes?', in Economic and Social Research Council, *How People on Low Incomes Manage their Finances*, ESRC, 2002

60 W Paxton, 'Asset-based welfare – a solution to child poverty?', *End Child Poverty Newsletter*, Winter 2002, Issue 3

61 Department for Work and Pensions, *Family Resources Survey 2001/02*, 2003

62 See note 61

63 C Holmes, *Housing, Equality and Choice*, The Institute for Public Policy Research, 2003, piv

64 Institute for Public Policy Research, Press Release, *Housing Gap UK's Biggest Social Inequality*, 2003

65 *The Guardian*, Money section, 29 May 2003

66 W Peterson, *Housing and the Dynamics of Wealth-Holding in the UK, preliminary report for BHPS User Group*, July 2003, p18

67 See note 8

68 See note 8

69 See note 8

70 See note 8, p10

71 C Giles and P Johnson, 'Tax Reform in the UK and Changes to the Progressivity of the Tax System, 1985–1995', *Fiscal Studies*, Vol 15 No 3, 1995

72 See note 71

73 J Hills, *Income and Wealth: the latest evidence*, Joseph Rowntree Foundation, 1998

74 S Bond and M Wakefield, 'The distributional effects of fiscal reforms since 1997', in *IFS Green Budget*, Institute for Fiscal Studies, January 2003

75 M Brewer, *The New Tax Credits*, Briefing Note 35, Institute for Fiscal Studies, 2003

76 F Bennett, 'The New Tax Credits', in F Bennett, J Ginn, J Grieve Smith, H Land, R Madeley, P Spicker and A West, *Budget 2002: a Catalyst response*, April 2002, p30

77 T Sefton, *Recent Changes in the Distribution of the Social Wage*, CASE Paper 62, STICERD, LSE, http://sticerd.lse.ac.uk/publications/ casepapers.asp

78 See note 77

79 See note 77

80 W Paxton, Institute for Public Policy Reform press release, May 2003

81 See note 60

82 M Barnes, 'Reaching the Socially Excluded?', in C Kober and W Paxton (eds), *Asset-Based Welfare and Poverty: exploring the case for and against asset-based welfare policies*, 2002, p13

83 In response to Peter Hain's suggestion that taxes needed to be reviewed, Tony Blair stated that his concern was not to take money from high earners but to raise the incomes of the poorest (*The Guardian*, 20 June 2003). This reflects his earlier position stated on 'Newsnight' in June 2001; when asked if a widening gap between the rich and poor was acceptable the Prime Minister would only answer that the lowest incomes must be raised.

9

Geographical divisions

More than just a North–South divide, Britain suffers from pockets of poverty in every country and in every region in England.
(Trades Union Congress, *Half the World Away: making regional development work*)[1]

Poverty is not evenly spread across the United Kingdom. Measured in terms of contribution to Gross Domestic Product the UK ranks second only to Mexico in the industrialised world in terms of its regional inequality.[2] Although some regions and countries are poorer than others, each contain diverse areas and cities with different poverty levels.

Since 1997, the UK's countries and regions have become increasingly important in the policy-making process. At the same time, smaller territories have become the focus for area-based initiatives, such as neighbourhood renewal schemes and Sure Start. More data than ever before is now available at sub-regional and 'neighbourhood' (ward) level. One example is the provision of information relating to the number of families and children reliant on out-of-work benefits in different wards.[3] However, despite the increasing availability of local-area data, there is still a demand for more detailed, up-to date information at a regional and sub-regional level, with poverty, deprivation and social exclusion identified as important areas of concern.[4]

This chapter is an overview of data on poverty at different geographical levels, starting with the UK; then, following the lines of devolved powers, the smaller nations within the UK and London as the capital city are examined. This is followed by consideration of poverty by constituencies, districts and wards, and finally rural poverty.

Here both Great Britain (excluding Northern Ireland) and the UK are referred to, depending on the source; 'regions' are the government office regions of England, following the convention in the Office for National Statistics' *Regional Trends*.

GEOGRAPHICAL DIVISIONS ACROSS THE UK

INCOMES

The Department for Work and Pensions' *Households Below Average Income* (HBAI) statistics now include a breakdown by countries and regions within Great Britain (GB). During 2001/02, individuals in Wales, the North East, Inner London, and Yorkshire and the Humber were more likely to have a low income. Those with incomes at the

---

TABLE 9.1: **Percentages of quintile groups of individuals, after housing costs, including self-employed, Great Britain 2001/02**

Quintile	I (lowest)	2	3	4	5 (highest)
North East	20	25	22	20	13
North West	21	23	21	21	15
Yorkshire and Humberside	22	24	23	18	14
East Midlands	20	22	22	20	16
West Midlands	21	21	23	20	15
East	16	17	19	23	24
London	24	14	15	18	29
Inner	32	16	10	14	29
Outer	19	13	18	20	29
South East	17	17	18	20	29
South West	19	21	22	20	18
England	20	20	20	20	21
Wales	22	23	22	20	13
Scotland	19	21	20	22	19
GB total	**20**	**20**	**20**	**20**	**20**

Percentages do not sum due to rounding

Source: Department for Work and Pensions, *Households Below Average Income 2001/02*, The Stationery Office, 2003, Table 3.2

higher end of the distribution (after housing costs (AHC)) were more likely to be located in Outer London and the South East (see Table 9.1). Over the period 1998–2001, average gross weekly incomes for households in London were more than one and a half times those of households in Northern Ireland, Wales and the North East of England.[5]

Some of the poorer areas of the UK also had a higher proportion of their income from benefits, especially Northern Ireland and the North West.

As described in other chapters, the *Poverty and Social Exclusion in Britain* (PSE) survey defined poverty as being unable to afford two or more basic necessities.[6] On this definition, the pattern is different from income data – see Figure 9.1.

EARNINGS

Some income disparity may be explained by regional differences in earnings. London has considerably higher average earnings than any other region or country in the UK, £624 per week. This is partly attributable to the concentration of high-paying occupations in the capital. The lowest levels of pay are found in the North East and in

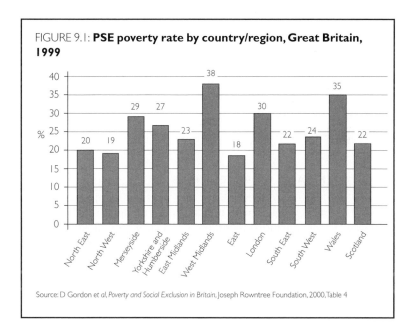

FIGURE 9.1: **PSE poverty rate by country/region, Great Britain, 1999**

Source: D Gordon *et al, Poverty and Social Exclusion in Britain,* Joseph Rowntree Foundation, 2000, Table 4

TABLE 9.2: **Average gross weekly household income and proportion of income from social security benefits across the UK, 2001/02**

	£ per week	% of income from benefits
North East	494	15
North West	443	17
Yorkshire and the Humber	469	15
East Midlands	517	12
West Midlands	488	14
East	577	10
London	761	7
South East	687	8
South West	511	13
England	567	11
Wales	459	15
Scotland	478	13
Northern Ireland	445	20
UK total	551	11

Source: Office for National Statistics, *Family Spending: a report on the 2001–02 Expenditure and Food Survey*, 2003, p142

Wales, with average rates of around £399 per week.[7] The North East is also the most likely to have earnings at, or just above, the national minimum wage – 6.7 per cent of jobs pay less than 10p above the minimum wage in the North East, compared with 2 per cent in London.[8] Average annual rates of pay also reflect the regional earnings pattern (see Table 9.3).

EMPLOYMENT AND WORKLESSNESS

As with poverty, employment is not evenly spread; a Trades Union Congress report concluded that there was a clear 'jobs divide' between the level of worklessness in the south of England (excluding London) and the rest of the UK.[9] In 2003 the highest proportion of workless households were in the North East (22 per cent). Wales and Northern Ireland also had a high proportion of workless households, each over

TABLE 9.3: **Average annual levels of pay by region in Great Britain, 2002**

	Average gross annual pay (£)
North East	20,716
North West	22,487
Yorkshire and the Humber	21,503
East Midlands	21,772
West Midlands	22,387
East	24,099
London	34,762
South East	26,449
South West	22,359
England	25,079
Wales	20,758
Scotland	22,016
Great Britain	**24,603**

Source: Office for National Statistics, *Labour Market Trends*, Vol. 111, No. 4, The Stationery Office, April 2003

19 per cent. The lowest proportion of workless households was in the South East (11.3 per cent) (see Figure 9.2).[10]

There is a 'regional jobs deficit' in many areas that suffer high worklessness and unemployment, such as the North of England, Wales and Scotland. This is largely a consequence of the collapse of heavy industry in these areas and a lack of any alternative, unskilled, manual work.[11]

The employment rate also varies; Northern Ireland had the lowest proportion of adults in employment in 2001/02, followed by Wales and the North East. Many inner city areas and former industrial areas have low rates of employment.[12] Figure 9.3 shows that differentials in employment exist not only between regions but also within them. The broadest spread of employment rates was in London, which ranged from 53.9 per cent employment in Newham to 82.2 per cent in Sutton.

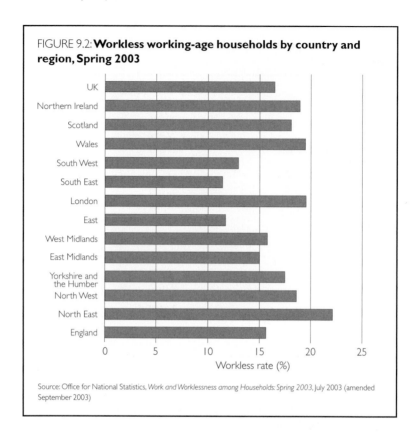

FIGURE 9.2: **Workless working-age households by country and region, Spring 2003**

Source: Office for National Statistics, *Work and Worklessness among Households: Spring 2003*, July 2003 (amended September 2003)

DEATH RATES

The poorest GB countries and regions experience poorer health and higher death rates. Deprived areas within regions suffer considerable health inequalities, health-related unemployment and higher mortality rates[13] than their more affluent neighbours in the same region. Some wards have death rates comparable to those of the national average in the 1950s.[14]

Table 9.4 shows death rates in the UK and England by region, measured as an average number per thousand. Wales and Scotland have higher rates than England and the UK average. Death rates in Scotland are the highest in the UK and among the highest in the EU.[15] Looking at the regions of England, the North, especially the North East, has the highest mortality rates overall and the highest death rates from cancers, heart disease and suicides.[16]

FIGURE 9.3: **Employment differentials within and between regions, 2001/02**

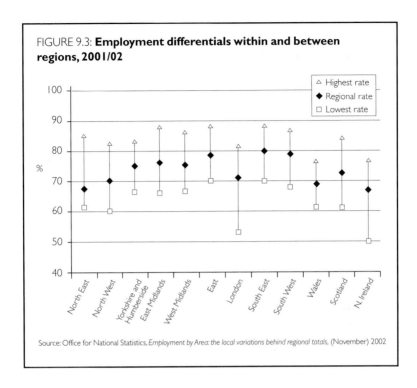

Source: Office for National Statistics, *Employment by Area: the local variations behind regional totals*, (November) 2002

POVERTY IN SCOTLAND, WALES AND NORTHERN IRELAND

Levels of child income poverty, at around 30 per cent, are similar in England, Wales and Scotland. While this figure demonstrates a slight fall in numbers for England and Wales, it shows that child income poverty in Scotland has barely altered over the period from 1997/98 to 2001/02.[17]

Individuals in Wales are more likely than those in Scotland and England to be living in the lowest income bracket, and Wales had the highest proportion of households living on income support[18] and the highest percentage of children living in workless households in the UK in 2000/01 (see Table 9.5). However, Northern Ireland had the highest proportion of children eligible for free school meals.[19] In all countries, data for primary schools reveals that more pupils were eligible for a meal than took it up (see Table 9.6).

TABLE 9.4: **UK death rates, Scotland, Wales, Northern Ireland and regions of England, 2002***

	All deaths (Rate per 1,000 population, of all ages)
UK total	**10.2**
North East	11.3
North West	11.1
Yorkshire and the Humber	10.6
East Midlands	10.3
West Midlands	10.3
East	10.1
London	8.0
South East	10.0
South West	11.2
England	10.1
Scotland	11.5
Wales	11.4
Northern Ireland	8.6

Source: Office for National Statistics, *Health Statistics Quarterly 20*, Table 2.1 and Table 6.2, Winter 2003

TABLE 9.5: **Proportion of children living in workless households by UK country, 2000/01**

	per cent
England	16.0
Scotland	16.7
Wales	19.5
Northern Ireland	18.2 *
UK	**16.0**

Source: Chris Ruane: Parliamentary Question to the Chancellor of the Exchequer, 30 Jan 2002, *Column 364W*; *Office for National Statistics, *Households in Northern Ireland 1997–2001* (spring of each year), 2001

TABLE 9.6: **Eligibility and take-up of free school meals, primary* and secondary schools, 2001/02**

	Primary (per cent)		Secondary (per cent)	
	Eligible	Receiving meals	Eligible	Receiving meals
England	17.1	14.0	14.9	10.9
Scotland	20.1	16.9	15.9	10.9
Wales	19.4	17.7	16.8	13.4
Northern Ireland	22.1	18.0	21.4	16.7

* Figures are for maintained nursery and primary schools.

Source: Department for Education and Skills, *Education Statistics: Education and Training Statistics for the United Kingdom 2002 edition*, DfES, 2002

SCOTLAND

About a quarter of people in poverty in Scotland live in rural areas but there are also notable concentrations of poverty in the larger cities. More than half the council wards in Glasgow and Dundee were within the worst 10 per cent of multiply deprived wards across Scotland.[20]

A major cause of poverty has been high levels of unemployment and economic inactivity, particularly due to the erosion of manufacturing industries from the early 1980s.[21] Again, major cities are particularly affected; 32 per cent of the most employment-deprived wards are located in Glasgow.[22] In spring 2002, nearly 210,000 working-age households in Scotland had been without work for three years or more, the highest number for more than a decade.[23] In February 2003, 29 per cent of the working-age population in Glasgow were claiming a key benefit, compared to 18 per cent of the working-age population in Scotland as a whole and higher than the Great Britain figure of 14.2 per cent.[24]

The risk of living on a low income has recently increased in Scotland, in contrast to the rest of Great Britain, which has seen a decline. There has also been a rise in the number of the 'working poor' – low-income households containing someone who is working; in 2001, 40 per cent of households in poverty had at least one a working adult.[25] Employment appears to be particularly insecure; 45 per cent of those making a claim for jobseeker's allowance in spring 2002 had previously claimed less than six months earlier.[26]

In 2002, 20 per cent of the Scottish population reported having a disability, long-term illness or health problem that limited their daily activities.[27] A higher proportion of income support claimants in Scotland (30 per cent) were disabled, compared to Great Britain as a whole (26.4 per cent).[28] As well as an increased risk of poor health, the Scottish population have a higher risk of premature death, especially in the Glasgow area, which has the lowest life expectancy for men and women in the UK.[29] Glasgow is also where 43 per cent of the most health-deprived wards in Scotland are to be found.[30] Mortality rates in the 10 per cent most deprived areas of Scotland were more than twice as high as those of the least disadvantaged 50 per cent.[31] A more in-depth analysis of the Scottish situation can be found in CPAG's *Poverty in Scotland 2002*.[32]

WALES

Two-thirds of the Welsh population lives in South Wales, where levels of deprivation are high. Wales has higher rates of economic inactivity, sickness and early childbearing (births to women under 20), and lower numbers of young people in post-16-year-old education than in England.[33] According to the New Policy Institute, 'Wales is both somewhat poorer and somewhat less unequal than GB as a whole'.[34] Over a quarter of the working-age population is economically inactive, with very high rates of health-related inactivity.

- The Welsh Index of Deprivation showed a high concentration of deprivation in the South Wales Valleys, although concentrated pockets of deprivation were found even in the least deprived wards.[35]
- A report by Save the Children found high rates of child poverty in certain districts. While in Swansea 3 per cent of children were in poverty, in nearby Townhill over 80 per cent of children were poor.[36]

Although employment levels have recently increased in Wales, from 68.5 per cent in spring 2002 to 72.9 per cent in 2003, there is a lower employment rate in Wales compared with the UK (74.7 per cent in spring 2003).[37]

In 2001/02, a quarter of individuals in Wales had incomes below 60 per cent of the median, a higher proportion than in England (22 per cent) and Scotland (21 per cent).[38] Not only are there concentrations at the lowest end of the income distribution but the distribution as a whole is poorer than that of England. The income distribution in Wales is skewed towards the bottom income groups, with only 12 per cent of individuals in the top fifth income bracket (AHC) compared to 21 per cent in England.[39] Benefits make up a larger proportion of total gross income in Wales than in England or Scotland, with a higher proportion of children living in households claiming income support – 18.9 per cent – compared to the UK-wide figure of 13.5 per cent.[40]

- In Wales 23 per cent of adults of working age lived in households below 60 per cent of the median income (AHC) in 2001/02 compared to 19 per cent in England – higher than any GB country.[41]
- Wales had the lowest gross weekly earnings in 2002, at 14 per cent below the UK average.[42]

NORTHERN IRELAND

As many statistics are Great Britain-based, Northern Ireland is often excluded from a wider analysis. It is the smallest UK country, with a younger population containing a higher proportion of children and lone parents. There are long-standing demographic differences between the two communities, the Catholic community being younger and with larger average household size and lower incomes than Protestant households. A recent report examining poverty and social exclusion in Northern Ireland found Catholics to be 1.4 times more likely than Protestants to live in poverty.[43] The report also found that in 2002/03:

- more people were living in poverty in Northern Ireland than in Great Britain or the Republic of Ireland;
- more than a quarter, 29.6 per cent, of households were defined as poor;
- 37.4 per cent of children lived in a 'poor' household.[44]

Other studies have found considerable variations in levels of multiple deprivation across Northern Ireland, with particular concentrations of deprivation in large cities such as Belfast and Londonderry; 12.2 per cent of the population live in the most multiply-deprived 10 per cent of wards.[45]

Northern Ireland has the lowest regional employment rate in the UK, 69.2 per cent in spring 2003, with very low employment in some areas such as Strabane, which had an employment rate of just 49.7 per cent in 2001 (the latest local labour market data available) in addition to significant levels of deprivation.[46]

Wages in Northern Ireland are 84 per cent of the UK average. Over a quarter of all full-time employees (26.8 per cent) receive less than £250 per week;[47] there are also fewer high earners than in Great Britain.

POVERTY IN THE CAPITAL CITY

As the capital, London attracts much wealth, but also has many areas of high deprivation and poverty. The division between Inner and Outer London is particularly marked, with 33 per cent of the Inner London population in income poverty in 2001/02, compared to 20 per cent in Outer London.[48] In 2002, around 40 per cent of secondary school pupils in Inner London were eligible for free school meals, compared with 15 per cent nationally and 17.5 per cent in Outer London.[49] The three million residents of Inner London experience far higher rates of income poverty for children, working-age adults and pensioners than in any country or region of Great Britain.[50] A 2002 report, commissioned by the London mayor, found acute levels of poverty, with over half of Inner London children – 53 per cent – living in income poverty. The report also found:

- 36 per cent of pensioners in Inner London were in income poverty, compared to 25 per cent nationally and 21 per cent in Outer London;
- 24 per cent of children in London are living in households in receipt of income support; this compared with 16 per cent for Great Britain overall.[51]

London is one of Great Britain's most severely affected regions in terms of unemployment. Of the 10 worst areas for unemployment in the UK, half are in London, with levels of more than 10 per cent in some boroughs.[52] Within the Bangladeshi community in London, one out of four men are unemployed.[53] A third of children in London lived in workless households in 2001, more than 10 per cent greater than the national average.[54]

Earnings in the capital have become increasingly polarised. In 2001, 10 per cent of men in London earned more than £1,204 per week but 10 per cent earned less than £267.[55] In 2001/02, 24 per cent of individuals in London were in the bottom fifth of incomes (rising to 35 per cent in Inner London) but there were also more in the top fifth (29 per cent) than the England average (20 per cent).[56] In London, 'high levels of deprivation exist side by side with the highest concentrations of the least deprived citizens in the country'.[57]

TABLE 9.7: **Poorest and least poor British parliamentary constituencies according to HPI-2 indicators**

| | HPI-2 indicator | | | | |
	1	2	3	4	HPI-2
10 poorest					
Glasgow Shettleston	27.2	2.3	35	26	27.1
Glasgow Springburn	25.3	2.6	34	25	26.0
Glasgow Maryhill	23.4	2.5	34	25	25.8
Birmingham Ladywood	18.6	2.9	35	27	25.7
Manchester Central	21.4	2.5	34	23	24.7
Camberwell and Peckham	17.1	2.6	34	25	24.6
Glasgow Bailleston	21.6	2.1	33	24	24.5
Liverpool Riverside	21.4	3.3	35	20	24.5
Hackney South/Shoreditch	17.0	2.3	34	23	24.0
Bethnal Green and Bow	17.8	1.6	32	24	23.6
10 least poor					
Beaconsfield	9.4	2.0	9	10	8.6
Rayleigh	9.7	1.9	8	10	8.5
North East Hampshire	9.2	1.2	9	10	8.4
Romsey	8.5	1.9	9	10	8.3
Chesham and Amersham	8.8	1.6	8	10	8.3
Buckingham	9.2	1.8	9	9	8.2
Woodspring	8.4	1.1	8	10	8.1
Cheadle	9.2	1.3	8	9	7.9
Northavon	9.1	0.9	8	9	7.9
Wokingham	8.4	1.0	7	9	7.5

Note: 1–4 refer to the numbered indicators listed in the preceding text

Source: J Seymour, *Poverty in Plenty: a human development report for the UK*, UNED-UK, 2000

High housing and childcare costs intensify poverty in the city. People in Inner London were 52 per cent more likely to report finding it difficult to manage financially than in any other part of the UK.[58]

POVERTY AT LOCAL LEVEL

Areas of severe deprivation range from major cities such as Manchester, Liverpool, Birmingham and London to parts of Cornwall and Cumbria to seaside towns.[59]

Many districts contain 'pockets' of deprivation in inner city areas and social housing estates.[60] As poverty and inequality grew during the 1980s and 1990s, people on low incomes became more concentrated in poor areas and the gap between richer and poorer wards widened.[61]

BRITISH PARLIAMENTARY CONSTITUENCIES

More statistics are being produced at constituency level; one example is *Poverty in Plenty: a Human Development Report for the UK*, using the United Nation's Human Poverty Index (HPI). The UN HPI for industrialised countries (HPI-2) consists of the following indicators:[62]

1. The percentage of people not expected to survive to age 60.
2. The long-term unemployment rate (12 months or more).
3. The percentage of people living below the income poverty line (50 per cent of median disposable income).
4. The functional illiteracy rate.

DISTRICTS AND WARDS

The former Department of the Environment, Transport and the Regions (DETR) produced deprivation indicators for English districts and wards, most recently in 2000. The Neighbourhood Renewal Unit, in conjunction with the Social Disadvantage Research Centre at Oxford University, is reviewing and developing these indices of deprivation and, at the time of writing, publication of the updated Index was expected in early 2004.

The 2000 Index comprises 33 indicators, with different weightings across six different 'domains'.[63] These domains and weightings are:

Income	25%
Employment	25%
Health deprivation and disability	15%
Education, skills and training	15%
Geographical access to services	10%
Housing	10%

Districts and wards can be ranked according to the extent and concentration of indicators in these domains. The top ten districts (ie, the most deprived) on the income scale tend to be mainly in the North and Midlands, whereas London appears more prominent on combined

TABLE 9.8: **Top ten (most deprived) English districts ranked by income, combined deprivation and extent of deprivation, DETR Index 2000**

Income ranking	Combined ranking	Extent ranking
1. Birmingham	1. Tower Hamlets	1. Hackney
2. Liverpool	2. Hackney	2. Tower Hamlets
3. Manchester	3. Newham	3. Newham
4. Leeds	4. Easington	4. Manchester
5. Bradford	5. Liverpool	5. Knowsley
6. Sheffield	6. Knowsley	6. Easington
7. Newham	7. Manchester	7. Liverpool
8. Kirklees	8. Islington	8. Middlesborough
9. Sandwell	9. Southwark	9. Islington
10. Nottingham	10. Hartlepool	10. South Tyneside

Source: derived from the DETR 2000 *Index of Deprivation* at district level

deprivation indicators. The extent order shows the most deprived districts according to the percentage of the population in wards that rank within the most deprived 10 per cent of wards in England.

According to the Neighbourhood Renewal Unit, 40 per cent of the population live in the 88 most deprived local authority areas.[64] The highest concentration of severe deprivation, defined by percentage of the most deprived wards, are found in four regions:

- the North East – 19 per cent;
- the North West – 25.7 per cent;
- London – 18 per cent;
- Yorkshire and Humberside – 9.4 per cent.[65]

When compared to the national average, deprived areas typically have:

- twice as many people living on means-tested benefits;
- three times as much child poverty;
- higher rates of ill-health and early mortality;
- more lone-parent households;[66]
- high levels of worklessness and low levels of work opportunities.[67]

Information at ward level can show the very localised nature of poverty or deprivation and variations within small areas. For example, within

Liverpool Local Authority, 72 per cent of children resident in Aber-
cromby were living in families reliant on out-of-work benefits in 2002,
compared to 12 per cent of children in the nearby ward of Church.[68]

POVERTY IN RURAL AREAS

Although urban areas do suffer from greater poverty, there are also
considerable levels of poverty and social exclusion in many rural
areas.[69] In 2002 nearly a fifth of rural households were defined as 'low
income'.[70] Rural poverty is more dispersed and therefore more hidden,
reinforced by a mistaken belief that poverty is an urban problem.

The gap between rich and poor may be wider in rural areas; in one
Wiltshire village, 40 per cent of households had annual incomes of over
£40,000 whilst a further 40 per cent had incomes below £8,000.[71]

Rural unemployment tends to be lower (3 per cent, compared with
5.1 per cent in England in 2002) but greater 'travel to work' distances
make finding new employment harder in rural rather than urban areas.
One study found a mismatch between people's skills and the jobs
available, together with difficulties getting to work and the costs of
working, including transport and childcare.

> So I was in a bit of a catch-22 situation, I couldn't get a job, I couldn't
> get a car until I got a job and I couldn't get a job until I got a car.
>
> (Andrew, Lincolnshire)[72]

Young people were also affected by poor transport and lack of
affordable housing; living in the parental home tended to disguise
personal poverty, and parents only nominally received 'digs money'.[73]

Children living in low-income families in rural areas have expressed
feelings of isolation, boredom and a growing conflict with adults, perhaps as a result of restricted opportunities locally; nearly half of rural
children in low income families had no family car.[74] Lack of access to
transport can reinforce social exclusion and restrict access to health and
education facilities.[75]

Factors influencing rural poverty include more older people retiring
to these areas, and the prevalence of low pay.[76] The *New Earnings Survey*
showed that, in 2002, average gross weekly pay in agriculture was
£330, 29 per cent lower than the national average for all industries
(£465).[77] Lack of affordable housing is also a significant problem in
many rural areas, especially for those on a low income.[78] Proposals for
the construction of an indicator to measure 'difficulty of access to

owner occupation' in the new English Index of Multiple Deprivation will show the number of households who are not able to afford to enter owner-occupation on the basis of their income, and may shed more light on this problem in rural areas.[79]

NEIGHBOURHOOD RENEWAL

In 2001, the Neighbourhood Renewal Unit implemented a National Strategy Action Plan for neighbourhood renewal across England. Extra resources were made available through the Neighbourhood Renewal Fund for 88 of the most deprived local authority districts. The core aim of the strategy is that 'in 10 to 20 years no one will be seriously disadvantaged by where they live'.[80]

One part of the regeneration strategy is the New Deal for Communities (NDC), a ten-year government programme to tackle multiple deprivation in the most deprived neighbourhoods.[81] New Deal for Communities partnerships have been established in 39 neighbourhoods across England and focus on five key themes: poor job prospects; high levels of crime; educational under-achievement; poor health; and problems with housing and the physical environment.[82] The NDC works through neighbourhood partnerships, particularly with local community organisations but also with business and voluntary groups.

Similar renewal plans for the most deprived communities are also underway in Scotland and Wales.[83] Northern Ireland has a more general approach to tackling disadvantaged areas via its new Targeting Social Need (TSN) policy.

In Scotland, targeted regeneration strategies are focusing on improving core public services in deprived areas and increasing the 'social capital – the skills, confidence, support networks and resources' – of individuals and communities in areas of deprivation.[84] In Wales, the new Minister for Social Justice and Regeneration will be responsible for the Communities First programme, which concentrates on regeneration of the most disadvantaged communities in Wales.[85]

The NDC in England does claim to be making some progress, although spending delays, community tension and frequent management changes have caused setbacks.[86] A separate problem with neighbourhood renewal initiatives is that spotlighting specific areas may well be at the expense of examining the wider structural inequalities that contribute to such localised disadvantage.[87]

CONCLUSION

A precise 'geography of poverty' is hard to define, as regions, countries and large cities contain wide variations in poverty and wealth, and even seemingly idyllic rural areas contain poverty, although this is often less visible.

With devolution to countries within the UK, and the prospect of regional assemblies in the North East, the North West, Yorkshire and the Humber, better information may emerge about poverty within these areas and aid the process of policy development.

Through the Neighbourhood Renewal Unit the Government is attempting to reduce disadvantages connected to location within 10 to 20 years.[88] Regional and sub-regional inequalities are vast and the undertaking to diminish them is an essential task if opportunities both to avoid and escape from poverty are to be realised.

NOTES

1 Trades Union Congress, *Half the World Away: making regional development work*, TUC, July 2002

2 OECD Territorial Outlook 2001, cited in J Rowlands, *Alive and Kicking: women's and men's responses to poverty and globalisation in the UK*, Oxfam GB, 2002

3 Department for Work and Pensions, *Work and Pensions Statistics* – 2003, 31st edition, 2003; Office for National Statistics, www.neighbourhood.statistics.gov.uk; for Scotland's neighbourhood statistics: www.sns.gov.uk/

4 A E Green and D Owen, Regional and Sub-regional Information/ Intelligence: needs, uses, gaps and priorities, Department of Transport, Environment and the Regions, March 2002, www.local.odpm.gov.uk/ research/needs.pdf

5 Office for National Statistics, *Regional Trends 37*, 2002 Edition, 2002

6 D Gordon *et al*, *Poverty and Social Exclusion in Britain*, Joseph Rowntree Foundation, 2000

7 J Bulman, 'Results of the 2002 Earnings Survey', *Labour Market Trends*, Vol. 110, No. 10, October 2002

8 D Heasman, 'Patterns of Low Pay', *Labour Market Trends*, Vol. 111, No. 4, April 2003

9 Trades Union Congress, *The Regional Jobs Divide*, TUC, March 2000

10 Office for National Statistics, *Work and Worklessness among Households: Autumn 2002*, January 2003

11 Trades Union Congress, *Half the World Away: Making regional development work*, TUC, July 2002

12 C Summerfield and P Babb (eds), *Social Trends*, No. 33, Office for National Statististics, The Stationery Office, 2003

13 Neighbourhood Renewal Unit, *Factsheet No.3*, 'Health and Neighbourhood Renewal', April 2002

14 Department of Health, *Tackling Health Inequalities: summary of the 2002 Cross-Cutting Review*, 2002, p8

15 Scottish Executive, *Social Justice: a Scotland where everyone matters: indicators of progress*, 2001

16 Office for National Statistics, 'Age-standardised mortality rates, by cause and sex, 2000', *Regional Trends 37*, 2002 Edition, 2002

17 P Kenway, S Fuller, M Rahman, C Street and G Palmer, 'Monitoring Poverty and Social Exclusion in Scotland', *Findings*, Joseph Rowntree Foundation, December 2002; Department for Work and Pensions, *Households Below Average Income 1994/5–2001/02*, Corporate Document Services, March 2003

18 See note 5

19 Free school meal entitlement is often used as a simple indicator of poverty. Free school meals in 2001/02 were only available to children living in a family in receipt of income support or income-based jobseeker's allowance.

20 The new Scottish Indices of Deprivation comprise indicators which are combined to form domains of deprivation. The domains in the Scottish index of multiple deprivation are: income deprivation, employment deprivation, health deprivation and disability, education, skills and training deprivation, and geographical access to services. The Social Disadvantage Research Centre, *Scottish Indices of Deprivation 2003*, Social Disadvantage Research Centre, University of Oxford, 2003.

21 House of Commons, Scottish Affairs Select Committee, *Poverty in Scotland*, Session 1999–2000, HC 59-I, July 2000

22 See note 20

23 See note 17, 'Monitoring Poverty and Social Exclusion in Scotland'

24 Department for Work and Pensions/Office for National Statistics, *First Release*, 'DWP Statistical Summary – June 2003', June 2003; Scottish Executive, *Benefits and Tax Credits in Scotland: report for February 2003*, Scottish Executive National Statistics, September 2003. Key benefits are jobseeker's allowance, incapacity benefit, severe disablement allowance, disability living allowance and income support.

25 See note 17, 'Monitoring Poverty and Social Exclusion in Scotland'

26 See note 17, 'Monitoring Poverty and Social Exclusion in Scotland'

27 Scottish Executive, *Health in Scotland 2002*, Report to the Chief Medical Officer, June 2003

28 U Brown, G Scott, G Mooney, B Duncan (eds), *Poverty in Scotland 2002*, CPAG, 2002

29 Office for National Statistics, *Life Expectancy at Birth: local and health authorities in the UK, 1991–1993 to 1999–2001*, August 2003

30 See note 20

31 See note 17, 'Monitoring Poverty and Social Exclusion in Scotland'

32 See note 28

33 J Bradshaw (ed), *Well-being of Children in the UK*, Save the Children, 2002

34 New Policy Institute, www.poverty.org.uk/W02/all.htm, May 2003

35 Communities Directorate, Welsh Assembly Government, *Annual Report on Social Exclusion in Wales 2002*, March 2002

36 See note 33

37 Office for National Statistics, *Labour Market Trends*, Vol. 111, No. 9, September 2003

38 See note 17, *Households Below Average Income 1994/5–2001/02*

39 See note 17, *Households Below Average Income 1994/5–2001/02*

40 Department for Work and Pensions, *Family Resources Survey 2001/02*, 2003

41 See note 17, *Households Below Average Income 1994/5–2001/02*

42 See note 7

43 P Hillyard, G Kelly, E McLaughlin, D Patsios and M Tomlinson, *Bare Necessities: poverty and social exclusion in Northern Ireland – key findings*, Democratic Dialogue No.16, 2003. People were defined as being in poverty if they lacked three or more 'necessary' items and had, on average, an equivalised income of £156.27 a week or less.

44 See note 43

45 Social Disadvantage Research Centre, *Measures of Deprivation in Northern Ireland*, University of Oxford, June 2001

46 See note 37 and note 45

47 See note 5

48 See note 17, *Households Below Average Income 1994/5–2001/02*

49 Department for Education and Skills, *Statistics of Education: schools in England*, 2002 edition, The Stationery Office, 2002

50 Mayor of London, *London Divided: income inequality and poverty in the capital*, Greater London Authority, 2002

51 See note 50

52 Trades Union Congress, *Pockets of Poverty,* Briefing Document, TUC, June 2002. Unemployment is the International Labour Organization definition, which is a count of all jobless people who want to work, are available to work and are actively seeking employment.

53 London Health Commission, *Health in London Report*, 2003

54 See note 50

55 See note 5

56 See note 17, *Households Below Average Income 1994/5–2001/02*

57 N Buck, I Gordon, P Hall, M Harloe, M Kleinman, *Working Capital: life and labour in contemporary London*, Routledge, 2002, p256

58 See note 57, p243

59 Office of the Deputy Prime Minister, *Factsheet 14: Housing and Neighbourhood Renewal*, 2003

60 G Smith, *Area-Based Initiatives: the rationale and options for area targeting*, CASE paper 25, STICERD, LSE, 1999

61 Described in J Hills, *Inquiry into Income and Wealth*, volume 2, Joseph Rowntree Foundation, 1995

62 J Seymour, *Poverty in Plenty: a human development report for the UK*, UNED-UK, 2000

63 Department of the Environment, Transport and the Regions, *Indices of Deprivation 2000*, Regeneration Research Summary No 21, 2000

64 Office of the Deputy Prime Minister, *Factsheet 1: What is Neighbourhood Renewal*, 2003

65 See note 64

66 See note 64

67 Office of the Deputy Prime Minister, *Factsheet 11: Employment and Neighbourhood Renewal*, 2002

68 Department for Work and Pensions, *Work and Pensions Statistics – 2003*, 31st edition, 2003 – 'Neighbourhood statistics', Table 1

69 A Harrop and G Palmer, *Indicators of Poverty and Social Exclusion in Rural England: 2002*, Countryside Agency, December 2002

70 Countryside Agency, *The State of the Countryside: summary of the key facts 2003*, 2003

71 P Milbourne with J Cursons and M Clark, *Poverty and Social Exclusion in Wiltshire*, Cheltenham and Gloucester College of Higher Education; quoted in Performance Innovation Unit, *Rural Economies Report*, Cabinet Office, December 1999

72 S Monk, J Dunn, M Fitzgerald and I Hodge, *Finding Work in Rural Areas: bridges and barriers*, Joseph Rowntree Foundation, 1999

73 S Pavis, S Platt and G Hubbard, *Young People in Rural Scotland: pathways to social inclusion and exclusion*, Joseph Rowntree Foundation, 2000

74 J Davis and T Ridge, *Same Scenery, Different Lifestyle: rural children on a low income*, The Children's Society, 1997; see also T Ridge, *Childhood Poverty and Social Exclusion: from a child's perspective*, The Policy Press, 2002

75 Social Exclusion Unit, *Making the Connections: final report on transport and social exclusion*, February 2003

76 Performance and Innovation Unit, *Rural Economies Report*, Cabinet Office, December 1999

77 Office for National Statistics, *New Earnings Survey 2002: Part A: UK streamlined and summary analyses*, Table UK 2, 2002

78 The Countryside Agency, *Social Exclusion: facts and figures*, www.countryside.gov.uk

79 Neighbourhood Renewal Unit, *Updating the English Indices of Deprivation 2000: proposals for the construction of the indicator 'Difficulty of Access to Owner Occupation'*, 2003

80 Office of the Deputy Prime Minister, *A New Commitment to Neighbourhood Renewal: a National Strategy Action Plan*, 2001

81 See note 64

82 See note 80

83 Scottish Executive, *Better Communities in Scotland: closing the gap, The Scottish Executive's Community Regeneration Statement*, 2002; National Assembly for Wales, *Plan for Wales, 2001*, 2001

84 See note 83, *Better Communities in Scotland: closing the gap*

85 See note 83, *Plan for Wales, 2001*

86 Office of the Deputy Prime Minister, *New Deal for Communities: The National Evaluation 2002/03*, Neighbourhood Renewal Unit, 2003

87 See note 28, p110

88 See note 64

10 International comparisons

For many countries the 1990s were a decade of despair. Some 54 countries are poorer now than in 1990. In 21 a larger proportion of people is going hungry. In 14, more children are dying before age five... In 34, life expectancy has fallen.

(UNDP, *Human Development Report 2003*, 2003)[1]

Many countries experienced rising income inequality during the 1980s and 1990s, 'most consistently and dramatically in the United Kingdom and the United States of America'.[2] Increasingly wide earnings dispersion was a major cause of rising inequality in the USA and the UK during the 1980s and early 1990s, with the richest seeing a significant increase in wealth whilst the income of the poor stagnated.[3] By 1997, the top 1 per cent of US families had an income 23 times that of the median US family income. However, such inequality was not an inevitable consequence of global economic and social changes and some countries, such as Canada and Denmark, saw a stabilising or reduction of inequality, largely achieved through the tax and benefits systems.[4]

In this chapter trends across the European Union (EU) are examined; poverty in other industrialised countries and across the world is also considered. As international data comes from a variety of sources, using a range of different methods and definitions, results can vary. Greater accuracy in assessing poverty and social exclusion across the EU will soon be available through a new EU-wide annual *Survey of Income and Living Conditions* (SILC), which began data-collection in 2003.

THE EUROPEAN UNION

In March 2000, the European Council at Lisbon agreed to create a strategy 'to make a decisive impact on the eradication of poverty and social exclusion by 2010' across the European Union (EU).[5] Common objectives were agreed upon by member states and subsequently endorsed by the European Council at Nice in December 2000. These endeavour to:

• facilitate participation in employment and access by all to resources, rights, goods and services;
• prevent the risks of exclusion;
• help the most vulnerable;
• mobilise all relevant bodies.[6]

These common objectives were the basis of the National Action Plans against poverty and social exclusion, usually known as National Action Plans on social exclusion (NAPs), first submitted by member states during June 2001.[7] Within the National Action Plans (revised every two years) each member state outlines its priorities and efforts in promoting social inclusion and combating poverty and social exclusion. The second round of plans for 2003 to 2005 was submitted by the 15 current member states in July 2003.[8]

Following on from Lisbon and Nice, the Laeken European Council (2001) approved 18 common statistical indicators to aid the monitoring of progress on the common objectives in tackling poverty and social exclusion. From 2003, these indicators were incorporated into the member states' National Action Plans. The Laeken indicators cover four elements of social exclusion:

• financial (or income) poverty;
• employment;
• health;
• education.[9]

The common objectives of the member states and the formulation of NAPs demonstrate a co-ordinated European approach in tackling poverty and social exclusion, and enable poverty and social exclusion to be monitored and comparisons to be made across the EU. Many of the latest NAPs, however, have been criticised by the European Anti Poverty Network (EAPN) for giving the impression that overall economic growth and greater employment alone will reduce or eliminate poverty.[10] The EAPN also notes that 'the fight against poverty and social exclusion seems to have a lower political priority in most Member States than two years ago, and this is reflected in the Plans'.[11]

PATTERNS OF POVERTY IN THE EUROPEAN UNION

The data available for income poverty in Europe primarily comes from the European Commission (Eurostat). Eurostat uses the measure of people living in households with below 60 per cent of national equivalised median income, after social transfers, as an income poverty line, now referred to as the 'at-risk-of-poverty rate' – the same measure used to determine income poverty in Great Britain. During the 1980s, poverty increased in all of the then 12 member states of the European Community, with Italy, Germany and the UK experiencing the sharpest rises.[12]

The latest figures, released in 2004, indicate that 15 per cent of the EU population were at risk of income poverty in 2001. The average figure, however, conceals the considerable variation in income poverty between EU countries, ranging from 10 per cent in Sweden to 21 per cent in Ireland.[13]

Table 10.1 shows the percentage of the population at risk of poverty across the EU15. The figures for those at persistent risk of income poverty – those people with an income below the 60 per cent poverty threshold in the 1999 and in at least two of the preceding three years – are also given.

Sweden has the lowest proportion of its population at risk of income poverty (10 per cent). Denmark, Finland and the Netherlands also have less income poverty than the EU average and have the lowest number of people at risk of persistent income poverty (5 per cent). By contrast, the proportion of persistent income poverty in Greece and Portugal is almost three times as much as in these countries, in addition to having one of the highest proportions of population at risk of current income poverty in the EU (20 per cent). Ireland had the highest proportion of its population at risk of income poverty in 2001 (21 per cent), a rise of 3 per cent since 1999. More than 33 million people, half the total number of people at risk of income poverty in the EU in 1999, were at risk of persistent poverty.[14] The duration of poverty is also very different between the northern and southern member states. The majority of those people in poverty in northern countries experience two to three years of living in poverty, whereas the most common duration in southern countries is 14 to 15 years.[15] It appears therefore that poverty is easier to escape from in the northern countries.

TABLE 10.1: **Poverty in the European Union**

	Population at risk of poverty in 2001 (%)	Population at persistent risk of poverty (in poverty in 1999 and at least two of the preceding three years) (%)
EU-15	15	9
Austria	12	7
Belgium	13	8
Denmark	11	5
Finland	11	5
France	15	9
Germany	11	6
Greece	20	13
Ireland	21	12
Italy	19	11
Luxembourg	12	8
Netherlands	11	5
Portugal	20	14
Spain	19	11
Sweden	10	–
UK	17	11

– ; No data available

Source: Eurostat, 'At-risk-of-poverty rate by age and gender', 2004; I Dennis and A C Guio, 'Poverty and Social Exclusion in the EU after Laeken – part 1', *Statistics in Focus*, THEME 3-8/2003, 2003

With the exceptions of Sweden, Finland, Greece, Denmark and Belgium, children in the EU are at a much higher risk of poverty than adults. In 2001, children in Portugal and Luxembourg stood close to twice the risk of adults of being in income poverty.[16]

NON-MONETARY INDICATORS OF POVERTY

A non-monetary indicator of poverty, such as child mortality,[17] also finds disparities between member states. The country with the lowest child mortality rate under 5 (U5MR) was Denmark (four per thousand) compared to 7 per thousand in the UK in 2001, the highest in the EU.[18]

TABLE 10.2: **Self-reported income poverty and deprivation among the EU poor**

	(per cent)	
	Having great difficulty making ends meet	Cannot afford one week's holiday
Austria	13	49
Belgium	12	47
Denmark	10	24
France	18	67
Germany	8	29
Greece	43	85
Ireland	29	68
Italy	15	70
Luxembourg	14	44
Netherlands	14	38
Portugal	31	86
Spain	36	80
UK	17	64

Source: Eurostat, European Social Statistics, Income, Theme 3, Poverty and Social Exclusion, 2000, cited in J Micklewright and K Stewart, 'Poverty and Social Exclusion in Europe: European Comparisons and the impact of enlargement', New Economy, Vol 8(2), Blackwell, June 2001

Indicators of deprivation, such as the inability to meet dietary, clothing or holiday needs, are used by the European Commission to measure the incidence of social exclusion among low-income households. Table 10.2 illustrates that a sizeable proportion of the income-poor in Greece, Spain, Portugal and Ireland report finding it 'very difficult' to make ends meet. Although the poor of other countries do not report difficulty to the same extent, a week's holiday away was financially out of reach of the vast majority of those in poverty across the EU.

Widening the focus beyond the current EU member states reveals even greater disparities in levels of poverty and deprivation, especially between the current EU countries and the acceding and candidate countries (those negotiating EU membership). The proportion of the population living in poverty in central and eastern European countries and the independent states of the former USSR, increased from 3.3 per cent in 1988 to 46 per cent by 1999.[19] This contrasts to an estimated

10 per cent poverty rate for Western Europe as a whole.[20] Enlargement from EU–15 to EU–25 will take place in May 2004 and the addition of eight central and eastern European countries, many with significant levels of poverty and inequality, will bring new challenges to the EU's anti-poverty agenda.[21]

INCOME AND INCOME INEQUALITY IN THE EUROPEAN UNION

Income inequality rose in most EU countries between 1980 and 1995. In 1999, the 20 per cent of the EU population with the highest income received 4.6 times as much of the total income as the bottom (lowest income) 20 per cent of the population.[22] Table 10.3 below shows two measures of inequality across EU countries:

- **S80/S20** (the income quintile share ratio) – the ratio of total income received by the 20 per cent of the population with the highest income (top quintile) to that received by the 20 per cent of the population with the lowest income (lowest quintile).[23]
- **The Gini co-efficient** – a more general measure of inequality, where the higher the figure, the greater the inequality.

The level of income inequality is informative about differential access to economic opportunities across EU countries and about the extent to which income is shared by different sectors of the national population. The figures reveal that the inequality gap, as measured by the Gini co-efficient, was widest in the UK, followed by Ireland and Portugal.[24] The income quintile share ratio (S80/S20) shows a different picture, with inequality greater in the southern countries: Portugal, Greece and Spain followed by the UK and Ireland.[25]

EMPLOYMENT AND UNEMPLOYMENT IN THE EUROPEAN UNION AND ACCEDING COUNTRIES

Employment policy in the EU reflects the principle that paid work is the best route out of poverty.[26] Employment is also seen as an important factor in both financial and social inclusion.[27] The initiation of the European Employment Strategy in 1997 consolidated an EU focus on employment policy priorities; annual NAPs on employment

TABLE 10.3: **Inequality measures in the European Union, 1999**

	S80/S20	Income inequality* (Gini co-efficient)
EU15	4.6	—
Austria	3.7	23.1
Belgium	4.2	25.0
Denmark	3.2	24.7
Finland	3.4	25.6
France	4.4	32.7
Germany	3.6	30.0
Greece	6.2	32.7
Ireland	4.9	35.9
Italy	4.9	27.3
Luxembourg	3.7	26.9
Netherlands	3.0	32.6
Portugal	6.4	35.6
Spain	5.7	32.5
Sweden	3.2	25.0
UK	5.2	36.1

– : No data available
Statistics are for 2001 or latest available data.

Source: Eurostat, 'Inequality of Income Distribution (S80/S20 quintile ratio)', *General Statistics*, 2002; *World Health Organization, *The European Health Report 2002*, 2002

have since been required from each member state, detailing how national policies implement the agreed EU guidelines. In 2000 the Lisbon council set EU targets of a 70 per cent overall employment rate by 2010 and an increase in the number of women in employment to more than 60 per cent by the same date.[28]

EU concern over unemployment is also associated with the EU's anti-poverty strategy and arises from a conviction that the risk of income poverty and social exclusion increases with length of time out of paid work.[29] Four out of the 18 Laeken indicators, implemented to monitor progress in the fight against poverty and social exclusion, relate to employment:

- the long-term unemployment rate (12 months and over);
- the long-term unemployment share;

- the very long-term unemployment rate (two years and over);
- the population living in jobless households.[30]

In 2002, 2 per cent of the active EU15 population were unemployed for at least two years and 3 per cent for more than one year.[31] Long-term unemployment was particularly high in Italy and Greece, countries that also had low employment rates (see Table 10.4). Long-term unemployment for women in Greece, Spain and Italy was more than twice that of men's.[32] The UK was above average in its International Labour Organization (ILO) employment rate and below average for long-term unemployment. Looking beyond the EU15, the long-term unemployment rate in 2002 was particularly high in some of the acceding countries, such as the Slovak republic (12.1 per cent) and Poland (10.9 per cent), posing significant challenges to the EU employment targets for 2010.

Another indicator covering the employment dimension of social exclusion is the proportion of persons living in jobless households (households with at least one member of working age but where no one works).[33] In 2002, one in eight people in the EU15 lived in jobless

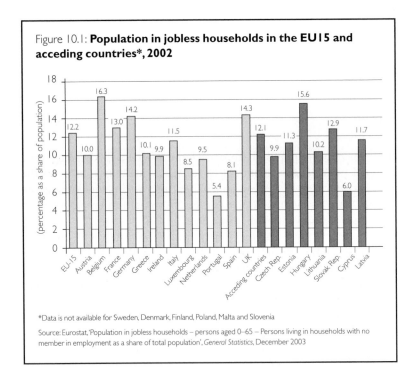

Figure 10.1: **Population in jobless households in the EU15 and acceding countries*, 2002**

*Data is not available for Sweden, Denmark, Finland, Poland, Malta and Slovenia

Source: Eurostat, 'Population in jobless households – persons aged 0–65 – Persons living in households with no member in employment as a share of total population', *General Statistics*, December 2003

TABLE 10.4: **Employment and long-term unemployment in the EU and acceding countries, 2002**

	ILO employment rate (per cent)	ILO long-term unemployment rate (per cent)
EU-15	**64.2**	**3.0**
Austria	68.2	0.8
Belgium	59.7	3.5
Denmark	76.4	0.9
Finland	69.1	2.3
France	62.9	2.8
Germany	65.4	5.1
Greece	56.9	5.1
Ireland	65.0	1.3
Italy	55.4	5.3
Luxembourg	63.6	0.8
Netherlands	74.5	0.7
Portugal	68.6	1.8
Spain	58.4	3.9
Sweden	74.0	1.0
UK	71.5	1.1
Acceding States	**56.1**	**8.1**
Cyprus	68.5	0.8
Czech Republic	65.6	3.5
Estonia	61.7	4.8
Hungary	56.5	2.4
Latvia	60.5	5.8
Lithuania	60.6	7.0
Malta	55.2	2.9 *
Poland	51.7	10.9
Slovak Republic	56.5	12.1
Slovenia	64.3	3.3

* Long-term unemployment rate for Malta is for 2001 as 2002 data was not available

Sources: Eurostat, 'Total long-term unemployment rate – long-term unemployed as a percentage of the total active population aged 15–64', *General Statistics*, December 2003; Eurostat, Eurostat News Report STAT/03/80, July 2003

households.[34] Belgium and the United Kingdom had the highest percentage of jobless households, 16.3 per cent and 14.3 per cent respectively (see Figure 10.1).[35] Of the acceding countries Hungary had the highest proportion of jobless households (15.6 per cent) and Cyprus the lowest (6 per cent) (see Figure 10.1).

By August 2003 the average ILO unemployment rate for the EU15 was 8 per cent, ranging from 3.8 per cent in Luxembourg to 11.2 per cent in Spain; the UK rate was below the EU15 average, at 4.9 per cent.[36] The long-term unemployment rate remained at 3 per cent for the current EU member states (EU15).

POVERTY IN INDUSTRIALISED NATIONS

CHILD POVERTY

Some of the worst levels of child income poverty exist in the richest countries of the world. A UNICEF study of 23 countries in the Organisation for Economic Co-operation and Development (OECD) showed that, in the 1990s:

- one in six children – 47 million – were living in income poverty (defined as below 50 per cent of the national median);
- child income poverty rates in the richest nations varied from 3 per cent to over 25 per cent.[37]

In the league table for relative child poverty (defined as income below 50 per cent of the national median), the bottom four places (ie, where child poverty was worst) were occupied by:

- the UK;
- Italy;
- the USA;
- Mexico.

The duration of child poverty in a number of industrialised countries was also examined in depth, tracking data on the poorest fifth of families over a period of ten years. In nearly all OECD countries, around 60 per cent of children in the poorest fifth remained there the next year and between 6 to 9 per cent remained in poverty for five consecutive years, with US children the least likely to move out of poverty.[38]

Using data from the Luxembourg Income Study[39] another analysis of child poverty across 25 nations showed a similarly wide variation, with Nordic and Northern European countries having low rates of child poverty and Southern European and English-speaking countries

TABLE 10.5: **Child poverty rates (percentages) in 25 countries by adult and child median**

Country	Year	50% of the overall median	50% of the child median
		(% rate)	(% rate)
Russia	1995	26.6	25.4
USA	1994	26.3	18.6
UK	1995	21.3	11.0
Italy	1995	21.2	15.7
Australia	1994	17.1	11.0
Canada	1994	16.0	11.2
Ireland	1987	14.8	6.5
Israel	1992	14.7	10.3
Poland	1992	14.2	10.9
Spain	1990	13.1	9.7
Germany	1994	11.6	7.1
Hungary	1994	11.5	10.1
France	1989	9.8	6.8
Netherlands	1991	8.4	5.8
Switzerland	1982	6.3	3.9
Taiwan	1995	6.3	4.1
Luxembourg	1994	6.3	1.9
Belgium	1992	6.1	4.2
Denmark	1992	5.9	5.1
Austria	1987	5.6	3.3
Norway	1995	4.5	3.5
Sweden	1992	3.7	3.2
Finland	1991	3.4	2.5
Slovakia	1992	2.2	1.5
Czech Republic	1992	1.8	1.6

Source: B Bradbury and M Jantti, 'Child Poverty Across Twenty-five Countries', in B Bradbury, S P Jenkins and J Micklewright, The Dynamics of Child Poverty in Industrialised Countries, 2001, p78

having significantly higher rates of income poverty during the 1990s.[40] The poverty measures used were: half of the equivalised median income for all persons within a country; half of the equivalised median for children only (ie, a child is poor if her/his disposable income is below half of that of the average child); and the US official poverty line.

The results of the measures of child and adult median are given in Table 10.5.

- On 50 per cent of the *overall* median, the UK was ranked as third worst, after Russia and the USA, with over a fifth of children in income poverty, having greater child poverty than Taiwan.
- For most countries child income poverty was about a third lower when measured against the *child* rather than the overall adult median, as the incomes of all children tend to be lower than those of the population as a whole. There were, however, differences, for instance between Russia (where the child median was high) and the UK and Ireland (where child averages were relatively low).

Although the research found that children were generally more likely to be poor if living with a lone mother, variations in rates of lone motherhood could not explain the differences. The authors concluded that higher market incomes (through access to paid work) marked out countries with the lowest levels of child income poverty, so low pay and worklessness may be significant factors in the UK.

While comparing child poverty levels usefully illustrates the cross-national variation of child income poverty, it has been argued that child poverty levels should not only be measured against the living standards of other children, but also compared with the population as a whole. If not it may '…lead to the adoption of a lower standard by which to judge children's poverty compared with that of any other groups'.[41]

LOW PAY IN INDUSTRIAL NATIONS

Research by Eurostat has estimated that around one in seven EU workers are low paid – a low-paid employee is one whose monthly wage is less than 60 per cent of the median salary in the country in which s/he resides.[42] The UK had the highest proportion of low-paid workers in 2000 – one in five; Ireland, Germany and Greece also had a high incidence of low pay. The lowest level was in Portugal, at around one in 17, followed by Denmark and Belgium.[43] With the notable exception of Portugal, countries with fewest low-paid workers also had lower poverty rates overall.

The UK is one of nine of the current 15 EU member states to have a national minimum wage and its introduction has had a significant impact on the most poorly paid workers.[44] A further 12 of the 13 candidate countries (those countries which have applied for EU

TABLE 10.6: **Monthly minimum wages in euros and Purchasing Power Standards (PPS) in some EU member states and candidate countries, and the USA**

Country	EUR	PPS ($)
Bulgaria	56	139
Czech Republic	199	389
Portugal	416	543
Spain	526	617
Greece	605	725
USA	877	826
UK	1,105	983
France	1,154	1,150
Netherlands	1,249	1,225
Luxembourg	1,369	1,338

Source: Eurostat: Statistics in Focus, 'Population and Social Conditions', *Minimum Wages EU Member States and Candidate Countries*, January 2003

membership, including the acceding states)[45] have a minimum wage, as does the US; but there are huge disparities in national levels. To compare living standards across countries, Purchasing Power Standards (PPS) can be utilised; price parity is established by comparing the cost of national consumption baskets, which are used to transform national incomes (per head) into a common currency, allowing for a comparable measure of purchasing power.[46] Even with price parity, a tenfold difference exists between the lowest and the highest minimum wage (see Table 10.6). It may be that low wages contribute to the growing phenomenon of the 'working poor'. However, although there is a causal relationship between low wages and poverty, the link is complex.[47]

POVERTY ACROSS THE WORLD

Poverty in developing countries can be seen as different in volume and depth from that in the industrialised world; but increasingly parallels between 'North and South' are recognised within policy debates, where the causes and consequences of poverty can be seen as similar.[48]

The United Nations (UN) has devised a Human Development Index (HDI) to rank countries development, and from 1997 included a Human Poverty Index (HPI). Whilst the HDI measures overall progress along a summary measure of three dimensions of human development – living a long and healthy life, being educated and having a decent standard of living – the HPI reflects the distribution of progress and the 'backlog of deprivation' that still exists.[49] Human poverty focuses on lack of capabilities – the inability 'to live a long, healthy and creative life, to be knowledgeable, to enjoy a decent standard of living, dignity, self-respect and the respect of others'.[50]

The HPI has been constructed separately for developing countries (HPI-1) and for industrialised countries (HPI-2), partly because human deprivation varies with the social and economic conditions of a community, and to reflect the additional data available in the latter countries.

The HPI-1 for developing countries includes indicators such as adult illiteracy rates and the percentage of underweight under-fives. The HPI-2 for industrialised countries includes the percentage of people:

- born today who are expected to die before age 60;
- whose ability to read and write is not adequate to be functional;
- living below an income poverty line (50 per cent of median personal disposable income);
- who are long-term unemployed (12 months or more).

The last dimension, long-term unemployment, is used as a basic indicator of social exclusion.

Figure 10.2 illustrates the variation in human poverty between industrialised countries. The UK has been ranked 15th out of 17 OECD countries for which the HPI was estimated, putting the UK third from bottom.[51] An important factor in this poor ranking seemed to be the high rates of functional illiteracy, 24 per cent on average. A study by the Department for Education and Skills in 2003 found that more than 10 per cent of adults could not read the instructions on a packet of seeds and 29 per cent, 11 million people, could not perform a basic mathematical task.[52]

A cruder poverty measure, used by the World Bank for the purpose of comparing income poverty on a global scale, is the US $1 and $2 a day yardstick (adjusted to local currency using purchasing power parities). The US $1 is set as a minimum standard of living for survival

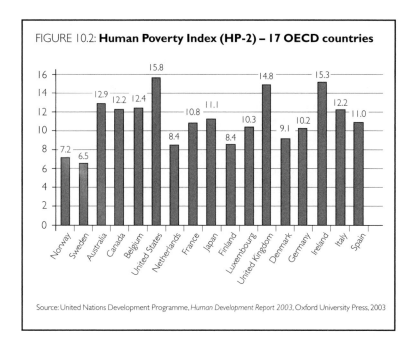

FIGURE 10.2: **Human Poverty Index (HP-2) – 17 OECD countries**

Source: United Nations Development Programme, *Human Development Report 2003*, Oxford University Press, 2003

and is generally used for the least developed countries, primarily African; the $2-per-day level is used for middle-income economies such as those of East Asia and Latin America.[53] Although offering a rudimentary estimate of international poverty, the $1 and $2 a day poverty measure fails to capture the multi-dimensional nature of poverty.

Since the early 1990s the concept of sustainable human development has gained ground within international institutions. Organisations such as the UN and World Bank recognise the failure of market-led solutions to poverty eradication and the need to address non-monetary aspects of poverty, such as education, health and partici-pation.[54] This 'new consensus', on the need to place people at the centre of development, was reflected in the ten commitments made by the 117 heads of State or Government at the 1995 World Summit for Social Development in Copenhagen.[55] Included in the inter-national commitments to social development was a pledge to eradicate absolute poverty by a target date to be set by each country, and to reduce overall poverty.[56]

Much of that committed to at Copenhagen was later reflected in the Millennium Development Goals (MDGs), agreed to by world leaders at the United Nation's Millennium Summit in 2000. For each goal one or more targets have been set – the target of the first goal is to halve the proportion of people living in extreme poverty (less than $1 a day) and to eradicate hunger by 2015.[57]

The United Nations Development Report 2003 claims that the proportion of the global population living in extreme poverty has reduced – declining from 29 per cent in 1990 to 23 per cent by 1999.[58] However, if China is excluded from the calculation, the number of people living in extreme poverty has actually *risen* by 28 million. At the current rate it would take more than 130 years to eradicate hunger.[59] The report also shows that:

- 2.8 billion people live on less than $2 a day, with nearly half – 1.2 billion – surviving on less than $1 a day – one in five of the global population;
- by 2000, Sub-Saharan Africa was 5 per cent poorer than a decade earlier; 49 per cent of the population currently live in extreme poverty;
- many transition countries[60] have seen a dramatic decline in living standards. In Eastern Europe and the Commonwealth of Independent States (CIS) poverty has tripled since 1990, from 31 million people in poverty to almost 100 million by the end of the decade;
- the richest 10 per cent of the US population has the same total income as the poorest 43 per cent of the world;
- the income of the world's richest 5 per cent is 114 times that of the poorest 5 per cent;
- an estimated 827.5 million people are undernourished.[61]

Foreign aid has been identified as an essential feature in poverty reduction, but most OECD countries gave less aid to developing countries in 2000 than in 1990, with 11 out of 22 countries on the Development Assistance Committee of the OECD (the world's largest donors) providing less than 0.3 per cent of their GNP.[62] The USA provides the lowest proportion of its wealth than any other country. However, since 2002, the EU and the USA, in addition to various individual countries, have pledged to significantly increase aid by 2006.[63] Nevertheless, even with the promise of increased aid, the problems of inequitable trade barriers, domestic subsidies and insurmountable debt remain relatively untouched, and as such continue to impoverish the poorest countries in the world.

TABLE 10.7: **The share (%) and number of people living on less than $1 a day, worldwide, 1999**

Region	Share of people (%)	Number ('000s)
Sub-Saharan Africa	49.0	315
East Asia and the Pacific	15.6	279
– excluding China	10.6	57
South Asia	36.6	488
Latin America and the Caribbean	11.1	57
Central and Eastern Europe and CIS*	20.3	97
Middle East and North Africa	2.2	6
Total	**23.2**	**1,169**
– excluding China	25.0	945

*CIS: Commonwealth of Independent States
Source: United Nations Development Programme, *Human Development Report 2003*, 2003; changes measured using the $2 a day poverty line – used as an 'extreme poverty' line for Central and Eastern Europe and the CIS, p41

Inequalities between and within countries, 'between rural and urban areas and between ethnic and income groups' are immense and these global inequalities appear to be growing.[64] Inequality in child mortality has dramatically increased. A decade ago, a child in Sub-Saharan Africa was 19 times more likely to die before the age of 5 than a child in a rich country; today the African child is 26 times more likely to die before the age of five.[65]

A recent study of child poverty in the developing world found significant levels of severe deprivation and poverty.[66] Based on a sample of 1.2 million children from 47 developing countries, the research examined children's lack of basic human needs using indicators of severe deprivation. These included: severe food, water, shelter, health, information and education deprivation and severe deprivation of access to basic services and sanitation.[67] The research defined absolute poverty as suffering from two or more forms of severe deprivation and found that:

- 674 million children – over a third of all children (37 per cent) in developing countries – were living in absolute poverty, with the highest rates in Sub-Saharan Africa (65 per cent or 207 million children);

TABLE 10.8: **Global comparison of child health, 2001**

	Infant mortality rate (under 1 year) per 1000	under-5s (1995–2001*) suffering from malnutrition (%) (moderate and severe)
Sub-Saharan Africa	107	29
Middle East and North Africa	47	14
South Asia	70	46
East Asia and Pacific	33	17
Latin America and Caribbean	28	8
CEE/CIS and Baltic States	30	7
Industrialised countries	5	–
Developing countries	62	27
Least developed countries	100	36
World	**57**	**27**

CEE – Central Eastern Europe. CIS – Commonwealth of Independent States. – Indicates that data are not available.
Source: UNICEF, *The State of The World's Children 2003: Official Summary*, 2003

- over half of all children in developing nations – one billion children – were living in conditions of severe deprivation;
- more than half a billion children in the developing world had no shelter (34 per cent) or any kind of toilet facility (31 per cent);
- girls were one and a half more likely to be severely educationally deprived than boys, especially girls in the Middle East and North African region, who were three times more likely never to have attended school than boys.[68]

Although considerable variation in levels of poverty and deprivation were found both within and across the developing nations, Sub-Saharan Africa had the highest rates of severe deprivation for shelter, water, education and health. However, countries within this region had divergent levels of deprivation; for instance, 19 per cent of children in Mali suffered severe water deprivation compared to 90 per cent of children in Rwanda. The research report concludes that a one-size-fits-all anti-poverty policy will not be effective in eradicating child poverty but that a tailored approach, which recognises the diverse national and regional conditions that exist, may be more successful in tackling poverty and severe deprivation.

CONCLUSION

The global picture of poverty is a complex one. What is clear-cut is that substantial levels of poverty continue to exist around the world, even within the richer nations, harming the health, well-being and development of those people it touches. The UK has a record of child poverty which remains among the worst in the EU and other industrialised countries, due partly to a political legacy that created high levels of poverty and inequality.

Although the fight against poverty in the developing countries is now firmly on the international agenda, the continuing inequalities in trade and debt must also be tackled if the goal of halving the proportion of people living in extreme poverty and eradicating hunger by 2015 is to be met. At the present time many of the world's poorest people are getting poorer.

NOTES

1 United Nations Development Programme, *Human Development Report 2003*, Oxford University Press, 2003, p3

2 United Nations Development Programme, *Human Development Report 2002*, Oxford University Press, 2002

3 J Hills, *Inquiry into Income and Wealth*, Vol 2, Joseph Rowntree Foundation, 1995

4 See note 2

5 European Anti Poverty Network, *National Action Plans on Inclusion 2003–2005: where is the political energy?* EAPN's response to the second round of plans, October 2003, p7

6 Council of the European Union, *Fight against Poverty and Social Exclusion: common objectives for the second round of National Action Plans – endorsement*, 14164/1/02 REV 1 SOC 508, Brussels, November 2002

7 For an example see the UK NAP for 2003–2005: Department for Work and Pensions, *United Kingdom National Action Plan on Social Inclusion 2003–05*, DWP, 2003. This document can be accessed at: www.dwp. gov.uk/publications/dwp/2003/nap/index.asp

8 European Anti Poverty Network, *National Action Plans On Inclusion 2003–2005: Where is the political energy?* EAPN's response to the second round of plans, October 2003

9 I Dennis and A C Guio, 'Poverty and Social Exclusion in the EU after Laeken – part 2', *Statistics in Focus*, THEME 3-9/2003, 2003

10 See note 8, p6 and p10

11 See note 8, p9

12 For a further discussion of trends during this time, see the 3rd edition of *Poverty: the facts*, CPAG, 1996

13 Eurostat, 'At-risk-of-poverty rate by age and gender', 2004

14 I Dennis and A C Guio, 'Poverty and Social Exclusion in the EU after Laeken – part 1', *Statistics in Focus*, THEME 3-8/2003, 2003

15 European Commission, *Social Precarity and Social Integration*, Eurobarometer 56.1, 2002

16 See note 13

17 Child poverty is associated with child mortality – D Quilgars, 'Child mortality', in J Bradshaw (ed), *Poverty: the outcomes for children*, Family Policy Studies Centre, 2001. Because of the link between child mortality and poverty, child mortality rates are sometimes used as a proxy for poverty, especially in an international context and by agencies such as the United Nations.

18 UNICEF, *The State of the World's Children 2003: official summary*, 2003

19 The poverty rate here is defined as living on less than $4 a day – see note 18

20 World Health Organization, *The European Health Report 2002*, WHO, 2002

21 European Commission, *The Social Situation in the European Union 2003 – in brief*, EC, 2003, p11. The eight acceding countries in Eastern and Central Europe are: Poland, Slovenia, the Slovak Republic, Latvia, the Czech Republic, Lithuania, Hungary and Estonia. The other two countries joining the EU in May 2004 are Malta and Cyprus.

22 See note 21

23 Income is equivalised disposable income

24 See note 20

25 The inconsistency between the results of the inequality measures may in part be due to the measures themselves; the S80/S20 ratio is only responsive to income changes in the top and bottom quintiles whereas the Gini co-efficient allows for the full income distribution to be taken into account

26 A Diamantopoulou, 'Policies, Partners, People: an integrated approach to fighting poverty', Address to Danish Presidency Conference on Social Inclusion, Denmark, September 2002

27 Eurostat, 'Poverty and Social Exclusion Indicators', 43/2003, News Release, April 2003

28 European Commission, 'Council Recommendation on the Implementation of Member States' Employment Policies' (2003/579/EC), *Official Journal of the European Union*, L197/22, August 2003

29 See note 9

30 See note 9

31 The total active population is the total population at work and the unemployed population. The International Labour Organization definition for employment and unemployment is used.

32 Eurostat, 'Total long-term unemployment rate – long-term unemployed as a percentage of the total active population aged 15–64', *General Statistics*, Eurostat, December 2003

33 The definition of jobless households – those persons living in households with no member in employment as a share of total population – is different from the UK's classification of workless households, which uses data from the *Family Resources Survey* (in *Households Below Average Income*) rather than the European Community Labour Force Survey (LFS)

34 Eurostat, 'Population in jobless households – persons aged 0–65 – Persons living in households with no member in employment as a share of total population (excluding persons in households where all members are aged less than 18 years, or 18–24 years and in education, or 65 years and more and not working)', Structural Indicators, *General Statistics*, December 2003

35 See note 34

36 Eurostat, 'Euro-zone unemployment', News Release, 138/2003 [should this be 13/8/2003?], December 2003

37 UNICEF, *A League Table of Child Poverty in Rich Nations*, Innocenti Report Card Issue No 1, June 2000

38 See note 37

39 The Luxembourg Income Study database provides household income surveys for various countries, adjusted to be as comparable as possible

40 B Bradbury and M Jantti, 'Child Poverty Across Twenty-five Countries', in B Bradbury, S P Jenkins and J Micklewright, *The Dynamics of Child Poverty in Industrialised Countries*, 2001

41 S Ruxton and F Bennett, *Including Children?: Developing a coherent approach to child poverty and social exclusion across Europe*, Euronet, 2002, p21

42 Only employees working at least 15 hours a week are taken into account – Eurostat, *Statistics in Focus*, 'Population and Social Conditions', No 11/2000, *Low Wage Employees in EU Countries*, 2000

43 See note 42

44 Low Pay Commission, *The National Minimum Wage: fourth report of the Low Pay Commission, building on success*, The Stationery Office, 2003

45 'Candidate countries' are those that have applied for EU membership: Poland, Slovenia, the Slovak Republic, Latvia, the Czech Republic, Lithuania, Hungary, Estonia, Malta and Cyprus will join the EU in May 2004. Bulgaria and Romania hope to join by 2007 and Turkey is currently not negotiating EU membership.

46 R Lafrance and L Schembri, 'Purchasing-Power Parity: definition, measurement, and interpretation', *Bank of Canada Review*, 2002, Autumn issue, pp27–33

47 See B Cantillon, I Marx, K Van den Bosch, *The Puzzle of Egalitarianism: about the relationships between employment, wage inequality, social expenditures and poverty*, Luxembourg Income Study Working paper No 337, December 2002; B Nolan and I Marx, 'Low pay and household poverty' in M Gregory, W Salverda and S Bazen, *Labour Market Inequalities: problems and policies in international perspective*, Oxford University Press, 2000

48 Terminology in this debate is developing, but the term 'developing countries' is used here, meaning those to which the UN Human Poverty Index-1 applies rather than HPI-2

49 United Nations Development Programme, *Human Development Report 2000*, Oxford University Press, 2000

50 See note 49

51 United Nations Development Programme, *Human Development Report 2003*, Oxford University Press, 2003

52 Department for Education and Skills findings from 'Get On' campaign, www.dfes.gov.uk/readwriteplus, May 2003

53 'Measuring Global Poverty', Infoplease.com, www.infoplease.com/ipa/ A0908762.html, 2003

54 United Nations, *Five years After the World Summit for Social Development*, www.un.lv/down/pover/5yearsafter.pdf, 2000

55 See note 54

56 United Nations, *The Copenhagen Declaration and Programme of Action: world summit for social development,* United Nations, 1995

57 United Nations Development Programme, *Millennium Development Goals and the UNDP Role*, 2003

58 See note 51

59 See note 2

60 Transition countries or 'transition economies' are former Communist countries

61 See note 51

62 See note 2

63 See note 51

64 See note 51

65 See note 51, p39

66 D Gordon, S Nandy, C Pantazis, S Pemberton and P Townsend, *Child Poverty in the Developing World*, The Policy Press, 2003

67 Household and individual survey data was collected from 47 countries, in addition to interview data from 500,000 households (380,000 were households with children). See note 66, pp7–8 for details on the measures of severe deprivation.

68 See note 66

Conclusion

Poverty is certainly difficult to define. Effort must be made because it is associated with the experience of a variety of negative consequences – not least the denial of the right to participate in mainstream society – which are the extreme manifestations of inequality, both of resources and fundamentally of power. Whatever the detailed arguments over particular measures of poverty, the bottom line is that we have a body of evidence which shows the association between low levels of income and other resources, relative to society, and a variety of negative consequences. This demands action.

High rates of poverty produce bad outcomes. Chapter 4 detailed research evidence on the effects that poverty and deprivation have on those directly affected, on both their lived experience now and their later life. Life is, as was noted in the Introduction, often shorter and more brutal for those in poverty than it is for the majority. Just as they are associated with individual costs, so too do poverty and deprivation cost society. Too often the expense of removing people from poverty is talked of without accounting for the cost of allowing them to remain in poverty. Among the issues are the following: if poverty is associated with poorer health, then this is a cost to the health service; if poverty is associated with worse educational outcomes, then this is a lost opportunity for employers and the wealth of the nation; and if poverty is associated with lower levels of participation, then this is a cost to social cohesion and community life.

The experience of poverty is patterned. Certain groups feel the effects much more than others. Chapters 5 (focusing on children), 6 (women) and 7 (ethnicity) specifically reinforce this point. The reason why certain groups are particularly prone to poverty is structural, due to factors beyond the control of the individual. Such factors are strongly associated with poverty and leave those affected in a weaker position relative to the rest of society. This is not to argue that individuals are unavoidably bound to particular trajectories of income or experience, but the statistical associations demonstrated in Chapter 2 bear witness to clear patterning. Where patterning is discovered, it is reasonable to look for what drives such experience. Where it is found to be structural, we have cause to act.

The levels of poverty rates are not inevitable. Chapter 3 demonstrates that we know a lot about what causes inequality and poverty. High levels of poverty are not inherent to the UK; we had much lower poverty rates before 1979. Neither can high poverty rates be cogently argued to be the inevitable price of the global economy; other countries have weathered the forces of global capital without it resulting in the chronic levels of poverty that we see here.

Redistribution has been shown to work. It may appear an obvious point, but it is one well worth making: data from the *Families and Children Survey* has been used to show that the redistributive policies of the Labour Government have brought about material improvements in the conditions in which children live.[1] Further data from the *European Community Household Panel* survey shows that the rates of child income poverty in the UK have been improving recently relative to other EU nations, from it being the worst performer in the European Union in 1998 to fifth from bottom in 2001.[2] Analysis of *Households Below Average Income* figures show that child income poverty rates are coming down;[3] much of this reduction is attributable to recent policy interventions.

What the analysis in this book amounts to is a moral case to reduce income inequality and poverty. Poverty can be shown to be associated with unacceptable experiences and outcomes for those enduring it. The experience of poverty is patterned, affecting certain groups more than others. Causation of poverty is best understood as the result of structural, predominantly labour market, factors over which individuals have less control than governments. Both historical and cross–national comparisons should tell us that there is nothing inevitable about poverty and that redistributive policies can be shown to work.

Poverty is about an inadequacy of resources. In the end it is as simple as that. Until this is effectively addressed, through changes in the labour market, social security/tax credit entitlements, tax policy, wealth ownership and/or action on the economy, it will not be remedied.

There is much to lose, both to those directly affected and to wider society if the government does not do more; but there is much to gain if it does.

NOTES

1 See S Vegeris and J Perry, *Families and Children 2001: living standards and the children*, Department for Work and Pensions Research Report 190, Corporate Document Services, 2003
2 Poverty is defined as living in households with incomes below 60 per cent of the median before housing costs. See Department for Work and Pensions, *Measuring Child Poverty*, DWP, 2003, p10 and p11
3 Using 60 per cent of the median disposable equivalised household income. See Office for National Statistics, *Households below Average Income 1994/5–2001/02*, Department for Work and Pensions, 2003, p64

Appendix

SUMMARY OF INDICATORS IN OPPORTUNITY FOR ALL 2003

CHILDREN AND YOUNG PEOPLE

1. Proportion of children living in workless households (GB)[†]

1997	1998	1999	2000	2001	2002	2003
17.9%	17.9%	17.3%	15.8%	15.2%	15.8%	15.2%

2a. Proportion of children living in households below 60% of median income (GB)

Before housing costs

1996/97	1997/98	1998/99	1999/2000	2000/01	2001/02
25%	25%	24%	23%	21%	21%

After housing costs

1996/97	1997/98	1998/99	1999/2000	2000/01	2001/02
34%	33%	33%	32%	31%	30%

2b. Proportion of children living in households below 60% of 1996/97 median held constant in real terms (GB)

Before housing costs

1996/97	1997/98	1998/99	1999/2000	2000/01	2001/02
26%	24%	22%	19%	16%	12%

After housing costs

1996/97	1997/98	1998/99	1999/2000	2000/01	2001/02
34%	32%	31%	28%	24%	20%

2c. Proportion of children living in households with persistently low income (below 60% and 70% median before housing costs in at least three out of four years) (GB)

Below 60% median in at least three out of four years

1992–95	1995–98	1996–99	1997–2000	1998–2001
17%	16%	16%	17%	16%

Below 70 per cent median in at least three out of four years

1992–95	1995–98	1996–99	1997–2000	1998–2001
29%	26%	26%	26%	25%

3. Proportion of 7-year-olds in Sure Start areas achieving Level 2 or above in Key Stage 1 English and Maths tests.

	2000	2001	2002
Reading			
All schools in Sure Start areas	75%	77%	85%
All schools in England	83%	84%	90%
Writing			
All schools in Sure Start areas	76%	78%	86%
All schools in England	84%	86%	91%
Maths			
All schools in Sure Start areas	76%	78%	86%
All schools in England	84%	86%	90%

4. Proportion of 11-year-olds achieving Level 4 or above in Key Stage 2 tests for literacy and numeracy (England)

English

1996	1997	1998	1999	2000	2001	2002	2003
57%	63%	65%	71%	75%	75%	75%	75%

Maths

1996	1997	1998	1999	2000	2001	2002	2003
54%	62%	59%	69%	72%	71%	73%	73%

5. Proportion of 16-year-olds with at least five GCSEs at grade A*– C (England)

1996	1997	1998	1999	2000	2001	2002
44.5%	45.1%	46.3%	47.9%	49.2%	50.0%	51.6%

6. Proportion of 19-year-olds with at least a Level 2 qualification[††] or equivalent (England)

1996	1997	1998	1999	2000	2001	2002
69.7%	72.3%	73.9%	74.9%	75.3%	74.8%	74.8%

7. Overall school attendance (England)

1995/96	1996/97	1997/98	1998/99	1999/2000	2000/01	2001/02
92.4%	92.8%	92.7%	92.9%	93.2%	92.7%	93.0%

8. Percentage of 16–18-year-olds in learning (England)

1996	1997	1998	1999	2000	2001
76%	75%	75%	75%	75%	76%

9. Proportion of children looked after by local authorities (England) who achieve 5 GSCEs (A*– C) (indicator – an improvement in the educational attainment and participation of children looked after by local authorities)

1999/2000	2001/02
7.3%	7.5%

10a. Under–18 conception rate (per thousand) aged 15–17 (England)

1996	1997	1998	1999	2000	2001
45.9	45.5	46.5	45.3	43.8	42.3

10b. Proportion of teenage parents not in education, employment or training (England)

1996	1997	1998	1999	2000	2001	2002	2003
85%	84%	72%	74%	69%	70%	67%	73%

11. Proportion of children registered on child protection register who have been previously registered (England)

1997/98	1998/99	1999/2000	2000/01
19%	15%	14%	14%

12. Admission rate of children under 16 (per thousand) to hospital as a result of unintentional injury (England)

1996/97	1997/98	1998/99	1999/2000	2000/01	2001/02
1.22	1.14	1.03	1.04	0.94	0.95

13. Proportion of children (aged 11–15) who smoke (England)

1996	1997	1998	1999	2000	2001	2002
13%	11%	9%	10%	10%	10%	10%

WORKING-AGE PEOPLE

14. Proportion of working-age people in employment (GB)

	1997	1998	1999	2000	2001	2002	2003
All	72.9%	73.5%	73.9%	74.6%	74.8%	74.6%	74.8%
Men	77.9%	78.5%	78.8%	79.5%	79.6%	79.2%	79.4%
Women	67.6%	68.1%	68.8%	69.5%	69.7%	69.8%	70.0%

15. Proportion of working-age people living in workless households (GB)

1996	1997	1998	1999	2000	2001	2002	2003
13.7%	13.1%	12.8%	12.3%	11.7%	11.7%	11.8%	11.5%

16. Proportion (millions) of working-age people in families in receipt of income support or income-based jobseeker's allowance for 2 years or more (GB)

1996	1997	1998	1999	2000	2001	2002	2003
2.28	2.03	1.86	1.76	1.76	1.74	1.75	1.76

17a. Employment rates of disadvantaged groups – people with disabilities, lone parents, ethnic minorities and the over-50s – and reduction in the difference between theirs and the overall rate (GB)

	1998	1999	2000	2001	2002	2003
All	73.3%	73.8%	74.6%	74.8%	74.6%	74.9%
Over-50s	65.7%	66.3%	66.9%	68.3%	68.1%	70.1%
Ethnic minority people	57.3%	57.6%	58.9%	58.6%	58.3%	58.3%
Lone parents	46.9%	48.6%	51.5%	51.7%	53.6%	53.4%
People with disabilities	43.5%	46.3%	46.8%	47.4%	48.0%	49.1%
Lowest qualified	50.7%	50.0%	50.9%	51.2%	50.1%	50.8%

17b. Employment rate gaps between disadvantaged groups and the overall rate (GB)

	1998	1999	2000	2001	2002	2003
Over-50s	7.6%	7.5%	7.6%	6.5%	6.5%	4.8%
Ethnic minority people	16.1%	16.4%	15.7%	16.3%	16.5%	16.7%
Lone parents	26.4 %	25.2 %	23.0 %	23.1%	21.0%	21.4%
People with disabilities	29.8%	27.6 %	27.7 %	27.4 %	26.6 %	25.7%
Lowest qualified	22.6 %	23.8 %	23.6 %	23.6 %	24.5 %	24.1%

18a. Proportion of working-age people living in households below 60% of median income (GB)

Before housing costs

1996/97	1997/98	1998/99	1999/2000	2000/01	2001/02
15%	15%	14%	14%	14%	14%

After housing costs

1996/97	1997/98	1998/99	1999/2000	2000/01	2001/02
21%	20%	19%	20%	19%	219%

18b. Proportion of working-age people living in households below 60% of 1996/97 median held constant in real terms (GB)

Before housing costs

1996/97	1997/98	1998/99	1999/2000	2000/01	2001/02
15%	14%	13%	12%	11%	10%

After housing costs

1996/97	1997/98	1998/99	1999/2000	2000/01	2001/02
21%	19%	18%	17%	16%	14%

18c. Proportion of working-age people living in households with persistently low incomes (below 60% and 70% median before housing costs in at least three out of four years) (GB)

Below 60% median in at least three out of four years

1991–94	1995–98	1996–99	1997–2000	1998–2001
8%	7%	7%	7%	7%

Below 70 per cent median in at least three out of four years

1991–94	1995–98	1996–99	1997–2000	1998–2001
13%	12%	112%	12%	12%

19. Proportion of working-age people without a qualification at NVQ 2 or higher (England)

	1998	1999	2000	2001	2002	2003
	39.1%	37.4%	36.3%	35.9%	35.1%	34.4%

20. The number of people sleeping rough (England)

	1998	1999	2000	2001	2002
	1,850	1,633	1,180	703	596

21. Smoking rates for adults 16 and over in all social classes (England)

1996	1998		1998	2000	2001
28%	27%		28%	27%	27%
Weighted data			Unweighted data, cannot be reliably compared with weighted data		

22. Proportion of death rates (per thousand) from suicide and undetermined injury for 16–64-year-olds (England)

	1996	1997	1998	1999	2000
	12.01	12.28	12.62	12.77	12.25

OLDER PEOPLE

23. Proportion of working-age people contributing to a state pension (GB)

	1996/97	1997/98	1998/99	1999/2000	2000/01	2001/02
Men	56%	55%	54%	51%	51%	50%
Women	38%	38%	39%	38%	37%	39%
All	64%	62%	62%	45%	44%	45%

24. Proportion of working-age people who have contributed to a non-state pension in at least three out of the last four years (GB)

	1994–97	1995–98	1996–99	1997–2000	1998–2001
Men	57%	57%	56%	57%	57%
Women	37%	39%	40%	41%	41%
All	46%	49%	48%	49%	49%

25a. Proportion of older people living in households below 60% of median income (GB)

Before housing costs

	1996/97	1997/98	1998/99	1999/2000	2000/01	2001/02
	21%	22%	23%	22%	21%	22%

After housing costs

	1996/97	1997/98	1998/99	1999/2000	2000/01	2001/02
	27%	27%	27%	25%	24%	22%

25b. Proportion of older people living in households below 60% of 1996/97 median held constant in real terms (GB)

Before housing costs

	1996/97	1997/98	1998/99	1999/2000	2000/01	2001/02
	21%	21%	20%	118%	15%	14%

After housing costs

	1996/97	1997/98	1998/99	1999/2000	2000/01	2001/02
	27%	26%	24%	19%	15%	11%

25c. Proportion of older people living in households with persistently low incomes (below 60% and 70% median before housing costs in at least three out of four years) (GB)

Below 60% median in at least three out of four years

	1991–94	1995–98	1996–99	1997–2000	1998–2001
	16%	17%	18%	17%	18%

Below 70 per cent median in at least three out of four years

	1991–94	1995–98	1996–99	1997–2000	1998–2001
	33%	33%	34%	34%	33%

26. Proportion of older people who live in a home which falls below the set standard of decency (England)

	1996	2001
	48%	34%

27. Proportion of older people whose lives are affected by fear of crime (England and Wales) (percentage of older people reporting fear of crime)

	1998	2000	2001	2001/02	2002/03
All	10%	10%	8%	8%	8%
Male	5%	7%	3%	6%	6%
Female	14%	12%	12%	9%	9%

28. Healthy life expectancy in years at age 65 (Great Britain)

	1995	1997	1999
Male	11.4	11.9	11.7
Female	13.2	13.3	13.3

29. Proportion of older people aged 65 and over being helped to live independently (England)
* Data on new basis. A change in definition took place in 1998/99. The new basis covers a wider variety of services and a wider range of people.

Helped to live at home through community-based services (people per thousand head of population)

1996/97	1997/98	1998/99	1999/2000*	2000/01*	2001/02*
83	81	71/82*	85	83	85

Intensive home care (more than ten contact hours and six or more visits a week per thousand head of population)

1998/99	1999/2000	2000/01	2001/02
7.8	8.8	9.3	9.9

COMMUNITIES

30. Difference between employment rates in the most deprived local authority areas and the overall employment rate, over the economic cycle (Great Britain)

	2000	2001	2002	2003
Employment rate for Great Britain	74.6%	75%	74.8%	75%
Employment 30 most deprived areas	62.2%	63.2%	63.7%	64.4%
Employment rate gap	12.4%	11.8%	11.1%	10.6%

31. Proportion of households who live in a home that falls below the set standard of decency (England)

1996	2001
45%	36%

32. Proportion of households in fuel poverty (England) (percentage of households in fuel poverty)

	1996	1998	2001
Total	22%	16%	8%
Vulnerable households	31%	20%	10%

33. Gap between the fifth of local authorities with the lowest life expectancy at birth and the population as a whole (England)

		1996	1997	1998	1999	2000
Men:	lowest fifth	72.6	72.8	73.0	73.3	73.6
	whole population	74.5	74.8	75.0	75.3	75.6
	difference	1.9	2.0	2.0	2.0	2.0
Women:	lowest fifth	78.3	78.3	78.4	78.6	78.8
	whole population	79.6	79.8	79.9	80.1	80.3
	difference	1.3	1.5	1.5	1.5	1.5

† Indicates which parts of the UK are covered by the data

†† Examples of a Level 2 qualification are: one A level, NVQ Level 2, Intermediate GNVQ

Source: Department for Work and Pensions, *Opportunity For All: fifth annual report*, The Stationery Office, 2003

Index

A

absolute poverty 6, 13-4, 15-7, 265-6
accommodation see bed and
  breakfast accommodation; housing
activation policies 80-2
asylum seekers 200-1
average income see Households
  Below Average Income

B

Bangladeshi people see
  Pakistani/Bangladeshi people
banking services 116-7
**bed and breakfast
  accommodation** 121, 122, 123
Black people see ethnic minority
  groups
Breadline Britain see Poverty and
  Social Exclusion in Britain
**budget approaches, to poverty
  measurement** 23, 24-5
budgeting 114-5, 180
  see also debt
budgets
  low cost but acceptable 24, 61-2
  modest but adequate 24, 62-3

C

carers 94-5, 112, 173-4
child benefit 89, 169
child development 148, 152
child tax credits see tax credits
Child Trust Fund 156
childcare 144, 152, 156-7, 172-3,
  178-9
children
  at risk of poverty 51, 53, 145-7
  clothes for 114, 148
  costs involved 142-4, 178
  deprivation in 54, 147-8
  effects of homelessness on 123
  effects of poverty on 133-4, 149-56
  and employment 154
  and food see food; free school
    meals
  and health 123, 151, 266
  and housing 119
  mortality of 124-5, 151, 152, 252,
    265, 266
  and parental sacrifice 63, 112,
    149-50
  persistent poverty in 48-9, 146-7,
    258, 275

and poverty statistics 39-43, 54,
55, 82, 274-7
changes over time 42, 44, 57,
63-6, 145
and income support 57, 58-60
international 252, 258-60, 265-6
regional 233, 234-5, 236, 237,
238
response to family poverty 154-5
spending on 63, 143-4
see also educational disadvantage;
young people
Children's Centres 152, 156-7
clothing 114, 148
costs
of children 142-4, 178
of disability 90-2, 118, 143
council housing see social housing
credit, access to 116
crime 134, 281
cycle of poverty 21, 155

D
death see life expectancy; mortality
debt 115-6, 117-9
see also budgeting; financial exclusion
deprivation 19, 54, 147-8, 265-6
see also necessities; Poverty and
Social Exclusion in Britain
deprivation indicators 24, 240-1
see also poverty indicators
deprived areas, living in 125, 126,
130-1, 152, 195-6
developing countries, poverty in
261-6
diet see food
direct taxes 220, 221
disability 98-9
costs 90-2, 118, 143
and housing 120
and regional variations 126, 236

and risk of poverty 51, 52, 55, 89,
145-6
and welfare benefits 84, 92, 93
and work 52, 92-3, 277-8
see also carers; sickness
district-level poverty 196, 236,
239-42, 282
see also deprived areas
divorce see relationship breakdown
domestic work 171-2
see also childcare

E
earnings
inequality in 175, 176, 213-6,
229-30, 231
regional variations 231, 237, 238
see also low pay
economic status, and poverty
32, 38-9, 44, 45, 52
education, statistics 275-6
educational disadvantage 79,
152, 153-4, 157, 194-6, 266, 279
educational maintenance
allowances 157
electricity see fuel
employment
of carers 94-5
of children 154
of ethnic minority groups 191-4,
277-8
'family-friendly' policies 172
international 254-5, 257
of lone parents 82, 85-6, 87, 119,
167-8, 277-8
of refugees 201
regional variations (UK) 231, 233,
235, 236, 237
statistics 32-3, 45, 277-8, 281
welfare benefits in 84-5
see also tax credits

of women 83, 85-6, 166, 167-8,
174-9, 193
*see also flexible working; in-work
poverty; labour market; New Deal
programmes; occupations;
unemployment*
England
homelessness in 121
mortality rates 125
poverty in 228, 230, 235
regeneration plans 243
see also London
ethnic minority groups
and educational disadvantage 194-6
effects of poverty on 194-9
and employment 191-4, 277-8
household composition of 189
and housing 197
living in deprived areas 195-6
and low pay 167, 193-4
poverty indicators 188-94
poverty statistics 145, 188-9
and sickness 197-9
and unemployment 190-2, 277-8
and welfare benefits 189-90, 199-201
European Union
child health in 266
concept of poverty 18
employment in 254-5, 257
low pay in 260-61
National Action Plans on social
exclusion 250-1
poverty in 250-60, 264, 265
unemployment in 255-8
*see also England; Northern Ireland;
Scotland; Wales*
expenditure *see spending*

F
'family-friendly' labour policies
172

family life 132-3
family spending *see spending*
family structure *see household
composition*
family support, policies 89
financial exclusion 116-7, 154-5
see also debt
flexible working 81-3, 172-3
see also part-time work
food 112-3, 148, 151, 152
free school meals 150, 153, 233,
235, 238
fuel 113, 128, 131, 132, 282

G
gender inequality *see women*
government *see Labour government*

H
health *see children, health; mental
health; sickness*
hidden poverty 34, 179-80, 242
homelessness 121-3, 197, 279
homeowners 120, 197
homeworkers 193-4
household composition 85-6, 147
of ethnic minority groups 189
and risk of poverty 37-8, 39-43, 45,
53, 54, 88
and wealth distribution 218, 219
and welfare benefits 59
see also lone parents
household items, lack of 111
household work *see childcare;
domestic work*
***Households Below Average
Income*** 19-20, 30-1, 35
context 32-4
critique 34, 121
on persistence of poverty 47-8
poverty line 35-7

statistics 31, 36-46, 145-6, 147,
228-9
housework 171-2
housing 119-21, 280, 282
and death rates 126
of ethnic minority groups 197
rent arrears 117, 120
and risk of poverty 51, 55
and wealth 218-19
see also homelessness
housing benefit 60, 85, 120-1
**housing costs, in poverty
measures** 36
Human Poverty Index 262, 263
humanistic discourses 12

I
illness see sickness
**immigration status, and welfare
benefits** 199-200
in-work poverty 38, 39, 82-5
see also low pay
income
regional variations 228-30, 235,
236-7, 242
trends 32
see also earnings; Households Below
Average Income; wealth, inequality in
income inequality 12, 44-6, 207-211
international 254, 255, 264-5
in pensioners 96-7
regional (UK) 228-30, 242
and women 83-4, 164-6, 175, 176,
178, 214, 215
see also low pay
income support 56-62, 63, 65, 88,
169, 277
indirect taxes 220, 221
industrialised nations
poverty in 258-61, 262, 263
see also European Union

inequality
of expenditure 212
in wealth 216-9
see also earnings, inequality in; income
inequality; low pay; social exclusion
infant mortality 125, 152, 198, 266
international poverty 26
see also developing countries, poverty
in; European Union; industrialised
nations

J
jobseeker's allowance see income
support

L
Labour government
developments under 1-2, 5-6, 63-7
targets 5, 49, 66, 122, 178
labour market 78-86, 192-3
see also employment; unemployment
leisure activities 129, 133, 148
life expectancy 96, 124, 281, 282
see also mortality
local poverty see district-level
poverty; London; rural areas
London 80, 121, 196, 229, 238-9, 241
lone parents
and debts 118, 119
and diet 112
and employment 82, 85-6, 87, 119,
167-8, 277-8
and income poverty line 37
income sources of 165-6
mothers 167-8
and persistent poverty 48
poverty statistics 38, 42, 54, 88, 145
changes over time 44, 45
Northern Ireland 55
risk of poverty 39-41, 51, 53
and sickness 126

spending on children 63
statistics on 33-4, 87-8
and unemployment 78, 87
and welfare benefits 58, 59, 62, 65,
  84, 88
low cost but acceptable budgets
  24, 61-2
Low Income Families statistics
  19, 56
low pay 82-4, 215-6
of ethnic minority groups 167,
  193-4
international 260-1
of women 82, 83-4, 166, 167, 175,
  176, 178, 214, 215

M
marginalisation *see social exclusion*
marital breakdown *see relationship
  breakdown*
market exclusion 18
material deprivation *see
  necessities, lack of*
mean income *see Households Below
  Average Income*
means testing 168
mental health 120, 127, 151, 198-9
minimum income guarantee 60,
  100, 169
see also pension credits
minimum income standards 24-6
minimum subsistence 12, 14-6,
  23-4
*see also low cost but acceptable
  budgets; Poverty and Social
  Exclusion in Britain*
minimum wage 46, 84, 167, 194,
  215, 260-1
see also social wage
modest but adequate budgets
  24, 62-3

mortality
of children 124-5, 151, 152, 252,
  265, 266
rates 124-6, 198, 232-3, 234, 236
see also life expectancy
mothers *see lone parents; parental
  sacrifice; teenage pregnancy; women*

N
**National Action Plans on social
  exclusion** 250-1
National Carers Strategy 95
National Childcare Strategy
  178-9
national minimum wage *see
  minimum wage*
necessities
definitions of 22, 52
lack of 6, 50-1, 52-5, 111-4, 147-8,
  253
*see also deprivation; low cost but
  acceptable budgets; services, lack of*
neighbourhood renewal 243
New Deal programmes 81-2, 93,
  168, 191, 243
Northern Ireland
homelessness in 121
mortality rates 234
poverty in 54-5, 111, 233, 234-5,
  237-8
*Poverty and Social Exclusion in
  Northern Ireland* 54-5, 111, 128,
  130, 147-8, 163
regeneration plans 243
nutrition *see food*

O
occupational pensions 97, 169,
  178, 279
occupations
of ethnic minority groups 192-3

and risk of unemployment 79, 80
of women 166, 174-7, 178, 193
OECD countries *see industrialised nations*
officials, dealing with 131-2, 201
Opportunity for All 66-7, 274-82

P
Pakistani/Bangladeshi people 167, 188-92, 193-4
parental sacrifice 63, 112, 149-50
parents *see lone parents; mothers*
part-time work 38, 39, 44, 45, 82-3
by women 166, 167, 177-8
pay *see earnings; low pay*
pension credits 100, 169-70
pensioners 96-100
and gender inequality 165
and poverty statistics 280-1
risk of poverty of 38, 39, 41, 44, 45, 98, 190
welfare benefits for 59, 60-1, 99-100
pensions 97, 169, 178, 279
persistent poverty 47-9, 83-4, 98, 278-9, 280
in children 48-9, 146-7, 258, 275
international 251-2, 258
poverty
at-risk groups 37-41, 44, 51-2, 53, 77-8, 251-2
see also children; pensioners; women
causes of 2-3, 118, 170-80
changes over time 31, 43-7, 49, 51, 82-3, 207-211
in children 42, 44, 57, 63-6, 145
characteristics of 13-4, 21-2
concepts 10-21
effects of 4, 131, 133-4, 149-56, 194-9
movements in and out of 47-8, 86, 88

perceptions of 129-31
and social trends 33-4
see also absolute poverty; deprivation; hidden poverty; inequality; persistent poverty; regional poverty; relative poverty; social exclusion
poverty cycle 21, 155
poverty indicators 6, 66-7, 188-94, 250, 262, 263
see also deprivation indicators; poverty measures
poverty lines 30-1, 35-7, 50-1, 55-6, 61
see also Households Below Average Income; minimum income standards
poverty measures 3, 6-7, 16, 23-6, 49, 56, 67-8
and housing costs 36
international 262-3
see also poverty indicators
Poverty and Social Exclusion in Britain 31, 49-51, 111, 147
statistics 31, 51-4, 111, 120, 128, 129-30, 148
regional variations 229
on women 163, 170
Poverty and Social Exclusion in Northern Ireland 54-5, 111, 128, 130, 147-8, 163
poverty trap 85
power imbalance 2-3
pregnancy, teenage 155-6, 276
prepayment meters 128, 132
primary poverty 16, 23
public opinion on minimum income 24-5
see also necessities

R
racial discrimination 193, 199, 201

refugees 200-1
regeneration plans 243
regional poverty 125, 228-30, 282
    district-level 196, 236, 239-42, 282
    rural 170, 242-3
    see also deprived areas; developing
        countries; England; European
        Union; industrialised nations;
        Northern Ireland; Scotland; Wales
relationship breakdown 85, 86,
    87-8, 118, 132-3
relative poverty 6, 15, 16-17, 31
rent arrears 117, 120
retired people see pensioners
rough sleepers see homelessness
rural areas 170, 242-3

S
savings gateways 117
school meals see free school meals
Scotland
    income statistics 228, 229, 231
    mortality rates 125, 234
    poverty in 152, 233, 234-6
    regeneration plans 243
secondary poverty 16
separation see relationship
    breakdown
services, lack of 128, 198
sickness 89-90, 123, 124, 126-7
    in children 123, 151, 266
    in ethnic minority groups 197-9
    and housing 120
    policies 93
    and risk of poverty 51, 52
    see also disability; mental health;
        mortality
single parents see lone parents
social exclusion 12, 17-8, 21, 153-4
    National Action Plans 250-1
    statistics 128-9

of women 170
    see also inequality; leisure activities;
        necessities; Poverty and Social
        Exclusion in Britain
social housing, and risk of
    poverty 51, 55, 117
social security benefits see welfare
    benefits
social security policies, effects
    220-2
social trends, and poverty 33-4
social wage 221-2
    see also minimum wage
spending 63, 143-4, 212
    see also market exclusion
stigma 130-1, 150
suicide 125, 279
supplementary benefit see
    income support
Sure Start 152, 156

T
tax credits 60, 65, 84-5, 93, 144,
    179, 221
    see also pension credits
taxation policies, effects
    220-2
teenage pregnancy 151, 155-6,
    276
temporary accommodation
    121, 122, 123
temporary work 81, 82-3
Third World see developing
    countries
truancy 153

U
unemployment
    and carers 94-5
    causes of 78-80
    and death rates 125

and debt 118
and disability 52, 92-3, 277-8
in ethnic minority groups 190-2,
    277-8
international 255-8
and lone parenthood 78, 87
policies 80-2
poverty statistics 38, 39, 41, 42, 51,
    52, 54, 274
regional variations 79-80, 230-2,
    234, 235, 236, 237, 238
and sickness 90
statistics 32-3, 277-8, 281
trends 78
of women 166, 177, 256
of young people 154, 276
**United Nations, definition of
poverty** 13-14
universal banking services
116-17

W

wages see *earnings; low pay*
Wales
income statistics 228, 229, 231
mortality rates 125, 234
poverty in 233, 234-5, 236-7
regeneration plans 243
ward-level poverty 240-2
wealth, inequality in 216-9
welfare benefits
adequacy of 65-6
for carers 95
deductions 117
for disabled people 84, 92, 93
for ethnic minority groups 189-90,
    199-201
for lone parents 58, 59, 62, 65, 84,
    88
for pensioners 59, 60-1, 99-100
regional variations 230, 237

take-up 60-1, 100
trends 33
for women 168-70
in work 84-5
see *also child benefit; educational
    maintenance allowances; housing
    benefit; income support; means
    testing; pensions*
welfare to work, see *also New Deal
    programmes*
women
causes of poverty 170-80
and childcare 172-3, 178-9
and costs of children 144
and domestic work 171-2
and employment 82, 83, 85-6, 166,
    167-8, 174-9, 193
and hidden poverty 179-80
and income inequality 83-4, 164-6,
    175, 176, 178, 214, 215
and low pay 82, 83-4, 166, 167, 175,
    176, 178, 214, 215
and mortality rates 124
occupations of 166, 174-7, 178, 193
poverty statistics for 163, 170
and risk of poverty 40, 51, 99, 163
and social exclusion 170
unemployment 166, 177, 256
welfare benefits for 168-70
see *also carers; lone parents*
work see *employment*
working families' tax credits see
    tax credits
worklessness see *unemployment*

young people 81, 83-4, 112, 154,
    191, 195-6, 276
see *also children; teenage pregnancy*